D1515854

REACHING the WORLD NEXT DOOR

Including a study guide for groups or individuals

◆ How to Spread the Gospel
in the Midst of Many Cultures

Thom & Marcia Hopler

INTERVARSITY PRESS
DOWNERS GROVE, ILLINOIS 60515

InterVarsity Press® *is the book-publishing division of InterVarsity Christian Fellowship*®*, a student movement active on campus at hundreds of universities, colleges and schools of nursing in the United States of America, and a member movement of the International Fellowship of Evangelical Students. For information about local and regional activities, write Public Relations Dept., InterVarsity Christian Fellowship, 6400 Schroeder Rd., P.O. Box 7895, Madison, WI 53707-7895.*

Cover illustration: Roberta Polfus

ISBN 0-8308-1661-5

Printed in the United States of America

Library of Congress Cataloging-in-Publication Data

Hopler, Thom, 1936-1978.
    Reaching the world next door: how to spread the gospel in the midst of many cultures/Thom Hopler and Marcia Hopler; including a study guide for groups or individuals.
      p. cm.
    Rev. ed. of: A world of difference: following Christ beyond your cultural walls. c 1981.
    Includes bibliographical references.
    ISBN 0-8308-1661-5
    1. Christianity and culture. 2. Ethnicity—Religious aspects— Christianity. 3. Reconciliation—Religious aspects—Christianity. 4. Evangelistic work. I. Hopler, Marcia, 1937- . II. Hopler, Thom, 1936-1978. World of difference: following Christ beyond your cultural walls. III. Title.
    BR115.C8H66   1993   93-38955
                                       CIP

15	14	13	12	11	10	9	8	7	6	5	4	3	2	1
04	03	02	01	00	99	98	97	96	95	94	93			

Introduction

Thom Hopler believed that urbanization would be the wave of the future. As the message of the gospel had ridden on the wave of colonialism centuries before, so it might do so again, but this time piggybacking on urbanization. But fifteen years ago, as farsighted as Thom was, he was not sure what form this piggybacking might take.

A decade and a half later, we are able to envision networks of communication that have grown tremendously in our ever-urbanizing world. Much of what would have appeared to be science fiction a short time ago is now a reality. The change is occurring so fast, even in the countries of the Two-Thirds World it is dizzying.

Our world is even more diverse and pluralistic than in 1981 when *A World of Difference* first came out. We do not need to cross an ocean to cross into a different culture anymore. Many different ethnic, religious and cultural groups may be represented across town or across the street.

Globally, there are strong ethnic tensions everywhere. We also see our economies becoming even more integrated, increasing the significance of the Two-Thirds World. With the demise of the Cold War and the collapse of the Berlin Wall, change has also swept Eastern Europe, the former Soviet Union and China.

In America there is moral corruption of heroes and heroines. We have whiplash from the 1960s—aftermath of the Vietnam War, assassinations, women's worldview and minority influence. Today we experience middle-class joblessness, the shadow of AIDS, refugees pounding on our door, an increase in single, female heads of households and educated BUPPIES

(Black Upward Professionals) who have not experienced much civil rights history.

But key among and embracing all of these changes, I believe, is urbanization. This century has been called the century of the urban revolution. In the more developed regions urban population doubled since 1950. In fact, in the last sixty years, urban population increased tenfold, while rural population only doubled.

Floyd McClung states: "Within the next 11 years 700 million people will immigrate to the teeming urban centers of our world." He goes on to say,

> Cities are the mountain peaks of society; trends, ideologies, and fashions are born in the fermenting caldron of city life, and spread throughout the whole globe. For example, in the late '70's, the fast flow of communication via television, fashion magazines, and pop music in the cities spread the "punk" movement which began spontaneously among alienated, unemployed youth in Liverpool and Amsterdam. Quickly it became a worldwide movement reaching into most western cities around the globe.[1]

Thom was more than a man of ideas, however. He was a unique person who called himself a bridge—a bridge between people, a bridge between truth and love in action. He shared his spiritual gifts of wisdom and knowledge, grasping otherwise mysterious problems and predicting possible solutions in the mode of a prophet. Once someone told me, "He answered all my questions." Others felt the same.

Marriage to such a rare bird as Thom might have been abrasive if he were not such a *human* person at home and outside the home. He slurped his coffee and laughed at himself in the midst of his profundity. Gentle and godly, he listened to us; he affirmed us. At an Urbana 79 meeting Pete Hammond said it completely when he spoke of Thom as one "who served me, as he served many of you."

In this book you may find a potpourri of ideas. That may be so because Thom himself was a mixture. He was like a mosaic with many pieces of truth. Yet his multifaceted vision formed a total image in an otherwise one-dimensional culture. It thrills me that the pages of writing here represent him in this way. This is due in large measure to the work and sensitivity of Andrew Le Peau, IVP editorial director, who compiled and molded this material into book form, which was first published in 1981 under the title *A World of Difference.*

In this new edition, I have added to the potpourri. In several new chapters

I have tried to portray the process of urbanization as I understand it from my experience. My viewpoint will be heavily Afro-centric because that is where I've been and where I've been taught. The relevant truths, however, align themselves with and apply to other minorities and the Two-Thirds World community.

Today Thom's call is more relevant than ever. "The urban mission must realize that the cries of America's minorities for identity, understanding, acceptance, and genuine love are the cries of what is in fact the majority around the globe."[2]

Thom's life was a remarkable combination of truth and love. He wore a gray suit, but his ideas were radically sharp. May this book be the same.

Marcia Hopler

Publisher's Preface

We at InterVarsity Press first met Thom Hopler when he attended our Writers' Workshop in August 1977. There we worked with him to develop his material on the book of Acts (much of which is found in chapters six and seven of this book).

At the time, we hoped his Acts material might be published as a pamphlet. But more work was needed. So we transcribed tapes of other talks Thom had given on Acts and did preliminary editing. His response to our work was positive. We asked him to send more tapes on other subjects, and he did. We also made plans to tape, transcribe and edit more material during his speaking engagements in the summer of 1978. He never gave those talks. Thom Hopler died of a heart attack on June 12, 1978.

After consulting with his wife, Marcia, and some of Thom's friends, we decided to search for other tapes by Thom, collect his writings and notes, transcribe the tapes and evaluate all the material for possible publication. This was done. The result was the publication in 1981 of *A World of Difference*. We especially appreciated the cooperation of Marcia Hopler at every stage of the production of the book. We also acknowledge the help and counsel of Neil Rendall, who was Thom's supervisor while he was on staff for InterVarsity Christian Fellowship. Many others sent us tapes, notes and papers from Thom, read the final manuscript for us, and offered their suggestions along the way. We are thankful for these as well.

Our goal was to make the book far more than a collection of talks and papers. We sought to make it a single, complete and well-reasoned presentation. The material was entirely based on Thom's work and thought. The organization of the chapters and of the material within some of the chapters is, however, the result of our work in consultation with Marcia and others. The transcribed talks were also edited to transform the material from spoken to written form. We conscientiously sought to maintain Thom's "voice" and perspective throughout and had the manuscript checked carefully by those who knew Thom's ministry best. Because Thom could not himself read this book, however, it is possible that his thinking has, on occasion, been misrepresented. The responsibility for such errors is ours.

As the years passed, many people told us how significant the book was. Even though it had gone out of print, it was still fresh. Thom, they said, was so far ahead of his time that the world was just beginning to catch up with the ideas he expressed years ago. Shouldn't the book be reintroduced? Maybe the time is even more right now for such a book.

So we began working with Marcia to update and expand the book. The result is the new edition that you hold in your hands. Most of the chapters from the original edition have undergone little change except to update statistics. Those chapters remain written in Thom's voice and perspective. In a separate section Marcia has added several chapters from her perspective of a dozen more years of ministry since Thom's death. These extend many of the themes in the original book and make it even more relevant for the nineties.

For a publisher, it is always a pleasure to produce a book with exceptionally fresh and challenging ideas. It is even more delightful to bring such a book back to life for a new company of readers who want to understand what God can do in our rapidly changing world.

1

"How Much Did You Pay for Your Wife?"

▼▼▼▼▼▼▼▼▼▼▼▼▼▼▼▼

"HOW MUCH DID YOU PAY FOR YOUR WIFE?" THE OLD MAN ASKED DURING the first month Marcia and I spent in Kenya. When I explained that we don't sell women in America, he laughed and said, squeezing Marcia's thin arm, "I wouldn't give a goat for her either."

People are different. Not only do individuals differ from one another, but groups of people differ as well. On another occasion in my first months in Africa, I waved hello to a friend across the street. Immediately he ran over to me asking, "What's the matter? What do you want?" I spent the next ten minutes trying to talk my way out of that innocent cultural misstep. My hand signal did not mean "Hello" but "Come here quickly. I need you."

Crossing cultures is difficult enough by itself. But when a person is a Christian who wants to communicate the lifegiving message about Jesus, the difficulty is greatly multiplied. What is culture? How does it affect my Christian life, my evangelism? What are the implications of culture for the church at large? In this chapter I want to introduce some preliminary responses to these questions and to set the stage for fuller answers in the rest of the book.

A Garbage Truck Is Culture

Because of differing geographies, differing histories, differing climates and differing languages, different groups have developed different cultures. The word *culture* is often used in the narrow sense of "high culture"—opera, sculpture and the like. But I am using the word in a broader sense that includes the total pattern of human life in society. That means garbage trucks, radios and paper bags are all a part of culture, at least Western culture. Whether we realize it or not, much of what we do is the result of our own culture.

This has profound implications for the church as it carries the gospel from one culture to another. How much of what we teach is culture and how much is gospel? Often we simply do not know because we have never thought about what our own culture is like.

Though the concept of culture is rich and complex, I want to focus on four specific aspects. First, culture is *a mental road map*. It helps us get from morning to night without running into dead ends or roadblocks. Those who have been in another culture know how terribly hard it is to get up in the morning and think, "What's the first thing I say when I meet someone? And if she responds, what do I say next? And if she offers to do a favor for me, what does it mean?" You realize that every movement, everything you wear, everything you say has a certain meaning that you have to make a conscious effort to figure out. The strain this can cause is called culture shock.

Our culture teaches us how to act in standard ways in normal situations. We do not have to think about what we are to do with forks and spoons and knives when we sit down to eat. Our culture has trained us. It has given us a series of shortcuts so we can function at a basic level every day. If two people from two different cultures were alone on a desert island, within weeks they would develop a third culture that would give them shortcuts for dealing with one another.

The sum total of our lived experience is another way of looking at culture. You may not know how to play the violin, but it is part of your culture if you recognize and appreciate it when you hear it. The five-toned flute of India, on the other hand, may sound strange to your ears. While it and the music an Indian plays on it may be just as sophisticated as violin music, you think it is peculiar because it is not part of your experience, not part of your culture.

Culture also provides us with *a system of values that directs our activities*. These are not absolute within each culture. Some people always insist on "breaking the rules." And cultures will often have slightly different values for different age groups, economic classes, localities or working groups. We allow children to act in a way adults are not to act.

Values (priorities in life) are important for Christians, of course, because God, too, has values that he wants us to learn. He does not wish simply to destroy the values of our culture or any culture and replace it with a "Christian" culture. Rather he wants to add to and redirect our values.

In this sense, culture is a gift from God that can keep us from destroying ourselves. It helps us maintain a low level of sociability until God is able to lift us to a higher level by his Word. From the very beginning God has built such protection into culture, as we will see in more detail in the next chapter.

This idea is illustrated by an incident from the early 1960s. There was a movement in Africa to remove anything associated with colonialism, including Christianity. The parliament of Kenya debated this issue quite seriously. At one point a non-Christian in the parliament said, in essence, "We are a tribalistic people. We each have our own gods, our own ideals, our own understandings of right and wrong. But these are not adequate to meet the needs of our nation. With Christianity has come a system of values that supersedes tribalism. We hold our young people accountable on the basis of the Bible. If we take away the Bible, whose tribal system will we adopt in its place?"

The parliament agreed. The people had stopped killing each other because the Bible said, "Thou shalt not kill." As they discussed it further, they decided to make it mandatory to teach the Bible in all the schools in Kenya. Other religions have come into competition with Christianity, but they still require that some more universal system of values be taught. They recognize that without values, people become dangerous. God does not desire to destroy our values but to lift them to a higher plane.

The opposite is happening in the West. As we secularize and move away from biblical values, we are finding it more and more difficult to maintain order, to maintain even a low level of sociability. Thus we should not encourage other cultures simply to dump their values, which allow for a degree of peace. Rather we should show a better way.

With Culture, Some Things Are Impossible

Lastly, culture defines for us *the limits of possibility*. For many years the four-minute mile was a barrier that people said could not be broken. It was impossible. Yet within two years after Roger Bannister ran a mile in 3 minutes 59.4 seconds, a half-dozen others did the same. It was no longer impossible.

In Africa, one of my students belonged to the Watusi tribe, who average between seven and eight feet in height. During track practice one day the coach was struggling to help the high jumpers over the 6'3" mark. The Watusi student, who was only seven feet tall, was standing to the side, arms folded, watching these efforts. He had never seen anything like it. But finally he asked the coach if he could try. So he walked up to the bar and started this Watusi dance which required keeping his whole body stiff except for his feet and ankles. Soon he was bouncing two feet off the ground. Suddenly he drew his knees up, cleared the bar and came down on the other side—on his feet! From a standing position he cleared 6'3".

What we could never get him to do, however, was to go over the bar horizontally. In his tribe they fight and throw spears from a standing position only. To him balance was very important, and you must stay erect to stay balanced. You never lie down horizontally. Consequently, it was outside his culture to do the high jump the way we see it in the Olympics. For him, it was impossible.

Culture can put similar limitations on our faith. The disciples thought feeding a huge crowd was impossible—even with two hundred days' wages. But it wasn't for Jesus.

They were limited in their understanding of what Jesus could do. In their culture—and in ours, too—no human being could perform such an act. But Jesus upset their expectations. He showed them he was more than they had thought. He had the capacity to break through such cultural limitations. This is the power and the commission that he has also given his church. If we, however, accept the limits of our culture as normative, we may also limit the gospel.

The church's temptation has always been to fall into such error. We have often emphasized the worth of every individual and the image of God in each person. Less frequently we have recognized the image of God in every group of people, every culture.

Who Is Really Backward?

"Western culture is more civilized than African culture." So goes the standard Western judgment. But is this right? While Christianity may have had a greater impact on one than the other, and while God's values may be more evident in one than the other, we cannot conclude that Western customs are appropriate or good to bring into other cultures. Yet read any newspaper. Are we really more advanced?

Think a moment about the old man's question about how much I paid for my wife. We find the bride price a strange, if not backward, custom. How primitive to buy wives, we say. But is it? When a man and woman are married in Africa, the giving of gifts from one family to the other binds them together. Several hundred people from one family in effect marry several hundred from another. Over the course of a year prior to the marriage, these families become acquainted and exchange gifts, which establishes communication between them. When the immediate family members finally give gifts, the marriage itself can take place. The only way divorce is possible is to return all the gifts. Therefore, because a thousand people will never agree to such a thing (they want to keep what they have), divorce is virtually unknown.

After an African explained all this to me he asked, "How do you do it in America?" I explained that often the mother of the bride meets the mother of the groom for the first time the night before the wedding. In shock he said, "Why, that's barbaric." He was right. Since then I have been to several wedding rehearsals that were quite painful. Within twenty-four hours two families were expected to put together one of the most important events in their lives, and there was no cultural procedure to make it work smoothly. Some of the bitter feelings that develop that night can take years to work out.

The notion that we are more advanced and more knowledgeable than ever before has contributed to our tendency to cut ourselves off from the past, from any cultural guidelines that might help us move into the future. Instead of having norms that help us move through minor problems, we are anchorless. Marriage, for example, becomes a series of crises.

Another factor, especially in America, clouds our ability to see God's general revelation in other cultures. This is a commitment to the idea of a melting pot, a society in which all peoples can share common values and customs. Chapter ten will expand on this. For now, suffice it to say that this has tended to blind us to the validity and vitality of cultural distinctions.

The church has not been immune to such blurred vision and ethnocentrism. But as we overcome these, new life will come to the church. As Arthur Glasser notes,

The new linkage between theologians, missionaries and national church leaders all over the world . . . will not be Western-dominated. Significant

stirrings are discernible among younger intellectuals in the churches of
Asia, Africa and Latin America. . . . This shall bring about the long
overdue transformation of a western religion into a universal faith. . . .
The deposit of truth Christ gave the disciples long ago is not confined to
any one segment of the structured church.[1]

One of the reasons missions can bring life to the church as a whole is that
carrying the gospel crossculturally forces us to peel off culture so that only
the core gospel remains. When this purer gospel is brought back to the home
churches, it brings renewal. In chapter seven we will see how Paul reported
back to Jerusalem what God was doing among the Gentiles (Acts 15). The
Jews suddenly got a larger view of who God is. Thus crosscultural ministry
brings us as Christians to the cutting edge of cultural change because we will
be pointing out where our culture has gone astray and where we have strayed.

Our cultural blindness has caused us to define missions as crossing
geographical barriers with the gospel. This is the great unfinished work of
the church, we say. In fact, the church has never had difficulty crossing
geographic barriers. From the very day the church was born, at Pentecost,
those who heard the gospel believed and were baptized, and returned to their
distant homes around the Mediterranean basin, in Africa and in Asia (Acts
2:5-11). The only problem was that they did not cross cultural barriers with
the gospel. Many of them only spoke to Jews (Acts 11:19). Indeed, Acts
8—15 records the great wrenching that had to take place before the church
broke through to the Gentiles. (This is discussed more fully in chapters six
and seven.) Ever since then, the church's difficulty has been to cross cultural
barriers. Even today there is hardly a geographic boundary the gospel has not
crossed, but there are hundreds of cultural groups that have not heard the
gospel. We need new eyes to see new fields that are ready for harvest.

Old Methods in a New Setting

Most of the experience the church has in crossing cultural barriers is in
traditional foreign missions. I believe, therefore, that what missions has
learned can be used profitably to reach the unreached cultures of today. We
agonize over our degenerating cities, not realizing that the tools to reach them
for Christ already exist. Yet many of the attitudes that prevent us from
penetrating the city were identified by foreign mission experience decades
ago. This book is an attempt to apply missionary insights to crosscultural
evangelism.

Take one example: If missionaries have learned to live with polygamy in the church, seeking to modify it slowly rather than immediately, why have we not learned to accept the transient urban Black male in the same way?[2] We will consider this question more in the next chapter. A more important lesson is that though isolated individuals can be won for Christ, churches must be built from people involved in the community itself. Few urban ministries are aimed specifically at the average citizen.

I was in Africa for ten exciting years—1960-70—when Africa went through tremendous turmoil. It was the end of the colonial era and the beginning of independence. I became involved in the vital African church which taught me much about faith and about my own cultural limitations.

I kept hearing two disturbing questions: What is the situation of Blacks and the Black church in America? And why are there no Black missionaries from America to Africa? I had no answers, but I knew I needed some. My search took me to Newark, where the Africa Inland Mission began its first urban ministry in America. This was a radical move for a "foreign" mission society. It meant redefining its call to include all crosscultural missions, whether foreign or domestic. But it is a direction that I believe more should move in.

My search also led me to find help from a variety of places. I suspect many readers will be frustrated in their attempt to label me as having one theological stance or another, or one missions strategy or another. I have purposely avoided such labels because I seek to bridge many different groups. My concern is for the vitality of the church, and I accept insights from any source that helps God's truth to reach more and more people.

Another perspective I bring to these issues comes from sociological and anthropological urban studies. Traditionally, sociologists study social structures within a single culture while anthropologists study whole cultures and compare them to each other. Early anthropologists tended to look for the simplest and purest cultures so they could be compared most easily. Primitive and small cultures were the most likely choices for accomplishing this. Anthropologists therefore tended to avoid the city because it was so complex.

On the other hand, sociologists do not spend time dealing with cultures with only two or three institutions. They have gravitated toward complex societies—such as America. But this has created a bias because they have assumed that America is one—a complex unity, but a unity nonetheless. As this has proven untenable, sociologists have begun looking to anthropologists for help. Urban sociology and urban anthropology are similar disciplines which have developed to account for both the diversity and the interrelations found in the city. While I find help in both approaches, my bias is toward anthropology because I find the city opens up to me if I come to it with a people orientation. If I come with a system orientation, I see only confusion.

A Look Ahead
My goal in this book is to highlight and focus on God's concern for reaching the many different cultures of the world. I begin, in part one, by considering what the Bible has to say about crossing cultures with God's Word. Here we will look at the Bible chronologically, but not from the standpoint of a traditional historical survey. We will focus on the cultural dimensions present in a few key books. This survey is not meant to be exhaustive, but rather suggestive. By focusing on the issue of culture in this way, I do not mean to imply that this is the only, or even the most important, issue in the Bible. But it is a neglected issue to which we need to pay special attention.

Part two then discusses how we can apply in practical ways the biblical teaching on culture to the world today. Chapter eight highlights urbanization as one of the main forces affecting cultures around the world. Chapters nine and ten then cover five main groups on which our evangelism should concentrate, illustrating how to reach each.

The next section, part three, further develops the issues of urbanization and ethnicity with special emphasis on Black culture, the Black church and racial reconciliation. Finally, part four discusses the overriding concerns that Christians in any culture should have. Truth and love are seen, in chapter sixteen, as the basis for a universal biblical value system. The book closes by looking at the characteristics of true disciples of Christ.

People are different. We can rejoice in our diversity because together we reflect the boundless creativity of our God. We need not fear our diversity because our God is One. The living truth that comes out of diversity is the mystery of his church.

Part 1

▼▼▼▼▼▼▼▼▼▼▼▼

A Cultural Survey of the Bible

2
Building
the Family:
Genesis

▼▼▼▼▼▼▼▼▼▼▼▼▼▼▼

GENESIS IS THE BOOK OF MANY BEGINNINGS—OF THE WORLD, OF HUMANITY, of sin, of reconciliation, of promise. The beginning of culture is here too. And culture, in Genesis, begins with the family. In Genesis God has much to tell us about what the family is and what it should be, even in a crosscultural setting.

Both Male and Female

Genesis 1—2 tells us how God wanted this world to be, in particular, how he wanted us as people to be. Genesis 1:26 reads, "Then God said, 'Let us . . .' " Immediately we see a hint of the plurality of God. In the New Testament the teaching becomes explicit. God is a triunity—Father, Son and Holy Spirit. This is a mystery, a unique doctrine. But we need to understand this plurality in Genesis because the passage goes on to say,

> "Let us make man in our image, after our likeness; and let them [notice: let *them*] have dominion over the fish of the sea, and over the birds of the air, and over the cattle, and over all the earth, and over every creeping

thing that creeps upon the earth." So God created man in his own image, in the image of God he created him; male and female he created them. (Gen 1:26-27)

The nature of man includes both male and female. The Bible often refers to the whole human race as *man*, just as I will. Usually the context makes it very clear if a specific male is being considered. But more often than not, we should assume that when the Bible refers to *man*, it means both male and female.

I did not understand this until I left America for Africa, because probably no society in the world is more individualistic than that of America. When I first held tryouts in Kenya for a track meet, I could not get the students to compete against each other. They said, "We will select the one among us who is the fastest runner. He will run against the other school." I asked, "Why?" They said, "If we pick the one who can run best for us, then we can all cheer him on to victory against the other school. But we could never cheer him on to victory if he had selected himself by his own qualities. If we compete against ourselves, we will divide ourselves, and we will not be able to compete against the other school." That's corporateness. That is the way a tribal society operates. They do not know what it means to be individual. God created us in this kind of corporateness; "male and female he created them."

Genesis 2:18-24 reinforces this concept. Remember that throughout the six days of creation God evaluated his work as being good. Yet suddenly we read, "Then the LORD God said, 'It is not good.' " What is not good? "It is not good that the man should be alone." Maleness is good, but is not good by itself. So he says, "I will make him a helper fit for him."

God helps Adam come to the same conclusion through an inductive process. In verse 19 he forms the animals and birds out of the ground and parades them before Adam, instructing him to name them all. In verse 20 Adam looks at each and every one of God's creatures and names them. This demonstrates that from the beginning God created maleness as a complete entity, able to function alone, by itself. Adam had the capacity to commune with God, to exercise some dominion over nature, to be creative in thinking up names. But it was not good that he should be alone. And as he began to function alone, in maleness, he discovered what God already knew—that this was not good. This was made especially vivid as Adam was introduced to every kind of living creature that existed yet found none that was like him. He realized that though he was in complete harmony with nature, there was nothing in nature like him. He was alone, and this was not good.

After God creates Eve, he brings her to Adam, just as God brought the animals. But this time Adam's response is quite different. "This at last is bone of my bones and flesh of my flesh" (2:23). Here is someone like me! This is just what I've been looking for! Adam then gives the woman a name. After looking at every kind of animal on the earth and discovering his uniqueness, he now sees that uniqueness in a mirror image. "Therefore a man leaves his father and his mother and cleaves to his wife, and they become one flesh. And the man and his wife were both naked, and were not ashamed" (2:24). This is what God thought was very good, man in a family which in its unity expresses the nature of God.

Breakdown Begins, Reconciliation Begins

In chapter 3 sin enters, and there is an immediate breakdown of the relationships which God has established in his creation. "And they heard the sound of the LORD God walking in the garden in the cool of the day, and the man and his wife hid themselves from the presence of the LORD God among the trees of the garden" (3:8). The first breakdown is that man and woman are alienated from God. They are now hiding from him.

Then, in verse 10 we read, "And he said, 'I heard the sound of thee in the garden, and I was afraid, because I was naked; and I hid myself.' " Sin has also broken down man's relationship with himself. He sees himself as inadequate. He is uncomfortable with himself. He is ashamed, and so he hides from God.

We see a third breakdown in verse 12. "The man said, 'The woman whom thou gavest to be with me, she gave me fruit of the tree.' " The relationship between the man and the woman has changed drastically because of sin. This is no longer the rejoicing of "At last . . . bone of my bones and flesh of my flesh." This is tension, alienation, separation. The unity that God intended is gone. The corporateness is gone.

Lastly we come to verse 17. "And to Adam he said, 'Because you have listened to the voice of your wife, and have eaten of the tree of which I commanded you, 'You shall not eat of it,' cursed is the ground because of you; in toil you shall eat of it all the days of your life.' " No longer will man and woman exercise dominion over nature by working with it but by working against it. They are alienated from creation.

The breakdown of the system moves God to intervene. He takes an immediate step of reconciliation. "The LORD God made for Adam and for his wife garments of skins, and clothed them" (3:21). God reached down in his mercy and acted to rebuild their relationship with him. The man and woman were incapable of taking the initiative here. So God acts on their behalf.

God also acts to rebuild the relationship between man and himself. God helps protect us from our own self-destructive tendencies. He also puts clothing around man, around woman, to care for their nakedness. In doing this God makes it possible for us to be comfortable with ourselves, to be in relationship with ourselves in a way that we can handle. Underneath, man and woman still have trouble accepting themselves, but God has provided a way so they can continue to function in at least a moderately normal and healthy fashion.

Then, in 3:22-23 we learn, "The LORD God said, 'Behold, the man has become like one of us, knowing good and evil; and now, lest he put forth his hand and take also of the tree of life, and eat, and live for ever'—therefore the LORD God sent him forth from the garden of Eden, to till the ground from which he was taken." God also protects the man and woman from themselves by putting out of their reach the temptation of taking that second fruit and living in eternal death.

This sending out is not merely a negative act of protection. It is also a positive act of commission. They are sent out for a purpose. They are sent out to till the ground. They are not allowed to sit around and vegetate or degenerate in self-loathing. They are given a task. In the task we see just the beginnings of re-creation or reconciliation between man and creation. It is obviously partial. But it is a foretaste of the full reconciliation God plans.

God then helps rebuild the relationship between man and woman. "Now Adam knew Eve his wife, and she conceived and bore Cain, saying, 'I have gotten a man with the help of the LORD' " (4:1). The sexual relationship between man and woman suddenly takes on a whole new meaning. Before it was part of God's creation, now it is the means by which man and woman who, because of sin need to keep skins on themselves, can now get those skins off and become united again. In other words there is a process by which God instills in man the ability to reunite that maleness and femaleness.

The Family of Cain
All of this, of course, is not adequate. Man is still alienated from God. Man

ıs still separated from self and from spouse and from creation. God therefore begins a long-term process of reconciliation as he builds family and community.

Genesis 4 concentrates on family, in particular on the family of Cain. But the example is a negative one, showing degeneration within a family rather than upbuilding.

"Now Abel was a keeper of sheep, and Cain a tiller of the ground" (4:2). Anthropologically, this is the basic division of humankind—the farmer versus the herdsman, the stable tribes versus the migrant tribes. Most of the wars of early history were fought between the herdsmen and the farmers. In the United States the homesteaders going out to the West had great battles with the cattlemen.

The same tension existed between Cain and Abel as well. God accepted Abel's sacrifice but refused Cain's (4:4-5). Apparently Abel had offered first fruits ("the firstlings of his flock") while Cain did not (merely bringing "an offering of the fruit of the ground"). Cain withheld from God the first portion while Abel gave it freely. Cain's response is one that psychologists might call misdirected anger. He's mad at God, but he takes it out on Abel. More simply, Cain is jealous of Abel, and so he kills him (4:8).

God responds to this by forcing him to quit farming and become a fugitive (4:11-12). Cain protests, "My punishment is greater than I can bear. Behold, thou has driven me this day away from the ground; and from thy face I shall be hidden; and I shall be a fugitive and a wanderer on the earth, and whoever finds me will slay me" (4:13-14). So the Lord says to him, "Not so! If any one slays Cain, vengeance shall be taken on him sevenfold" (4:15). So God punishes Cain, sending him out to live in fear of having his head bashed in. And God gives him one bit of security. If anybody kills him, there will be vengeance sevenfold.

By the end of Genesis 4 we come to the man who is at least the great-great-great-grandson of Cain, the last of Cain's line mentioned in the Scripture, Lamech. "Lamech said to his wives: 'Adah and Zillah, hear my voice; you wives of Lamech, hearken to what I say; I have slain a man for wounding me, a young man for striking me. If Cain is avenged sevenfold, truly Lamech seventy-sevenfold' " (4:23-24). This is how the line of Cain has degenerated. Kidner puts it this way:

> Lamech's taunt-song reveals the swift progress of sin. Where Cain had succumbed to it (7) Lamech exults in it; where Cain had sought protection

(14-15) Lamech looks round for provocation: the savage disproportion of killing a mere lad (Hebrew *yeled,* 'child') for a mere wound is the whole point of his boast (cf. 24). On this note of bravado the family disappears from the story.[1]

Sin takes its course and the family disintegrates.

The Family of Seth

In contrast, the very next verses, 4:25-26, read, "And Adam knew his wife again, and she bore a son and called his name Seth, for she said, 'God has appointed for me another child instead of Abel, for Cain slew him.' To Seth also a son was born, and he called his name Enosh. At that time men began to call upon the name of the LORD." In the next few chapters (Gen 5—7), we find that the line of Seth from time to time falls back and calls on the name of the Lord. We find that his descendant Enoch walked with God. And Enoch's descendant Methusaleh is noted to have had a special relationship with God. Also within the same line, Noah turns out to be a man righteous in the eyes of God.

In spite of Seth's family, there were other people on the earth who did not follow God. So God annihilated everybody except for one righteous man. But when God said, "I have seen that you are righteous" (7:1), in God's mind that meant Noah and his wife and their sons and their sons' wives. God does not break up families. The righteousness of Noah affects each individual in his family just as Cain's sin affected those in his. God is working through families to rebuild humankind's relationship with him.

Yet by the time we reach Genesis 11, there is another dilemma. "And the LORD came down to see the city and the tower, which the sons of men had built. And the LORD said, 'Behold, they are one people, and they have all one language; and this is only the beginning of what they will do; and nothing that they propose to do will now be impossible for them. Come, let us go down, and there confuse their language, that they may not understand one another's speech" (11:5-7). God is saying in effect, "I created human beings to be special. I gave them many gifts, many abilities. When they begin to use those gifts for themselves, however, for their own glory, it is incredible what they can do. But in the end they will self-destruct." So to protect man from himself, once again God intervenes. He scatters them all over the earth.

That is the last time within the book of Genesis that God deals with mankind as a whole. He says, "I am not going to deal with all of mankind anymore. I am going to select a family, Abraham's. I am going to bless that family and through him bless all the other families of the earth."

Abraham's family becomes a model for us. We need to look at the rest of Genesis in that light, because God is intervening in human history to establish his ideal of family.

The Family of Abraham

The Genesis story progresses through four more sections related to families. In Genesis 12—15 we see the preparation of Abraham's family. God once again calls a family, not just an individual. God tells Abraham to bring himself and all his responsibilities. That includes Terah, his father, who was too old to care for himself (11:31-32). It includes Lot, who was the son of Abraham's dead brother (11:27-28). It includes his wife. And it includes his possessions. Family relationships are not to be broken.

In the next section (Gen 16—23) the family is established. We have the well-known stories of Ishmael and Isaac, the promised birth of a son and the disbelief that accompanies it. When Isaac is older, God tests Abraham by asking him to sacrifice Isaac. The era ends with the death and burial of Sarah.

Genesis 24—36 covers the extended family of Abraham. It begins with the search for a wife for Isaac. Then we hear about the line of Esau and the line of Jacob; the latter God blesses and the other he does not. These chapters end with the genealogy of Esau, after which we hear nothing more about his family.

The last section is Genesis 37—50. We see the relationships of Jacob and his children and how those children interact as a family. Joseph is sold into slavery in Egypt by his brothers who envy the special treatment their father Jacob is giving their younger brother. Joseph works his way to the top of the Egyptian government and saves that country, as well as his own family, from famine.

We can draw a number of principles from these chapters. First is one I have already referred to: *family relationships are not to be broken.* In fact, God maintains these relationships in order to fulfill the promises he has given. This can be illustrated in Abraham's relationship with Lot.

After Terah dies, Abraham cares for Lot by setting him up with his own section of ground and making sure Lot is able to be self-sustaining (13:2-13). And God promises Abraham that the land he sees around him will be his own (13:14-16), and he commands Abraham, "Arise, walk through the length and the breadth of the land, for I will give it to you" (13:17). This is the Promised Land.

There is only one problem with the Promised Land: other people happen to live there. There are four kings on one side of the Valley of Siddim and five kings on the other side. The four kings on one side join together and grab up all of the surrounding villages. The other five kings decide they are not going to stand for this, so they go to war to see who will rule. And what about poor Abraham? He is wandering around in the middle of all that, an itinerant.

The four kings win, but they make a mistake in the process. They take Lot (14:1-12). After all these great warlike machinations, the Bible simply says Abraham "routed them and pursued them" (14:15). He wipes out the four kings. This says a great deal about God's concern for Abraham and God's concern for Lot (who is still part of Abraham's family). But it also says to Abraham, "I am going to fulfill my promise to give you this land as you fulfill your responsibilities to your family. Now you can live in this land in peace." We see the same theme in Genesis 37—50. Joseph maintains his relationship with his family despite their hostility, and God uses this to preserve Abraham's line, saving them from the drought.

Many people read the book of Genesis with their twentieth-century morality in mind. But we have to recognize that God plucked out of savage, alienated mankind a family that he chose to redeem. Keeping this in view we can see how God taught Abraham's family a second principle: *the sanctity of marriage.*

Abraham and Sarah's relationship was typical for the culture they came out of. Marriage was important but not sacred. In Genesis 12 the family goes to Egypt because of a famine. So Abraham says to his wife, "I'm sorry about this, Sarah, but you are a beautiful woman, and I'm going to lose my head if I say you are my wife. So let's just say you are my sister. So you'll be on your own. You can do whatever you want." That's how he views his commitment to marriage. That is how his culture views it. But since he does not know any better, God intervenes to teach him something new. God ratifies the sanctity of the sexual relationship in marriage.

After Sarah is accepted into Pharaoh's household, plagues follow, and Pharaoh discovers they are due to Sarah's presence. So Pharaoh sternly rebukes Abraham and drives him right out of the country (12:17-20). Yet Abraham has not yet learned his lesson and tries the same deception with Abimelech when the family travels to Gerar. God then works through another pagan king to teach him the importance of marriage (Gen 20). Later, in Genesis 26, we find Isaac employing the same deception as his father. And a third time the family of Abraham is rebuked for its low view of marriage (Gen 26:1-16).

It was a common pattern of the day. If you could not protect yourself, then you had better do whatever you could to save your neck. Three times God intervenes, once in each of the first three sections that I outlined. In the fourth section, however, we find Joseph saying to Potiphar's wife, "I'll go to jail before I'll violate the purity of a marriage relationship." Where did Joseph ever get an idea like that? From God, who had been building that into his family for four generations.

There is another factor accounting for Joseph's reaction. This brings us to the third principle in Genesis 12—50: *the importance of love in family relationships.* Abraham is promised a son. So he waits. And waits. No son. Sarah suggests he have a child by her maid, Hagar. Abraham agrees. But Sarah becomes upset when Hagar starts flaunting the fact that she has conceived and Sarah hasn't. Sarah demands that Hagar be thrown out, and again Abraham agrees. He is willing to expel this woman, who carries his son, into the barren desert. Yet God rebukes Abraham again by saving Hagar and her child. God has more concern for them than Abraham, a fact which is not lost on Abraham (Gen 16).[2]

By the time he has a son through Sarah, Abraham is desperate. When the son is born, therefore, a whole new relationship develops. He makes a great feast when the child is born. Yet God wants to develop the father-son relationship further. He says to Abraham, "Take your son, your only son Isaac, whom you love." Do you hear the buildup? Abraham is not just to take his son but his only son. And not just his only son but the son he loves, the son who will mean even more to him when this episode is ended. "And go to the land of Moriah, and offer him there as a burnt offering" (Gen 22:2). Of course God is accomplishing other things as well, but this is, I believe, an important aspect that is often overlooked.

The importance of love in family relationships continues to be built up in Isaac until he marries Rebekah, and he loves her (Gen 24:67). Remember that Isaac's wedding is arranged for him in contrast to Isaac's son, Jacob, who chooses his own wife on the basis of what he has seen to be so important in his parents' relationship—love. So Jacob endures seven years of labor under Laban so he can marry the girl he loves—Rachel. (And then seven more on top of that after Laban tricks him into marrying Leah first.) Jacob has an emotion in his breast that few others had expressed, an emotion that God has placed in him.[3]

Joseph, Jacob's son, is the result of the family that God has worked in. After four generations Joseph understands the purity of marriage. The biblical pattern is that sin follows to the third generation. It may also take about three generations to develop solid, godly family relationships. Does it happen in a day? Sometimes we think a marriage can become ideal within a few weeks or months. But it's not so. We are dealing with a basic institution that belongs to God and comes from God. He is building it into a means of communicating his personality to those around us.

A fourth principle we can draw from Genesis is what I call *the maintenance of a name*, the continuation of a family, its lineage. These chapters are full of negative examples. First, Lot's daughters decided to commit incest with their father "that we may preserve offspring through our father" (19:32). They bear sons who are the fathers of the Moabite and Ammonite nations, both of whom later lead Israel into idolatry (Num 25:1-5; 1 Kings 11:5) and harrass Israel throughout the Old Testament period. All of this originates with a case of incest. Another example is the rape of Dinah, Jacob's daughter, which is avenged by the massacre of the offending family (Gen 34:1-34). In yet another case Onan refuses to fulfill his duty to carry on his brother's name and so is put to death (38:8-9). Then Judah, Onan's father, goes to a prostitute only to find out it is his daughter-in-law, Tamar. God does not condemn all these, but neither does he sanction them. He allows the norms of the culture to work themselves through. Yet he also allows the contrasting examples to flourish. The line of Abraham, Isaac, Jacob and Joseph, conceived and nurtured in love and fidelity, is preserved and used by God to proclaim his true character.

The fifth and final principle from Genesis regarding families is *the importance of sibling relationships*. As with maintaining a lineage, we find negative examples—Isaac versus Ishmael and Jacob versus Esau. Even in the fourth generation Joseph's brothers are jealous and sell him into slavery after plotting to kill him. But God has finally broken through in the life of Joseph. He does not hold a grudge against his brothers but seeks to preserve them—and even to reunite the whole family under his care and protection in Egypt. Family ties are not to be broken. Through the years God built the family, allowing variations and sinfulness to run their courses, but never changing the ultimate purpose he had in mind. Cultures might change, but God's Word does not.

The Family Today

The importance of these principles will be seen much more clearly in chapters nine and ten when I discuss two of the key communication networks in our urbanized world—kinship and ethnicity. But allow me to draw a few preliminary conclusions about how the teaching of the book of Genesis on the family affects our witness. As the church, we are to witness to the world in light of the fact that we have a redeemed kinship and a redeemed volunteer association that all can come into if they will submit themselves to the person of Jesus Christ. God communicates himself through redeemed family relationships. The world should see our redeemed relationships, begin to admire them and say they want the same. Our response? "You can have the same if you will submit yourself to Jesus Christ."

Marriage then is a process of glorifying God; dating is a testing of that process and can glorify God as well. A vital part of our dating patterns should be witness as couples. In double-dating with an unsaved couple, for example, you can better express the fullness of God's personality than by a one-on-one friendship alone. Remember, "God created man in his own image, in the image of God he created him; male and female he created them. . . . 'It is not good that the man should be alone' " (Gen 1:27; 2:18). It is not what we as individuals do so much as how we relate to other people within the body. We witness through the two basic relationships: marriage and the family of God (the church).

If you are single, one way you might develop a witness is in partnership with a Christian family near you. For example, I have seen many families do what individuals could never do on campus. A dormitory dining hall is chaos. Trying to witness in that context is quite a challenge. But invite that same friend into the living room of a friendly Christian family, and you see how different it is. Many Christian families would be glad to have you use their homes as bases for evangelism. You invite your friends to meet a family you know, have them set you up with Coke and cookies, drift out and then let you use the living room. How quickly the conversation will turn. Let your friends see how this Christian family loves each other and loves you, and how you love them. Your friends may well learn to want to be part of that.

If you are from a Christian home, understand its importance in your witness. You are a product of that family. Take your friends home for a weekend and let them see that family. Let them be amazed. We do not realize the gift that we have in Christian homes. After we had been in Reading, Pennsylvania, just eight months, four people on the block asked us, "What is so different about your family?" The doors for witness were wide open.

God's Time Frame and Ours

Let me conclude this chapter by discussing one important principle in crosscultural witness: *God's time frame is not our time frame.* Satan has tried to have a strong influence in every culture, sometimes with more success than others. So when people become Christians within a culture, they may find that most of what they are doing is at odds with where God is going. One of the common mistakes that missionaries made in the colonial era was to encourage them to change immediately from their cultural patterns to Christian patterns of life. Condemning polygamy, for example, can destroy the family rather than build it as God intends. It can create divorcées who are forced into prostitution as their only form of livelihood. Too often missionaries have cut into a culture with a fixed value system, calling all people to that value system. But God is saying, "I'm going to meet all individuals where they are and begin to work a regenerative process within their lives. And it may take four generations to complete the regeneration as it did with the patriarchs." What missionaries are now learning and applying, we must also apply in other crosscultural ministries.

When Beth (not her real name) was sixteen, she had her first child. By the time she was twenty she had had three children by two different men. She had dropped out of high school. She never went anywhere. Her whole life was messed up. Then she met an African-American pastor in Philadelphia who met her where she was and introduced her to the power of the gospel.

But now what? She is on welfare; she has no education; she has three children with no husband; she's living with a man; she's in a Philadelphia Housing Authority house that is a mess; she's living in a neighborhood where her daughter will be pregnant (by force or otherwise) before she is fourteen. That's the nature of the neighborhood. Beth has to have a man in the house if she is going to have protection. That's the nature of the neighborhood too. She's been redeemed. She's been regenerated. But what do you do? Where do you start?

I know what I would like to do—snatch her and her lovely children right out of that nasty environment and put her out in some good, clean place. But reality says you cannot operate that way. So I asked Beth, "Where do you think God is taking you?" It was amazing how God's Spirit gave her insight light years beyond where one would expect.

She put together the following plan. "My daughter is now eleven. Within two years I have got to get her out of this neighborhood. I have no education and no money. But if I get one year of education and take a practical nurse's course, I can get a job that can provide me with enough extra income to put my daughter in a Christian school. There she can get an education and meet friends during the day which will help her learn to live by Christian values during off hours. Then if I continue my education, I can become an R.N. and get a better job which will get me enough money to get all of us out of here in four years."

I met Beth when she was halfway through her four-year plan. But it was my hope that she would not have to stay there for the remaining two years. So together we approached the housing authority about getting her into a better neighborhood. My strategy with the city was to say to them, "In the two years since Beth has become a Christian, her lifestyle has significantly changed. She has completed high school and her nursing course while keeping a full-time job. She has gotten her daughter into a Christian school. In two years she has begun to do everything that she hadn't done in the past ten. So it's obvious that here is a woman who has been turned around. Would you respond by getting her better housing?"

Three months and twenty-seven levels of administration later, I finally worked my way through to the woman at the top who said, "No. We won't move her." That looked like the end of the road. But we went back to the church community and said, "You've got to provide housing for this woman. It means that some of you are going to have to sacrifice to put up the money to get a mortgage. But it's the only way we are going to get her out of there." The church responded and bought her a house in Germantown despite the fact that she was, as we would say, living in sin. They recognized that God was doing a work in her and were content to let him continue at his own pace.

As it turns out, of course, Beth was struggling with her living situation at the same time. She had been talking to me a little, knowing that I was a white from suburbia with certain values. "The Bible says that I shouldn't be living with Lou, since I'm not married to him; however, if I don't live with him, I'm in trouble. If Lou moves out, anybody and everybody on the streets would move in. I would be raped every night. His being here is a kind of protection."

I responded by saying, "Look, if the Holy Spirit tells you to do something, you do it."

I also got to know Lou. He started sharing with me his dilemma of marrying. Now that she had become, in his words, a church woman, he shouldn't be living in the house with her. But he knew she needed the protection too. So I said, "Look, that's not my business. If she wants you out, she'll tell you."

A couple of years later I met her pastor and asked about Beth and Lou. "You know," he said, "he's coming around. He's going to be a Christian soon. They'll probably end up getting married."

God has a whole different set of values and a whole different time frame from you and me. He's going to fully regenerate both of them. If we had approached that situation from our moralistic stance of what is right and what is wrong, we would have interfered in God's plan for that family. A book like Genesis can help us gain God's long-range plan for the family, so we can work in concert with him to regenerate what is fallen.

3

The Impact
of a Minority:
Daniel

▼▼▼▼▼▼▼▼▼▼▼▼▼▼▼▼

GOD'S PROMISE TO ABRAHAM WAS THAT THROUGH HIS FAMILY ALL NATIONS
would be blessed (Gen 22:18). With Joseph we see the beginning of the
fulfillment of this promise. Egypt was saved from drought and famine
through Abraham's family. During the next four hundred years the Egyptian
people were brought into an understanding of the sovereign God through the
Hebrew people. As the nation left Egypt and went on to conquer the Promised
Land, the battles they fought were a witness to all nations of God's power.

During the period described in the books of Joshua and Judges, Israel
struggled to establish itself in the land. But a problem arose. While God had
ordained that the people of God should in time become the kingdom of God,
the Israelites had decided that they wanted to become the kingdom of Israel.
In the days of Samuel they started saying, "We want a king." God was
opposed to the idea. He was to be their king. But the people continued to
make the demand. "We want a dynasty. We want a human institution that
we can look to, to be proud of, to make us secure." God knew the problems
they would face if they followed this path. But as he often does, God

allowed his people to make their own choices. And in the process, he still made them into the people of his choosing.

He began by offering them Saul—their choice—who turned out to be a failure. Saul possessed virtually no religious discernment. He did not know the prophet Samuel existed until Saul's own servant told him. And even then Saul did not seek him out for religious reasons but because he thought Samuel might have some magical power to help him find his lost donkeys (1 Sam 9:5-10). In contrast God then offered the people David—his choice—who was a great success. God took an obscure shepherd with nothing to commend him and made him into a true king and a man after his own heart.

Out of David's kingdom came Solomon. And after that, God no longer was king. The people said, "The king is our ruler." For the next four hundred years God fought with the Old Testament people to recognize God as their king. But they would not. They came to the point of believing that they could not be destroyed. They were God's people and this was God's land, so they could not be beaten. From the time of Adam, the people of God had not been finally defeated. They had come to see themselves as culturally superior instead of as the people of God. God finally had to destroy his own temple and his own people to make the whole world aware of who he truly was.

We come, then, to the book of Daniel, with Judah in exile in Babylon. Daniel is probably one of the most abused books in the Bible. Many simply ignore it, choosing to focus on how God brought Israel back out of exile and missing what he did in it. Others see Daniel as a string of fascinating Sunday-school stories about praying hard and not being burned up or eaten by lions. Still others allegorize the book out of history or see it solely as a prophecy of the future. We fail to see its plain significance: the story of God's people in Babylon and of how God wants to reveal himself to the world.

Each of the first six chapters of Daniel is a separate story with a final concluding paragraph. Rather than concentrating on the stories, however, I will focus on these final verses which give us the thread of continuity through the book.

Daniel Stands Out

The first chapter tells of the conquest of Judah and of how a few of the people were brought to Babylon. Among them, Daniel was recognized as a leader. He and a few of his countrymen were given some special training by the Babylonians. In Daniel 1:20 we read this: "And in every matter of wisdom and understanding concerning which the king inquired of them, he found them ten times better than all the magicians and enchanters that were in all his kingdom." The king recognized that Daniel and his friends were exceptionally bright. Why do you suppose this was so?

In the wilderness God had given his people a system of law. When the law was obeyed and the people followed their God, they had inside information on truth—on science, on social institutions, on psychology. The Israelites were not a bunch of ignorant nomads. A powerful military king conquered the nation of Israel and brought the best of the defeated people back. But in every matter of wisdom and understanding the king found them ten times better than the best of Babylon. Why? Daniel was simply being obedient to his culture, the culture that God had given him. In other words, he had developed a biblical way of life. Daniel did not make the same mistake his countrymen had. He did not credit himself or his culture with superiority. He credited God. We too must be careful not to confuse the two.

Daniel's God

Daniel 2 is the story of Nebuchadnezzar's dream of a statue which Daniel interpreted. The king's response is in the last paragraph.

> Then King Nebuchadnezzar fell upon his face, and did homage to Daniel, and commanded that an offering and incense be offered up to him. The king said to Daniel, "Truly, your God is God of gods and Lord of kings, and a revealer of mysteries, for you have been able to reveal this mystery." Then the king gave Daniel high honors and many great gifts, and made him ruler over the whole province of Babylon, and chief prefect over all the wise men of Babylon. Daniel made request of the king, and he appointed Shadrach, Meshach, and Abednego over the affairs of the province of Babylon; but Daniel remained at the king's court. (2:46-49)

In chapter 1 he saw Daniel as a superior man. Now he had seen why Daniel was superior—because he had a God that is superior. We should not read too much into this chapter. The king was not yet following God. Nonetheless, God was at work. The king had recognized that Daniel's God was good for Daniel. So he made Daniel a leader.

The third chapter of Daniel explains why we should not read too much into the second chapter. For here we read the story of Nebuchadnezzar ordering everyone to worship the huge gold statue he has made of himself. While he agreed that Daniel's God was a great God, he still saw himself as greater because, after all, he had destroyed the nation of Daniel's God. Anyone who would not worship the statue would be thrown into the fiery furnace. God, however, takes this opportunity to reestablish his claim as the God of the whole earth—despite what people might think because of the destruction of Judah—and, as he had promised to Abraham, to proclaim his sovereignty to all peoples.

As soon as Nebuchadnezzar made his proclamation, what happened?

Therefore at that time certain Chaldeans came forward and maliciously accused the Jews. They said to King Nebuchadnezzar, . . . "There are certain Jews whom you have appointed over the affairs of the province of Babylon: Shadrach, Meshach, and Abednego. These men, O king, pay no heed to you; they do not serve your gods or worship the golden image which you have set up." (3:8-9, 12)

The Jews had begun to rise to power, and the Chaldeans became jealous. It was like any political conflict. If you are on top, people are going to take pot shots at you whether you have done anything wrong or not because they do not want you on top. They want to be on top. Here, however, was a real opportunity for the Chaldeans to make some gains on these upstart Jews. They were ignoring a direct command of the king.

As we know, they were thrown into the furnace but were saved by God. As a result Nebuchadnezzar made another decree recorded at the end of the chapter. "Therefore I make a decree: Any people, nation, or language that speaks anything against the God of Shadrach, Meshach, and Abednego shall be torn limb from limb, and their houses laid in ruins; for there is no other god who is able to deliver in this way" (3:29). That decree went out to every people, nation or language. Abraham was called from among the nations to be a witness to the nations. The people had failed to do this; so God said, "If you won't speak to the nations from Jerusalem, you'll do it from Babylon."

Put yourself in the position of a Jew in Babylon—captured, abused, your land lost, sent some place to work in slavery. All of a sudden the word comes through: The God of the Jews is a powerful God. Anyone who says anything against this God will be torn to pieces. What do the Babylonians do? They turn to the nearest Jew and say, "You'd better tell me everything you can about your God. I don't want to say anything against him—even by mistake! And I don't want you to go around to some of your government friends and say, 'Listen, I think I heard so-and-so say something against my God.' " So instantaneously the Jews, scattered throughout the Babylonian Empire, are conferred with tremendous political power.

Something else happens as well. It quickly becomes apparent who among the Jews really knows God and knows the law. Those who had been disobedient, who had not learned the law but had been the fat cows of Bashan enjoying their riches up on the hill are suddenly nothing. But those who do know the law, who had gone to the temple school and could teach the law to the people begin to gain some power and prestige in the land. Through this decree God is calling out for himself a people—those who know the law.

Critics have disregarded this decree, claiming that it could not have been implemented. Why? Because the Jews were insignificant at the time. The whole point of the book of Daniel thus far has been the exact opposite—the Jews had grown in power. It would in fact be Jews at the top of the government who would implement the edict.

What about at the bottom of the ladder? Remember that Babylon was not a thriving industrial state of the twentieth century. As soon as you were outside the city, life deteriorated quickly. It would be like the remote villages of today's Third World. The real leaders are the small shopkeepers and teachers who read, write and occasionally visit the big city.

Once when I was in such a village in Kenya, I walked into a shop owned by an Indian. The shopkeeper was explaining to an African that the price of sugar suddenly went up because "your government just added a new transport tax." The Indian had just read this in the paper the day before and was interpreting the African's law to the African. What he did not choose to explain was that the tax would not be put into effect for two months and would not affect the price of sugar for four months—if at all!

There is evidence that long before the exile Jewish traders, educators, merchants and soldiers were not only in Babylon but also in India and China. "In a thousand and one ways the Jewish people were thrown into daily contact with their environs, and along with his goods the Jew frequently carried his religion."[1]

Nebuchadnezzar's God

Nebuchadnezzar had come a long way toward God since chapter 1. But notice that his edict in 3:29 is stated negatively: punishment was to be meted out only to those who spoke against God. People were not required to worship God. And not till Daniel 4 do we have any indication that the king himself finally bowed to Yahweh.

The writer in chapter 4 seems so excited that he has to give the end at the beginning:

King Nebuchadnezzar to all peoples, nations, and languages, that dwell in all the earth: Peace be multiplied to you! It has seemed good to me to show the signs and wonders that the Most High God has wrought toward me. How great are his signs, how mighty his wonders! His kingdom is an everlasting kingdom, and his dominion is from generation to generation. (4:1-3)

Then Nebuchadnezzar proceeds to tell the story of how he was reduced to madness and then returned to his throne by God. In the last verse he concludes, "Now I, Nebuchadnezzar, praise and extol and honor the King of heaven; for all his works are right and his ways are just; and those who walk in pride he is able to abase" (4:37).

The most powerful king of one of the most powerful kingdoms that has ever ruled the earth sent out a decree that everybody should recognize that he, the king, bows to the Lord God Jehovah. A pagan emperor suddenly did what the Hebrews themselves did not: he proclaimed to all nations that God is Lord. The kings of Israel and Judah did not do anything like this king of Babylon. The sovereign God had acted and put his man on the throne. Right under him were men who also worshiped Yahweh. The influence of the Jews was enhanced still further.

This, I feel, also helps explain why the people came out of the exile as monotheists. Before they had played the harlot with any number of gods. Afterward idolatry was no longer a problem for Israel. Synagogues started to pop up all over Babylon, Africa and Asia.[2] Again, in contrast to critics, it is unlikely that a defeated, insignificant minority group could have come out of the exile in such a strong position if the kind of transformation described in Daniel did not occur.

An Upstart King

Years pass, perhaps twenty or thirty, during which much of the kingdom has been ruled by Jews. But the author skips all this. Eventually Nabonidus becomes king of Babylon. He is away from the capital on a military campaign against the invading Persians. He has placed his son, Belshazzar, on the throne to rule in his absence on a limited basis. (Although Daniel 5:2 calls Nebuchadnezzar Belshazzar's father, this is probably a general term indicating that Belshazzar was descended from or related to Nebuchadnezzar.) Belshazzar is a young Turk who is a little fed up with all the Jewishness in the country.

The author lands us in Daniel 5 with Belshazzar's feast. It is the end of the empire, seventy years after the destruction of Jerusalem. The historical record is unclear, but we can piece together a probable scenario.

Belshazzar throws a party for all his young friends in the royal household and during the evening asks that the "vessels of gold and of silver which Nebuchadnezzar his father had taken out of the temple in Jerusalem be brought, that the king and his lords, his wives, and his concubines might drink from them" (5:2). He thus abuses these sacred treasures and mocks the decree of Nebuchadnezzar years ago that Yahweh be respected. "They drank wine, and praised the gods of gold and silver, bronze, iron, wood, and stone" (5:4). But on the wall a hand appears that starts writing, and he realizes that this god does not play games (5:5-9). In verse 10 Belshazzar's mother, the queen, enters. She has not been at the banquet (and as we shall see, neither has Daniel) because this is a party for the new breed of rulers. But she approaches her son, the king, respectfully, "O king, live for ever! ... Let Daniel be called, and he will show the interpretation" (5:10, 12).

Daniel is brought in. His approach is quite different from the queen mother's. "Let your gifts be for yourself, and give your rewards to another" (5:17). Is that a way to talk to a king? The picture painted here is of a young, frightened king facing a senior statesman, a retired prime minister, who has had a lot of power in Babylon. Daniel, in fact, still has enough authority and influence and commitment to God to rebuke this upstart king for abusing Yahweh. Belshazzar reverses direction and a "proclamation was made concerning [Daniel], that he should be the third ruler in the kingdom" (5:29). (Belshazzar is only the second ruler.) But it is too late. "That very night Belshazzar the Chaldean king was slain" (5:30). In other words, the proclamation never got out of the room. Why? What happened? The next verse tells us merely that "Darius the Mede received the kingdom, being about sixty-two years old" (5:31).

We can try to piece together what happened. Darius, probably a key general in the army of Cyrus the Persian,[3] had been moving across the plains and had encountered Nabonidus and defeated him. Nabonidus then backed off into a walled city. Darius saw that it would take months to complete the seige and finish off Nabonidus. By that time the people in the capital city would have heard about the defeat of Belshazzar's father. So thinking that surprise was more important than strength, Darius left part of his army to guard Nabonidus and raced across the plains with the rest of his army to the city of Babylon.

History records that the city fell with no resistance or by a surprise attack on the palace, meeting with little resistance.[4] Either case suggests the use of spies which Darius probably had planted months before. He had learned, no doubt, of the strategic role of the Jewish community scattered throughout the empire. He knew the Jews had a major influence on Babylon's economy. He knew Daniel was their leader. If he did not win Daniel over, the Jews might turn against him, and his control would be gone. He might have approached Daniel prior to the takeover. Daniel's response? "Belshazzar isn't helping us one bit; in fact, he's against us. If you can guarantee us the same kind of religious and economic and political freedom we had under Nebuchadnezzar, I am willing to help you overthrow the kingdom." Even if Daniel had not been approached beforehand, he certainly was as soon as the kingdom fell. How do we know? Because it was standard procedure to take the heads off of every leader when you conquered a city. That's what happened to Belshazzar. Daniel was not killed, however, because he was needed. Otherwise it would have been a perfect time for a counterrevolution by the nation of Israel, with a return to Palestine.

When a general, weakened in battle, has taken over a large kingdom, if there is a second people, a fifth column, inside who counterattack, they can easily obtain their freedom. Darius was a shrewd man. He had been commissioned by Cyrus to put the new government on its feet. He counteracted the possibility of counterrevolution by making Daniel one of the most important leaders of his kingdom (6: 2-3). This alone gives some indication of the extent of the power that Daniel had in that nation and the kind of control that the Jewish people had.

The pattern of Daniel 6 is the same as Daniel 3; only the names have changed. The Persian leaders, jealous of Daniel's power, set a trap for him, forcing him to disobey an edict of Darius which gets Daniel thrown into a den of lions. God rescues Daniel, and

> then King Darius wrote to all the peoples, nations, and languages that dwell in all the earth: "Peace be multiplied to you. I make a decree, that in all my royal dominion men tremble and fear before the God of Daniel, for he is the living God, enduring for ever; his kingdom shall never be

destroyed, and his dominion shall be to the end." (6:25-26)
God was getting a lot more mileage out of these pagan kings than he did out
of his own.

Two Models of Salt and Light

What does Daniel mean to us? God has always been a universal God. His
people are present throughout the world. They always have been. Abraham
wandered around from Mesopotamia to Egypt. He was just one man, but
through him the word about God got out to all people. The Jewish people
wandered around and did amazing things. Their reputation and God's reputation went out to all people. When they ceased doing that, God changed
tactics and scattered them forceably. Through Daniel and other exiles word
about God spread to all people.

I get a little troubled when people ask, "What happens to the heathen who
don't hear?" While God may be using you and me to bring his word to a
specific people, he has not abandoned the rest. God has used some unique
ways many times in history to make sure that people can have access to him.
People have always been found guilty of rejecting God because God has not
withheld his word from them. It is harder for some people to get at it than for
others. Nonetheless, God's word has always been universal (Rom 1:18-19).

Second, even today the Jewish nation is reflecting a way of life that they
learned in Babylon. Since the time of Daniel, there has hardly been a nation
on the earth that has not had a handful of Jews that worked their way into the
economic and political superstructures of that nation and controlled it to the
point that some rulers persecuted them.

Some may question how much power the Jews have had because of a lack
of archaeological evidence. But archaeology rarely tells us anything about a
minority people living within foreign boundaries. If the whole of America
should collapse today and a thousand years from now people come and look
at our buildings or read our history books, would they learn much about the
thirty million African-Americans living in our country? Not as much as they
should. Much of it is unrecorded. Or would they know the true significance
of even the Jewish people who exist within our boundaries? We build
buildings that manifest our own culture. So obviously, people would get the
impression that mostly white, Anglo-Saxon Protestants lived in this country.
When you go back to the Babylonian Empire, you will not find the archaeological traces of the power of Daniel. But there are the other traces that I

have mentioned in this chapter. The Jews have always had power beyond their numbers because they learned a style of life that was taught to them by God. And we should learn from them.

Jeremiah has an interesting prophecy which reads,

> Thus says the LORD of hosts, the God of Israel, to all the exiles whom I have sent into exile from Jerusalem to Babylon: Build houses and live in them; plant gardens and eat their produce. Take wives and have sons and daughters; take wives for your sons, and give your daughters in marriage, that they may bear sons and daughters; multiply there, and do not decrease. But seek the welfare of the city where I have sent you into exile, and pray to the LORD on its behalf, for in its welfare you will find your welfare. (Jer 29:4-7)

That is the kind of people we should be—spreading all over the world and working our ways into the economic and political structures of every kind of nation and capturing it for Jesus Christ. Not necessarily by becoming the prime minister, but by just being there and having influence. The Jewish model today is still the model that we should follow.

Another equally valid model is that of the Blacks. The Black migrant people cover the entire Atlantic seacoast, from Brazil and Argentina to Jamaica and Nova Scotia, from Iberia to South Africa. They are a people that for over three hundred years have been shifting and drifting around the earth, learning to live as a visible minority in a hostile environment. We need to learn from them what it means to be salt, what it means to hang on when the world is against you. The existence of the African-American community against tremendous persecution for over three hundred years and the existence of the Jewish community against tremendous persecution for over two thousand years should teach us something about the kind of life to which Jesus Christ is calling us.

4

The Center
of History:
Jesus Christ

▼▼▼▼▼▼▼▼▼▼▼▼▼▼

WHEN THE KINGS OF ISRAEL AND JUDAH, WHOM GOD HAD ESTABLISHED, lost sight of the fact that God's message is to all people, God laid them aside. He then reestablished himself and the revelation of himself to the world through the Babylonian Empire. It was not the structure, however, that was important but the people—God's people—who were to go out to all nations. Indeed, the structure of the kingdom of Israel proved to be an impediment which God removed.

In place of the Israelite kings God began to use people we would not call "committed Christians" to spread his name. As noted in the last chapter, some of the Jews carrying that message were probably cynical. Some must have been embarrassed when others came to them and said, "Hey! The king says I better not offend your God. Tell me about him." They might have scratched their heads and thought, "Well, I should have paid more attention in temple school. I really don't know very much about my own God. But I know a few things." They at least knew enough to say that the Lord God is One; the Lord God is righteous; and the Lord God must be worshiped. This was not the whole message of redemption. But it was what we could call preevangelism. It was preparing the whole world to receive the message of redemption, to receive the Messiah himself.

Prepare the Way

Another group of unlikely missionaries, as we also began to see in chapter three, completed the preparation. To look at this group more closely, let's first go back and consider in more detail the second chapter of Daniel.

Nebuchadnezzar had a vision of a giant with a gold head, a silver breast and arms, a brass midsection and iron legs with feet that were iron mixed with clay. Daniel then interpreted this dream. "You, O king, the king of kings, to whom the God of heaven has given the kingdom, the power, and the might, and the glory, and into whose hand he has given, wherever they dwell, the sons of men, the beasts of the field, and the birds of the air, making you rule over them all—you are the head of gold" (2:37-38). Note that it says, "wherever they dwell . . . you rule." God's message went out to *all* people via Nebuchadnezzar. There was no question about the interpretation. Babylon was the head of gold. Then Daniel says,

> After you shall arise another kingdom inferior to you, and yet a third kingdom of bronze, which shall rule over all the earth. And there shall be a fourth kingdom, strong as iron. . . . Just as you saw . . . a stone was cut from a mountain by no human hand, and that it broke in pieces the iron, the bronze, the clay, the silver, and the gold: A great God has made known to the king what shall be hereafter. (2:39-40, 45)

This vision of the statue is about four kingdoms which will ultimately be destroyed when a stone carved without hands hits the feet and topples the whole structure. Then that stone will grow into a kingdom that "shall stand for ever" (2:44). After Babylon, the first kingdom, was the Medo-Persian Empire; following that was the Grecian Empire established by Alexander the Great; after that was the Roman Empire which was supplanted by the church of Jesus Christ—the Stone.

How was the stage set for Christ? First, as we saw in chapter three, Babylon was used by God to proclaim his word. Daniel was the prime minister of Babylon. Second, Daniel also became the prime minister of the Medo-Persian Empire. This pattern continued with Ezra and Nehemiah, both high officers in the Persian government, who solicited and received help from the Empire to rebuild the walls and the temple of Jerusalem.

In the book of Esther we also see how God preserved his people despite the plotting of Haman, a jealous rival of the powerful Jews in Persia. In the end Haman hangs from the gallows, a Jew is queen (Esther), a Jew is prime minister (Mordecai) and all the Jews are getting special privileges from the king.

Not only the Persian Empire, but the Greek Empire begun by Alexander continued this practice of granting the Jews within their borders special rights. DeRidder writes,

> The Greek world also granted a special status to the Jew, although (1) this was not uniform and the extent of the Jews' rights depended on when, how and for what purpose they came to a given community outside Palestine, (2) the organized Jewish community as a whole stood juridically outside the Greek city and the Jews who lived in it had no civil rights there, (3) isolated Jews could acquire civil rights individually. The focus of Jewish life in the Diaspora must be found in the privileges of the Jewish communities, not in citizen rights in Greek towns.[1]

Rome was purely and simply iron, a military force covering the earth that had no ultimate commitment to a religious system. Consequently, it was perfectly all right for Jews to continue the process which was begun in Babylon.

> In 161 B.C. the Jews had received the status of *peregrini* in the Roman Empire, enabling them to be judged by their own laws and follow their own customs in marriage and inheritance. In 110 B.C. this status was secured for Jews everywhere in all states and kingdoms controlled by or allied with Rome. . . . It was Julius Caesar who said that "Jews might live according to their Torah," implying two things: (1) recognition of the Torah as part of the public law of the Empire, and (2) acceptance of any Jewish community anywhere within the Empire as part of a single Jewish people. This was a unique concession.[2]

Nestled in the heart of every community across the Roman Empire was a small group of Jews who were highly missionary in their attitude—proselytizing people, establishing synagogues—out of which came the whole Hellenistic (that is, Greek-speaking) Jewish movement.

It has been estimated that at the time of Christ one-tenth of the Roman Empire was Jewish. Two and one-half million lived in Palestine, but possibly twice that number were scattered elsewhere. There were a hundred thousand Jews in Cyrenaica, a million in Egypt, a million in Mesopotamia, a million in Asia Minor and a hundred thousand Jews in Italy.[3] There were Jewish communities in China, India, Europe, Ethiopia and along trade routes that covered Africa south of the Sahara. These offered Christian apostles an open door into virtually every area of the world.

Thomas likely went to India. The Ethiopian eunuch went to his home in North Africa. Paul went to Asia, Macedonia, Greece and Rome. The Hellenists who heard the gospel on Pentecost split to the four corners of the earth. The church has been universal from the beginning.

The meaning of all this is clear. God said through Daniel that he intended to set up four kingdoms to prepare the world for Christ. By the time Rome was established, the situation was unique in history for the rapid spread of the gospel.

Rome had one language, one system of roads, one system of law maintaining peace under one huge army that had all people under its control. The roads of Rome went from the Himalayas to Spain and from Persia to the coast of North Africa. The speed with which the Roman soldiers were able to move was phenomenal. But the speed with which the gospel was able to move was more phenomenal.

God had prepared the world logistically to communicate his message further and more rapidly then than at any other previous time. And it was into the center of that Empire, the geographic center, Palestine, that God sent his Son.

Let us consider the factors in Christ's life that are important for our discussion of crosscultural ministry.

Christ the Message

Paul puts the first factor this way:

> He [God] has made known to us in all wisdom and insight the mystery of his will, according to his purpose which he set forth in Christ as a plan for the fulness of time, to unite all things in him, things in heaven and things on earth. In him, according to the purpose of him who accomplishes all things according to the counsel of his will, we who first hoped in Christ have been destined and appointed to live for the praise of his glory. (Eph 1:9-12)

That is what missions is all about. The messengers are those who glorify Jesus. Jesus himself did not come merely to communicate the message. He *is* the message.

We should be careful not to just analyze the life of Jesus Christ to find out how to do missions. He was not here primarily to teach us or merely to demonstrate how to present the message. He is the incarnation of the message of redemption. He came to restore the broken relationships we discussed in chapter two. He lived this message in each area.

First, he lived a fully harmonious relationship to his Father. He prayed regularly to his Father. He taught, "I and the Father are one. . . . If you had known me, you would have known my Father also; henceforth you know him and have seen him" (Jn 10:30; 14:7). His life and his death exemplified this unity with the Father which Adam broke. Christ was "obedient unto death" (Phil 2:8) despite his desire that it not be so.

Second, he lived a fully harmonious life in relationship to himself. Jesus Christ was not an ambivalent person. He did not have inner doubts or confusion. He spoke with authority (Mt 7:28-29; Mk 1:27). He had a tremendous singleness of purpose and certainty about his mission (Lk 4:16-21). He was here to do the will of his Father (Jn 5:19). He demonstrated what a redeemed life is like.

Third, Christ, through his relationship as Son to his Father, incarnates for us a living model of redeemed family relationships. He was the beloved Son in whom the Father was well pleased. He also demonstrated redemption in marriage, although he was never married, through his husbandlike relationship to the church.

In Ephesians Paul says, "Be subject to one another out of reverence for Christ" (5:21). The theme is Christian subjection of one to another. Paul goes on to say that there are two models for this: the church and marriage. "Be subject to one another out of reverence for Christ. Wives, be subject to your husbands [in marriage], as to the Lord [in the church]. For the husband is the head of the wife [in marriage] as Christ is the head of the church, his body, and is himself its Savior" (5:22-23). This pattern continues for the next several verses. We understand what marriage is all about because we have seen Christ's relationship to the church.[4]

Christ built a community based on reconciliation. He unified the oddest assortment of disciples that you could imagine—intellectuals, nonintellectuals, wealthy, poor. Matthew, the tax collector, was a reprobate. He had sold himself out to the Roman system. On the other side was Simon the Zealot, a guerrilla dedicated to the destruction of Rome, a man who not only hated the Romans but who hated every Jew who sold himself to the Roman system.

How did Simon the Zealot and Matthew the Traitor come together and form a community? Certainly there was conflict between them. Jesus Christ demonstrated the redemption of community by building reconciliation that superseded individual wants and concerns. Marriage is also a community based on reconciliation. It does not accuse ("that woman you gave me") but forgives and binds together in love (Gen 4:1).

Finally, Christ lived in harmony and had dominion over his environment. The miracles proved that he had rule over disease (Mk 1:31-34), over nature (Mk 4:35-41) and even over death (Jn 11:1-44). He did not have to hurry from one sick person to another, afraid he would not make it in time to do any good (Lk 8:40-56). He had dominion over the world around him. We hear a tremendous amount from psychology about the effect and even the control that environment has on people. But Jesus Christ has redeemed us in such a way that we do not *have* to be controlled by our environment.

In summary, the first factor in Christ's life with important implications for crosscultural ministry is the way he lived the message of redemption. We too are called not merely to tell others about the gospel but to live it before them as well. We are to live in harmony with God, with ourselves, with others and with our environment.

A Cosmic Cultural Barrier

Another factor important to crosscultural ministry is the Incarnation, the full humanity which Christ took on. Paul writes, "Christ Jesus, . . . though he was in the form of God, did not count equality with God a thing to be grasped, but emptied himself, taking the form of a servant, being born in the likeness of men" (Phil 2:5-7). Jesus is fully God. Yet he chose to set aside the cloak of deity and become fully human. He crossed a cosmic cultural barrier. He identified totally with those he came to minister to and left behind his divine heritage.

Jesus chose willingly to accept the limitations of his adopted culture. Under Roman rule, his family was forced by the government to leave their home to go pay taxes in Bethlehem, where he was born. A mad king wanted to kill him, so once more the family was uprooted, and he was carried as an infant to Africa where he spent the first years of his life. Later, they moved back to a small area of Palestine where Jesus became a village carpenter, a role of low social standing. He was of a royal line, but his family was quite poor.

We are often concerned about the limitations a culture might place on us—fewer Christians to gain support from, fewer Christian books in the native language, less money, fewer physical comforts, greater governmental restrictions. Christ accepted all these limitations and more.

Why should the King of Glory reject all his power and wealth? Why should he accept restrictions of time, space, humanness and culture? Why shouldn't he openly proclaim himself as God and present the simple truth of salvation? To answer these questions let us first look at the temptations of Christ in the desert.

Jesus has been fasting for forty days and is hungry. So the Tempter comes along with the first temptation and says, "If you are the Son of God, command these stones to become loaves of bread." Satan challenges Jesus' divinity. "If you are the Son of God, then prove it by doing a miracle. Turn these rocks into bread. Show us you've got divine power." But Jesus refuses and answers, "It is written, 'Man shall not live by bread alone, but by every word that proceeds from the mouth of God' " (Mt 4:3-4). Notice, "*man* shall not live by bread alone." He does not appeal to any powers or abilities beyond the accepted limitations of humanity.

Again Satan tempts Jesus to perform (almost like a circus high-dive act) another miracle: "Throw yourself down from the top of the temple and let the angels catch you." Once more Jesus could have drawn on any resource to combat Satan, but he stayed within the bounds of what is available to us. "The Scripture says we are not to tempt God. We are not to try to make him perform miracles like a trained animal to increase our faith."

Lastly Satan decides to match his great power and wealth against that of a seemingly destitute God. "I will give you all the kingdoms of the earth if you will worship me." Satan says he will give these to us as well if we will give him the one thing he requires. Jesus rebukes Satan as we can, without an appeal to divine power. "It is written, 'You shall worship the Lord your God and him only shall you serve' " (Mt 4:10).

This also offers us hope as we cross cultures. We can accept what may seem to be tremendous limitations from other cultures and still live a life of full obedience to God. As I said earlier, Christ was not controlled by his environment. He willingly submitted to certain restrictions and yet overcame them to accomplish his mission. If the limitations are human, we too can supersede them as humans. "For as by a man came death, by a man has come also the resurrection of the dead. For as in Adam all die, so also in Christ shall all be made alive" (1 Cor 15:21-22). Through Jesus' conquest of sin and death, we too can be conquerors in life.

Beyond Human Limits

Not only *can* we take part in Christ's victory, it is God's plan from eternity that we should. As I quoted Ephesians 1 earlier, God intends to unite all things in Christ. How? "In him [Christ], according to the purpose of him [God] who accomplishes all things according to the counsel of his will, we who first hoped in Christ have been destined and appointed to live for the praise of his glory" (Eph 1:11-12). God plans to fulfill his plan through us! As Paul writes later in the book, "The plan . . . [is] that through the church the manifold wisdom of God might now be made known" (Eph 3:9-10).

This is why I believe that Christ did not come primarily as an evangelist. If he had, he certainly would not have passed by all the people he did, and he would have presented a much more straightforward message. Unlike many Jews he did not make proselytes and bring people into a Jewish setting. Instead, he came to reveal the kingdom of God, to build a community. He developed a small group of people who lived with him and ate with him and talked with him. Even in the upper room (Jn 14) he was still teaching them, and they still did not understand. But he would not give up on them despite this, despite the betrayal of one of the inner circle and despite his impending death.

Eventually, it became necessary for Jesus to return to his Father so his church remaining here on earth could fulfill its task. Jesus did this in order to send the Spirit to take up residence in all his followers. Now in and through us he is able to be young and old, rich and poor, educated and uneducated, black, yellow, red and white. As a body, we now can overcome all limitations of time, space, humanness and culture. Let us live to the praise of his glory.

5
Reaching an Oppressed and Open People: John 4

▼▼▼▼▼▼▼▼▼▼▼▼▼▼▼

AFRICANS ARE ESSENTIALLY A PROVERBIAL PEOPLE, A PEOPLE WHO TALK IN proverbs. So the Scripture often means much more to them than to us because even Jesus Christ taught in proverbs. When I was a missionary in Africa, the Africans pointed out to me that anybody who teaches in proverbs also talks in proverbs. Proverbs in Scripture are found not only in the specific parables that Jesus taught but also in the way Scripture itself is put together.

People who think in proverbs or parables often view history differently than we do. We think history is this event and that event strung like beads on the string of time. But all historians know that mere chronology is not history. Our opinions, our biases, our humanness skew or distort history.

Africans recognize from the beginning that history embodies truths which are far more important than the mere recording of facts. They also know that stories convey meaning in life-giving ways that far exceeds a list of principles. It surprised me how much truth in Scripture is conveyed in just this way. The story of the Samaritan woman in John 4 is one such story. It is truth about life embedded in history.

The key to understanding John 4 is parallel thinking. A parable begins with two lines of parallel thought. For example, we might start talking about the consequences of overconfidence and tell the story of the tortoise and the hare. Immediately, people are transferring the story into their real experience as it is being told. At the end, of course, the storyteller will explicitly tie the two together and make an application. "Like the hare, you could lose the football game tomorrow if you are overconfident." John 4 is, of course, more complex than that, but the principle holds.

Through the Ghetto

As the chapter opens, Jesus is in Judea, antagonizing the Pharisees because of his success in making disciples. He knows his time has not yet come, so he decides to go north to Galilee and let things around Jerusalem cool off for a while. The quickest way to Galilee from Judea was through Samaria. But most Jews insisted on making the trip by going the long way around the east side of the Dead Sea. They felt Samaritans were semipagan, semicivilized half-breeds. They would make themselves religiously unclean if they had anything to do with these people. And besides that—it was dangerous!

Samaria was like a ghetto. No one likes to go through someone else's ghetto. It makes us uncomfortable because the people there are different—not worse, just different. We develop myths about the ghetto to justify our actions. "Everybody that goes there gets mugged." The Jews had created the same myth about Samaria because, being cultural beings like ourselves, they did not like to be someplace that is culturally different. This is a form of ethnocentricity, the belief that your people are the good people—the best people—and no one else matches up.

Jesus, however, "had to pass through Samaria" (4:4). Now the heat might have been on from the Pharisees, and he had to get out of town as quickly as possible. But Jesus also had to be consistent with truth. If he had accepted the ethnocentricity that rejected the Samaritans, he would not be consistent with who he was. It was indeed necessary for him to go the direct route, right through the heart of Samaria.

He came to a town in Samaria called Sychar with a well and a field that once belonged to the patriarch Jacob who later gave them to Joseph's family (4:5; see Josh 24:32). We have a true story in a historical context about a real place. It reminds us that the Samaritans and the Jews have a common past. They both claimed Jacob as their father. There is a basis here for communication. This fact is ignored by the Jews, but not by the narrator.

In verse 6 we are told that "Jesus, wearied as he was with his journey, sat down beside the well." Perhaps Jesus wanted to test his disciples, so he said, "I'm tired and want to rest awhile. Why don't you get us something to eat in town?" Or it might have been that Jesus said, "We're all tired; let's sit down," but the disciples responded, "No, we're not too tired. We think we'll check out the town." In either case, they probably had the wrong attitude. It may have been necessary for Jesus to go through Samaria, but it wasn't for them.

The Well and the Town

This is where the two parallel lines begin. "There came a woman of Samaria to draw water. Jesus said to her, 'Give me a drink.' " This is immediately followed by, "For his disciples had gone away into the city to buy food" (4:7-8). Jesus is at the well. The disciples are in the town. In both cases we have a confrontation between Jew and Samaritan. John 4 only gives details of one of these stories, assuming readers will draw parallels to the other story on their own. Let me make some of the parallels explicit.

Jesus is at the well asking the Samaritan woman for a drink. Apparently the disciples are in the town asking some Samaritan vendors for food.

The woman responds to Jesus, "How is it that you, a Jew, ask a drink of me, a woman of Samaria?" (4:9). How do the Samaritans in town respond to the disciples? Imagine twelve big, bearded Black men walking up the street of a modern, Anglo, suburban community. Some residents will call the police, some will say, "May I help you?" and some will just peek out of their windows. Or reverse the situation. What if twelve white police officers start strolling down a Puerto Rican neighborhood? How will the residents react? They will have the same kind of suspicion and curiosity and concern that the woman expresses. It's a human reaction regardless of time and place.

Jesus answers, "If you knew the gift of God, and who it is that is saying to you, 'Give me a drink,' you would have asked him, and he would have given you living water" (4:10). He asks for water but says living water is what matters. The disciples might have done the same, though they didn't. They could have gone into town looking for bread and telling people about the bread of life. "The bread of life is waiting for you just outside the gates. There's no way we would have come here on our own. You're right. Jews and Samaritans don't get along. But this man out there is changing our lives—and everyone else's too." Yet nothing like this happened.

Out at the well the woman responds,

"Sir, you have nothing to draw with, and the well is deep; where do you get that living water? Are you greater than our father Jacob, who gave us the well, and drank from it himself, and his sons, and his cattle?" Jesus said to her, "Every one who drinks of this water will thirst again, but whoever drinks of the water that I shall give him will never thirst; the water that I shall give him will become in him a spring of water welling up to eternal life." (4:11-14)

He is raising her consciousness of spiritual truth and rousing her curiosity and interest.

"The woman said to him, 'Sir, give me this water, that I may not thirst, nor come here to draw.' Jesus said to her, 'Go, call your husband, and come here' " (4:15-16). The hour is noon. No one is around but the two of them. In the hot Middle East, the time to go to the well is in the cool of the morning or the evening. It is a social time as well when women talk and children play. Those who come to the well at other times are those who do not want to be at or who are not welcome at such gatherings; that is, the outcasts, the cripples, the disreputable. The woman is not sick or crippled. Neither does she want total solitude since she's willing to converse with a man sitting alone at the well. This is a disreputable woman cast out by society. She could be a prostitute, a woman of the street. Jesus, of course, perceives her social standing and reputation. This does not bother him at all, however. Indeed, he even begins to broach this most sensitive area of her life, her point of greatest need, because he is concerned about her as a person and not about how uncomfortable it might be to discuss such things with such a person.

How many of us have thought of going to certain sections of town to witness to prostitutes? These women are in a cultural group that has been totally rejected by many Christians. Fear jumps inside us when we even think of meeting them. "Oh, what would my fellow Christians say?" Many Jews had quite a lot to say about Jesus hanging around with publicans and sinners. They even called him a drunkard because of the people he associated with (Mt 11:19). That did not stop Jesus from having daily contact with them. But it stops us.

Others, however, will object, "But you don't want to put yourself in a place of temptation!" Yet if our commitment to God is so low that in the process of serving him we can be sidetracked easily by a woman on the street, then we probably need to examine whether or not our faith is true. Has it really changed us? Has it given us power or not?

These excuses, these fears, keep us from seeing that these women are lonely and in tremendous need. They are often very willing to engage in serious conversation. At the beginning they will assume that a man's interest is purely motivated by business. It will take a little time before they realize you have other things on your mind. Jesus likewise allows time to converse, even about "business" matters. "Go, call your husband, and come here," he says (4:16). This may have been a prophetic statement about the woman's marital status, but it might also easily be interpreted as a way for this potential customer to find out if she really was a prostitute. And she says, "I have no husband" (4:17), which is a way of saying, "Yes, I'm available."

All this would be quite normal for a man and a woman conversing at the well at noon until Jesus' next comment: " 'You are right in saying, "I have no husband"; for you have had five husbands, and he whom you now have is not your husband; this you said truly.' The woman said to him, 'Sir, I perceive that you are a prophet' " (4:17-19). The woman now realizes, "He's not interested in business. He's interested in me as a person and wants to talk about important things. He knows my reputation and isn't repulsed. He wants to discuss spiritual truth with me." So she goes on to say, "Our fathers worshiped on this mountain; and you say that in Jerusalem is the place where men ought to worship" (4:20).

A prostitute in our society might say, "You know, if I ever went to your church, I'd be thrown right out." And I would have to say, "You're right." In a way, Jesus does too. But he is not daunted and moves on. "Woman, believe me, the hour is coming when neither on this mountain nor in Jerusalem will you worship the Father. You worship what you do not know; we worship what we know, for salvation is from the Jews. But the hour is coming, and now is, when the true worshipers will worship the Father in spirit and truth, for such the Father seeks to worship him" (4:21-23).

In effect he says, "I'm a Jew, yes. And I know Jews have been keeping you out of Jerusalem. I also know truth is in Jerusalem with the Jews. Because you Samaritans don't come to Jerusalem, you don't have all the truth you could have. You worship in ignorance. But soon it won't matter where you worship. In fact, you can worship God right here and now because God's only requirement is that you worship in spirit and truth."

When Two Cultures Meet

Jesus has overcome two of the great difficulties inherent in crosscultural witness. First is the problem we have in speaking. There comes a time in our witness to those in other cultures when we have to honestly acknowledge our own background. Indeed, we must accept our own heritage—its good points and its bad—before we can gain a hearing. The danger exists that we might unconsciously present the gospel with our cultural accretions dominating rather than being submitted to God's truth. This can be overcome, though, if we know our own heritage (African, Anglo, Hispanic, Chinese, Polish, Italian, Indian, whatever) and understand how it affects our Christianity as well as our communication with others. It is apparent that Jesus has come to terms with his background, both in its positive and negative aspects.

The second problem Jesus has overcome is that of our audience's ability to listen. Let's say you are an Anglo Christian who approaches a Black person. Without saying a word you have automatically communicated something about your Christianity which makes it difficult for a Black person to listen to you. You may not like it, but it is a fact that African-Americans will associate your Christianity with the maintenance of slavery and of a social system that oppresses people. Christianity has been one of the big whips used to lash the back of the African-American community. You, as a white Christian, are therefore the enemy.

How can we deal with this? It is the same problem as a Jew saying, "I want to share the truth with you," and a Samaritan responding, "Who says! You've had the so-called truth all these years and wouldn't let us be part of it. What's so different now?"

Jesus acknowledges that this debate has raged and that his culture is in error. It is not important where one worships. What is important is truth and how we respond to it. Great things are about to happen in this regard, he says. In fact, they have already started.

The woman then responds, "I know that Messiah is coming (he who is called Christ); when he comes, he will show us all things" (4:25). This Samaritan woman who had been rejected by the Jewish system is still willing to buy the notion of a coming Messiah. Jesus takes this hint of openness and runs with it. "I who speak to you am he" (4:26).

How often do we respond instead like the disciples may have? In town they probably said, "We want some bread," to which the baker might have replied, "What would Jews want to buy bread from Samaritans for?" "Just shut up and give us some bread, half-breed." The conversation would no doubt have ended there.

Whatever happened in town, you can see the rejection the disciples exude when they return from this town trip. "They marveled that he was talking with a woman, but none said, 'What do you wish?' or 'Why are you talking with her?' " (4:27). They are afraid to ask Jesus these questions. The woman picks up their racism and recognizes that Jesus is in an awkward situation. But he continues to identify with her, socially unacceptable as she is. He does not break off the conversation. But she is getting uncomfortable enough that she decides this might be a good time to leave, at least for the moment. Still, she does not bring her water jar along, indicating that she intends to come back to get it and continue her talk with Jesus.

The Ripe Fields

At this point in the story the two parallel lines of the parable shift. While the story in view was Jesus and the woman, now it is Jesus and the disciples. And while the parallel story was the disciples and the townspeople, now it is the woman and the townspeople.

The disciples begin, "'Rabbi, eat.' But he said to them, 'I have food to eat of which you do not know.' So the disciples said to one another, 'Has any one brought him food?' Jesus said to them, 'My food is to do the will of him who sent me, and to accomplish his work' " (4:31-34). He rejects the food they probably obtained in an ungodly manner and says, "There is something more important in this world than food. But you've been more concerned with eating than with doing God's will."

Jesus goes on to make his point more clearly. "Do you not say, 'There are yet four months, then comes the harvest'? I tell you, lift up your eyes, and see how the fields are already white for harvest" (4:35). The scene is Jesus sitting with his disciples just outside the village. He gestures toward the gates of the town and says, "Lift up your eyes," as the woman and a group of townspeople begin to emerge. "I sent you to reap that for which you did not labor; others have labored, and you have entered into their labor" (4:38). He is rebuking the disciples. "The same people you passed by, ignored or snubbed were ready to respond to the good news. I sent you into town to share the truth with them. But you walked right through a ripe field and didn't even know it was ready to be harvested. I've had a short conversation with a woman who is an outcast even in her hometown. But she's in there telling them about me, and they're responding. They want to know more."

Many Samaritans from that city believed in him because of the woman's testimony, "He told me all that I ever did." So when the Samaritans came to him, they asked him to stay with them; and he stayed there two days. And many more believed because of his word. They said to the woman, "It is no longer because of your words that we believe, for we have heard for ourselves, and we know that this is indeed the Savior of the world." (4:39-42)

They believed first because of the words of the woman and then because of the words of Jesus. Significantly, the words of the disciples are absent. They played no part in this evangelism. If the disciples had expressed any concern to the Samaritans, any compassion, any hint that there was a man out at the well who was concerned about them and their spiritual condition, the Samaritans would have responded. But the disciples rejected their relationship with Jesus and chose not to get involved.

Who Sowed the Seed?

Jesus told them, "For here the saying holds true, 'One sows and another reaps.' I sent you to reap that for which you did not labor; others have labored" (4:37-38). Who had been sowing the seeds of the gospel in Sychar? Not the Jews. They rejected Samaritans. Not Jesus. He had not been there before. Certainly not the disciples. Who was it then?

God, in his concern for all people, has allowed truth to infiltrate every culture. In particular, the Samaritans had a culture that identified with Jacob and the well and with much Old Testament law. While they had many gaps in their theology, much truth had already been sown in their midst, and they were ready to receive more.

God has done the same thing within other culture groups in our country and around the world. The African-American community is one such group. When Africans were first brought to this country, slave masters used Christianity as a tool to maintain a submissive spirit among the slaves. But God had planted the seed, and he used this evil practice for good. Out of slavery came a vibrant African-American church.

Today many white Christians in this country believe that the African-American church needs to come to Jerusalem—out in the suburbs. We say that the Blacks, like the Samaritans, have been cut off from the truth, thus they hold only a partial gospel. "After all," we say, "the Black church has a rather emotional gospel. That is only part of the story." The irony is that while many of us believe that we possess the whole truth which Blacks need, we will not allow them to join in our fellowship, despite their efforts to do so.

The irony does not end there, for we are wrong in thinking that Jerusalem is in the suburbs, in the middle-class mentality. The white church, too, needs to come to the true Jerusalem—we have not yet arrived. We, too, hold only a partial understanding of the truth. Certainly we have absolute truth in God's word, but we do not have exhaustive or total truth in the Bible or in our understanding. If all people—Black, Anglo, Hispanic, Asian—will share the partial truth we each have, then we will all have a more complete picture.

There are many culture groups which have the seeds of truth. They are fully ripe for the harvest. We can join that harvest if we will be compassionate, sensitive and humble. Our task is to discover what truth God has already given to a people, emphasize that, and lay aside cultural differences. Jesus says, "The issue is not Jerusalem. In fact, I just came out of Jerusalem, and they don't accept me either. Let's talk together about God and his truth and how we can have greater access to him." We should not arrogantly assume that we have all the truth and that it is our God-ordained duty to enlighten the ignorant everywhere. Nor should we reject people and refuse to have contact with them because we feel they are inferior. Rather, by God's grace, after the example of Christ, let us go in humility and love to the harvest he has prepared.

6
Dividing Power, Multiplying Disciples: Acts (Part One)

▼▼▼▼▼▼▼▼▼▼▼▼

A KEY GOAL OF GOD'S PEOPLE ON EARTH IS ONENESS IN CHRIST. WE ALL want unity in truth and love—as long as it is unity on *my* terms. Many Christians, especially in America, believe that in Christ all our differences should disappear. We should think alike, act alike, feel alike. This belief is tied to the myth of the Great American Melting Pot, in which everyone becomes part of one uniform identity. Our tolerance for diversity is therefore often quite low. If some people do not have exactly the same theology or order of worship or type of music, or the same views on the military or homosexuality, then they may not be Christian at all, we say.

"Why can't we be like the New Testament church?" some ask. "After all, they were all united. They lived together in brotherhood and peace. The church was truly one then, as God intended. Why can't we be like that now?" The early church was *unified*, but it was not *uniform*. And there was brotherhood, but not without struggle and misunderstanding. Yet the book of Acts as it actually stands is more helpful to us than if it merely presented an idealized church. It shows us how by the Spirit we can come to terms with cultural differences and work through resulting tensions.

A Division Among the Jews

As I mentioned in chapter four, Jews were to be found in significant numbers throughout the Roman Empire as well as in Africa, India and even China. This was known as the Diaspora or the Dispersion of the Jews. Jerusalem remained, to a great extent, the focus of the Jewish religion, as well as an international center of trade. Some Diaspora Jews took on many of the customs of those they lived among. Hellenists (Jews influenced by the Greek culture, speaking the Greek language) probably constituted the largest subgroup within the Diaspora. There were also Mesopotamian Jews, Egyptian Jews, Asian Jews and others.

Some of the Diaspora Jews, however, did not accommodate to their surrounding context. They held steadfastly to their own culture, traditions and language (Aramaic). This united them with like-minded Jews who predominated in Palestine (Judea and Galilee). These Palestinian Jews, as I call them, considered themselves superior to other Jews because of their association with the traditional land of King David dominated by the Holy City of Jerusalem. The Pharisees, who epitomized this group, held to what they felt was the purest form of Judaism. Hellenistic Jews, for example, would still consider Judaism superior, but they were more open to other peoples, more "missionary-minded" and prepared to accept proselytes than Palestinian Jews.

Among the Hellenists, the synagogue, which developed after the Babylonian exile, was often a center for Jewish evangelism, especially when services were conducted in Greek. The Jewish monotheism, moral values and way of life appealed to Gentiles, who underwent instruction, circumcision and baptism. Nonetheless it could take two or three generations to become fully identified as a Jew. Thus, even in Jerusalem, synagogues developed around language groups, cultures, classes and even trades.

Many Gentiles, repulsed by the requirement of circumcision, would not become full proselytes (though they might have their sons circumcised). Instead these so-called God-fearers would hang around the edges of Judaism, learn from it and support it. Cornelius (Acts 10:1-2), whom I will consider more in the next chapter, was one such man, as was the centurion with the sick slave whose faith Jesus commended (Lk 7:1-10).

This tension arose among the Jews, especially among the different groups living in and around Jerusalem. To summarize this pecking order, Palestinian Jews were on top, followed by the Diaspora Jews (principally Hellenists), with proselytes and God-fearers next, and Samaritans (whom Jews regarded as heretics) and Gentiles at the bottom. Of course this order held true only for those who believed Judaism had some value. A pagan Roman soldier would not have cared a mite that he was at the bottom of the local religious system. He was on top of the international political system. But within Judaism, and in the context of Acts, this social order was very important.

Luke, the writer of Acts, was likely a Gentile from Syrian Antioch, writing to Theophilus, a fellow Greek (1:1). Thus the issue of culture and religion was bound to influence Acts because both its author and its recipient had non-Palestinian backgrounds.

Narrow Apostles, Broad Spirit

The book opens just after the resurrection and moves quickly to Christ's last appearance to the apostles. Our Lord's final words before his ascension are recorded in Acts 1:8: "You shall receive power when the Holy Spirit has come upon you; and you shall be my witnesses in Jerusalem and in all Judea and Samaria and to the end of the earth."

As we saw in the last chapter, early in Jesus' ministry he had taken the disciples with him into Samaria (Jn 4). He had observed, however, that they were not yet ready to deal with the Samaritans. They still considered the Samaritans second class. So when Jesus later sent the disciples out two by two, he instructed them, "Go nowhere among the Gentiles, and enter no town of the Samaritans" (Mt 10:5). In Acts 1:8, however, he says explicitly that when the Holy Spirit has come upon them, they will then be ready to go both to the Samaritans and to the Gentiles. Jesus had already told them that it was necessary that he leave in order that the Spirit could come (Jn 16:7). The Spirit would do through Jesus' disciples what Jesus himself could not. Jesus could not go out to all the ends of the earth, but his body, the church, can.

Today it is still the Spirit of God who does his work through us. Only as we are sensitive to where (literally) that Spirit is taking us is our work significant. Jesus wants us to be empty vessels that God can enter and use, to be present in and to be sensitive to cultures quite different from our own. This incarnational evangelism, this unique partnership through which God builds his worldwide church is the subject of Acts.

The work of the Spirit in us, however, does not obliterate our personality or eliminate our limitations. The humanity of the apostles is evident even in Peter's first sermon at Pentecost.

The disciples were together for this feast, one of the three major events of the Jewish calendar. While Jerusalem was already a multiethnic town, it was even more so at Pentecost when Jews from around the world made pilgrimage to the Holy City. Who were these people? "Parthians and Medes and Elamites and residents of Mesopotamia, Judea and Cappadocia, Pontus and Asia, Phrygia and Pamphylia, Egypt and the parts of Libya belonging to Cyrene [way over in North Africa], and visitors from Rome, both Jews and proselytes, Cretans and Arabians" (2:9-11).

They did not only come for religious purposes, but also to find out what was going on in the rest of the world and to bring that news back. This formed a communication network, much of it centered around Jerusalem. The pilgrims usually came to Jerusalem for the Passover feast and stayed until the time of Pentecost (fifty days later).[1] This international group, temporarily in Jerusalem, was soon to return to their nations scattered around the world. But while they were in Jerusalem, they observed the crucifixion and heard the preaching of the apostles. Many of these Diaspora Jews would have carried this news of the Messiah quickly over long distances when they returned to their homes, almost immediately fulfilling the Great Commission of Acts 1:8.

Peter, however, even after being filled by the Spirit, did not have God's work so clearly in mind as the Spirit did. A crowd had gathered around the disciples.

Now there were dwelling in Jerusalem Jews, devout men from every nation under heaven. And at this sound the multitude came together, and they were bewildered, because each one heard them speaking in his own language. And they were amazed and wondered, saying, "Are not all these who are speaking Galileans? And how is it that we hear, each of us in his own native language?" (2:5-8)

Peter's limited viewpoint is seen in his opening statement of explanation to this crowd of people from over fifteen nations: "Men of Judea and all who dwell in Jerusalem" (2:14). He then proceeds to quote an extended passage from the Old Testament (Joel 2:28-32) to explain that the disciples are not drunk but Spirit-filled. What this multinational crowd hears in this Spirit-inspired choice of words is, "I will pour out my Spirit on all people. . . . And everyone who calls on the name of the Lord will be saved" (2:17, 21 NIV).

They applied this invitation to themselves. But Peter's myopia continues: "Men of Israel, hear these words: Jesus of Nazareth . . ." (2:22). Nonetheless, the Spirit moved three thousand to respond to the message (2:41), and we can assume they included many of the nations represented in the crowd.

A Case of De Facto Segregation

This cultural myopia continued to plague the apostles in the early days of the church. As I already mentioned, not only were there synagogues for different language groups (Aramaic, Greek and so on) and different ethnic groups (Egyptians, Mesopotamians, Cretans and so on) but even for different trades (such as copperworkers). The pattern of house churches within the early Christian community tended to preserve this cultural diversity as believers gathered to worship in already de facto segregated neighborhoods and synagogues. Since all the apostles came from synagogues of Palestinian Jews, they also unintentionally remained isolated from Christian converts who attended synagogues of Hellenistic Jews.

This situation eventually threatened to divide the growing Christian community as it had the Jewish community. The problem surfaced when "the Hellenists murmured against the Hebrews because their widows were neglected in the daily distribution" (6:1). The Hellenists were likely Christian converts from among Jews belonging to Greek-speaking synagogues. The Hebrews mentioned most probably were Christian converts from among the Aramaic-speaking Palestinian Jews, of which the apostles were twelve.

The Hellenists quite naturally began to feel isolated from the power and communication network of the early church. When goods were being handed out to those in need in the Christian community, the Hellenists did not get the word until it was too late. But the word got out quickly among those who were close to the power structure of the apostles—Aramaic-speaking Palestinians. Even if the Hellenists did get the message, they felt the distribution was weighted unfairly and neglected their needy ones.

The communication problem was compounded, however, among those Hellenists who did not attend temple services. Even before the time of Jesus, a radical attitude toward the law and the temple had developed among some of them. They felt that the letter of the law could be loosened if its spiritual lessons were kept and that prayer could substitute for temple sacrifices.[2] With this devalued view of what Palestinian Jews held in high esteem, the Hellenists were likely to go to the temple far less often than the Hebrews.

And as Acts 5:42 reveals, the apostles were regularly in the temple as well as in their segregated house churches. "Every day in the temple and at home they did not cease teaching and preaching Jesus as the Christ."

This same sort of de facto segregation and isolation happens all the time today. A group of two dozen Korean pastors fellowship together regularly in one eastern city, but no one else knows they exist. There are also vast numbers of minority and urban churches that are blocked out of the entire evangelical communication system; for example, six or eight white evangelical presses compete to sell more and more literature to the suburban churches who can afford to buy. Meanwhile, the African-American churches are saying, "There is no literature for our people." The question is, What is our response?

Splitting Power with a Minority

The apostles were men of God. I am not criticizing them. I am only saying what the Bible says. They were human beings who failed. They knew it. And when they saw their failure, they said, "Okay, Lord. What do you want us to do about it? How should we respond?"

The twelve summoned the body of disciples and said, "It is not right that we should give up preaching the word of God to serve tables. Therefore, brethren, pick out from among you seven men of good repute, full of the Spirit and of wisdom, whom we may appoint to this duty. But we will devote ourselves to prayer and to the ministry of the word." And what they said pleased the whole multitude, and they chose Stephen, a man full of faith and of the Holy Spirit, and Philip, and Prochorus, and Nicanor, and Timon, and Parmenas, and Nicolaus, a proselyte of Antioch. (6:2-5)

Notice the names. Stephen and Philip are not Jewish names. Prochorus is certainly not a Jewish name, nor are Nicanor, Timon and Parmenas. Then notice this last fellow, Nicolaus, a proselyte from Antioch. Nicolaus was not even a Jew; he was a Gentile who had become a Jew through circumcision. The apostles were not simply having people chosen to distribute the goods. They recognized that the Hellenists felt isolated from the power structure of the whole community. The Aramaic-speaking converts were already well represented, so the apostles established a second power structure. They pulled out from the Hellenists a group of leaders who would be recognized by the apostles. They changed the structure. They split the power to overcome the de facto segregation.

Some may be wondering how you can reach Blacks on campus or through your church. Have you ever thought of putting two of them in your top leadership or creating a second leadership group for Blacks? You may find that other Blacks are much more willing to become involved if they have a piece of the power structure. If you simply ask them to come in at the bottom, you are implying that they must work their way up. We should imitate the apostles. They saw that right from the beginning they had to give equality of power.

They were not establishing two churches but simply delegating authority. The important fact is that they recognized cultural diversity as a valid reason for division of power. Mission societies around the world are faced by irate national churches who want the right to have power over their own affairs. Why must money given by American churches be spent only by American missionaries? The conflict lies not in their ignorance but in our unwillingness to accept a Spirit-filled national who is responsible directly to the Holy Spirit. Giving them this right and power frees the national to use national values and lines of communication. Similarly, the racial rift in this country will not be settled by inviting African-Americans merely to join white churches, but rather by recognizing a Black power structure that is responsible directly to the Holy Spirit.

Many evangelical Blacks are saying, for example, "Why is it that we can't get any students into Christian schools?" A Christian school could respond by saying, "Okay. We'll establish a quota system. Four or five Black leaders from, let's say, the National Black Evangelical Association can select any twenty-five Black students that they want trained, send them to us, and we will accept them, carte blanche, without any further selection process." Doing this would begin to train the real leaders within the African-American community. Now that's radical, but it's biblical.

What was the result of the apostles' action? "The word of God increased; and the number of the disciples multiplied greatly in Jerusalem" (6:7). The men who were chosen to distribute the food because they were "of good repute, full of the Spirit" also became filled with grace and power (6:3).

Philip, one of the seven men, went on to preach in Samaria where the apostles had not gone since the resurrection. The apostles became a bit concerned and decided to send an investigative delegation (8:4-25).

Now when the apostles at Jerusalem heard that Samaria had received the word of God, they sent to them Peter and John, who came down and prayed for them that they might receive the Holy Spirit; for it had not yet fallen on any of them, but they had only been baptized in the name of the Lord Jesus. Then they laid their hands on them and they received the Holy Spirit. (8:14-17)

Peter and John stayed around a while observing, recognizing their faith to be genuine. As a result, the faith of the apostles was stretched.

I suggest that the reason the Spirit of God came on the Samaritans only after the apostles laid hands on them was more for Peter and John, who were not quite sure that the Samaritans were fit for inclusion in the church, than for the Samaritans. Only when they saw the Spirit of God active in people outside their own tight Judean context did they believe that extending the gospel to those who were not strictly Jews was proper. They returned to Jerusalem and broadened the vision of the believers there by including the Samaritans, a socially outcast people, among the faithful. They recognized them, without distinction, as full-fledged members of God's family. This view is confirmed in that Jerusalem never sent another delegation or imposed their leadership on the Samaritans. Rather they were allowed to continue to grow and develop as an indigenous movement without outside intervention.

But the understanding of those in Jerusalem was still inadequate. While the apostles were preaching in the temple every morning, Philip met an Ethiopian (probably a Black) and told him that he too could believe. Presumably the man returned to his own land to preach the gospel there (8:26-39).

Stephen, another one of the seven, "did great wonders and signs among the people" (6:8), and then he went to the "synagogue of the Freedmen (as it was called)" (6:9).[3] This is the first time Acts mentions that somebody went with the gospel to the Diaspora community in Jerusalem. Notice it was a man who came out of this community. Apparently the apostles had never been there. As soon as he was given authority, Stephen began to use it to communicate the gospel.

Suddenly, in the act of sharing power and authority with a minority, the church burst its cultural bonds and reached not only that minority, the Hellenists, but also the Samaritans and the Ethiopians. The full implications of this had not fully dawned on the apostles, but God was doing a work, the completion of which will be seen in the next chapter.

Although Philip received an open response to his message, the reaction Stephen received in the synagogue of the Freedmen was quite different.

Stephen the Hellenist

The synagogue Stephen addressed included people from Cyrene (in North Africa), Alexandria (in Egypt), Cilicia and Asia (in what is now Turkey). They were either proselytes or they were brought up in Jewish homes in these different countries. They were Jewish, but they were considered second-class Jews who were struggling to become part of the first class.

From their midst arose a reaction to Stephen far more heated than even the Pharisees' response to the apostles. Some of his opponents interpreted his teaching as an attack on the law and the temple. But he preached with such wisdom that none of them could stand up to him. They were so enraged that they trumped up charges against him and brought him before the Sanhedrin. This at first may seem surprising, since I have already indicated that some Hellenistic Jews had their own radical views of the law and the temple. Understanding this tension among Hellenistic Jews themselves begins with a basic understanding of the nature of ethnicity.

The most red-white-and-blue Americans are often second-generation people out of an ethnic community. Those with strong ethnic identity have a name for them. If they are Chinese, they call them bananas (yellow outside, white inside). If they are Indians, they call them apples (red outside, white inside). If they are Black, they call them Oreos or Uncle Toms. Those who are trying to move out of a second-class ethnic community and become part of a first-class melting-pot community are the most defensive of the rights and sanctity of the first-class community. They are also the quickest to dismiss and reject unique aspects of their background that reveal their second-class ethnicity.

Of course if you ask these second-generation peoples about the others, they'll say, "Oh, they are just radicals trying to take us down the road of nonexistence. We're trying to build peace in society." So there are two points of view which frequently show up as culture develops and changes. The nature of culture is to define in-groups and out-groups because that's how culture gives us security. We have a way to tell who is safe and who is not.

This tension among those who were changing over to the dominant culture may well have been a principal cause of the reaction to Stephen's message. While Diaspora Jews tended to devalue the temple, some were even more attached to it than even the Pharisees and rabbinate. They also tended to accept less from their surrounding culture than other Hellenists.[4] Stephen had come into this synagogue preaching something that was not pure Judaism.

These Hellenists got angry and accused him. They wanted to please, to make points with the Palestinians. They were not concerned with being Egyptian. They were giving up their Egyptianness in order to try to become more Palestinian. So when they brought Stephen to the Sanhedrin, they were saying in effect, "We want to show you how much we identify with you. Here is a bad man; we're accusing him before you. Listen to him, and then you'll see how good we are and how committed to you we are." They were so intense in this that they even "set up false witnesses who said, 'This man never ceases to speak words against this holy place and the law' " (6:13).

Stephen now stands before the high priest. He has been brought by the Freedmen out of the synagogue to defend himself in the temple courtroom against the charges of condemning the temple and the law. On one side sits the high priest and the Sanhedrin. On the other is a motley group of Hellenistic Jews, from all over the world, who are angry because Stephen is not speaking the truth as they see it. They have brought him in before the Jewish establishment. Stephen is given an opportunity to defend himself. That is a tight spot for a Hellenist to be in.

In 1970 Tom Skinner was asked to come to the Urbana Student Missions Convention and talk about what Black Christians are thinking. A lot of white people heard for the first time what Black Christians have been saying for a long, long time. It shocked them. Many people were unhappy with Andrew Young as our ambassador to the U.N. But when Young, for example, said that there were political prisoners in the United States, he was saying nothing more than what people in the African-American community have been saying for many years. In fact, he was extremely conservative in the way he spoke. But when it came through to the white community, it sounded radical. Andrew Young may not have been able to understand why people were getting so confused and upset. After all, he was only saying what he had always heard and what he knows to be true.

Stephen does the same when he stands up before the Sanhedrin: he begins to say some of the things that he has heard ever since he was a boy. "Brethren and fathers, hear me. The God of glory appeared to our father Abraham, when he was in Mesopotamia" (7:2). Immediately Stephen is on the offensive. Abraham was not from Palestine. In fact God's glory first appeared to him outside this land, considered so important. "And [God] said to him, 'Depart from your land and from your kindred and go into the land which I will show you.' Then he departed from the land of the Chaldeans and lived in Haran [near Asia Minor]" (7:3-4). Even after receiving the promise Abraham did not go straight to Palestine. He was in no rush to get to the so-called sacred land. Maybe his father had greater priority at that time.

And after his father died, God removed him from there into this land [Israel] in which you are now living; yet he gave him no inheritance in it, not even a foot's length, but promised to give it to him in possession and to his posterity after him, though he had no child. And God spoke to this effect, that his posterity would be aliens in a land belonging to others [Egypt], who would enslave them and ill-treat them four hundred years. . . . And he gave him the covenant of circumcision. And so Abraham became the father of Isaac, and circumcised him on the eighth day; and Isaac became the father of Jacob, and Jacob of the twelve patriarchs. (7:4-8)

Abraham, the founding father of Judaism, never got one foot of his land. It was promised only to his children. So much for the Palestinian claims on Abraham, argues Stephen. Not only that, but it was after God appeared to Abraham, after the promise was given and after God began moving Abraham, that the sign of circumcision was given. The issue for Gentiles seeking to become Jews was, "Will you be circumcised or not?" This was a fixture of Jewishness that Stephen claims is only important in the context of an ongoing relationship with God—quite a contrast to the Palestinian position.[5]

Stephen continues. "And the patriarchs, jealous of Joseph, sold him into Egypt; but God was with him, and rescued him out of all his afflictions, and gave him favor and wisdom before Pharaoh, king of Egypt, who made him governor over Egypt and over all his household" (7:9-10). Stephen is drawing a comparison between Abraham who never got a piece of his land and Joseph who was booted out of the land by his brothers, the patriarchs. While this bunch of rumscullions sent him down into Egypt, it was the Egyptians who gave him proper honor. Joseph was identifying with Egyptian culture. He was absorbing their wisdom while helping them to survive as a nation by overcoming the seven-year famine.

Remember some of the people in the synagogue are Egyptians. Stephen reminds them that Abraham was a Mesopotamian and that it was the Egyptians, not the patriarchs, who lived in Palestine, who took good care of Joseph. Imagine how this is beginning to sit with the Pharisees!

Stephen keeps on building his case. "And Joseph sent and called to him Jacob his father and all his kindred, seventy-five souls; and Jacob went down into Egypt. And he died, himself and our fathers, and they were carried back to Shechem [in Israel]" (7:14-16). In other words, the early home of the nation, the place where even the patriarchs died, was Egypt. They too became Egyptian. And that, Stephen was implying, is who many of us Hellenists are. We are full Jews, nonetheless.

After four hundred years of Egyptian rule,

Moses was born, and was beautiful before God. And he was brought up for three months in his father's house; and when he was exposed, Pharaoh's daughter adopted him and brought him up as her own son. And Moses was instructed in all the wisdom of the Egyptians, and he was mighty in his words and deeds.

When he was forty years old, it came into his heart to visit his brethren, the sons of Israel. And seeing one of them being wronged, he defended the oppressed man and avenged him by striking the Egyptian. He supposed that his brethren understood that God was giving them deliverance by his hand, but they did not understand. And on the following day he appeared to them as they were quarreling and would have reconciled them, saying, "Men, you are brethren, why do you wrong each other?" But the man who was wronging his neighbor thrust him aside, saying, "Who made you a ruler and judge over us? Do you want to kill me as you killed the Egyptian yesterday?" At this retort Moses fled, and became an exile in the land of Midian. (7:20-29)

Not only had the nation been influenced by being in Egypt four hundred years, but Moses, the greatest leader and prophet of the Jews, was so Egyptian that his contemporary Jews (the fathers of Stephen's listeners) rejected him (as is seen in 6:36). Even when Moses fled, did he go the Promised Land of Palestine? Not even then. He went to Midian. That did not set well with the Pharisees either.

Stephen has more. "Now when forty years had passed, an angel appeared to him in the wilderness of Mount Sinai" (7:30). Where is God? He is out in the wilderness. And God says to Moses, " 'I am the God of your fathers, the God of Abraham and of Isaac and of Jacob.' And Moses trembled and did not dare to look. And the Lord said to him, 'Take off the shoes from your feet, for the place where you are standing is holy ground' " (7:32-33). Stephen has made it clear that this holy ground is not Palestine. Stephen is still not making any friends in the Sanhedrin.

Courageously he proceeds with his Hellenistic interpretation of Israel's history. "This Moses whom they refused, saying, 'Who made you a ruler and a judge?' God sent as both ruler and deliverer by the hand of the angel that appeared to him in the bush. He led them out" (7:35-36). Moses was an Egyptian-styled leader, rejected by his brothers because of this, who God ordained as just such a leader. The irony is clear to Stephen's audience.

"This is the Moses who said to the Israelites, 'God will raise up for you a prophet from your brethren as he raised me up.' " Stephen means Jesus. "This is he who was in the congregation in the wilderness with the angel who spoke to him at Mount Sinai, and with our fathers; and he received living oracles to give to us" (7:37-38). What were those "living oracles"? They were the law, given by God to this Egyptian leader, Moses, in the Sinai wilderness far from the "holy land."

Not until Stephen has firmly established that the patriarchs and Moses were a universal and international group does Stephen identify with his listeners: "*Our* fathers refused to obey him, but thrust him aside, and in their hearts they turned to Egypt" (7:39). In fact, they made a god like they had seen in Egypt. They were more Egyptian than they were Jewish. These were our fathers, Stephen insists.

Stephen concludes his defense on the first accusation against him: that he had condemned the law. He has taken forty-two verses to explain that the earliest part of Jewish history starts in Mesopotamia, continues in Egypt and ends in the wilderness. And the law came in the wilderness. The Jewish nation was made up of people who came from Mesopotamia and who were more Egyptian in their hearts than anything else. He is not against the law, just concerned with where it came from and who it came to.

Stephen then defends himself against the second charge: that he had condemned the temple. "Our fathers had the tent of witness in the wilderness, even as he who spoke to Moses directed him to make it" (7:44). In other words, not only does the law originate in the wilderness outside the holy land, but the first tabernacle—God's dwelling place—was also in the wilderness.

Stephen then dismisses the long period of the judges (from Joshua to the monarchy) in two sentences: "Our fathers in turn brought it in with Joshua when they dispossessed the nations which God thrust out before our fathers. So it was until the days of David" (7:45). The Palestinlan Jews, in contrast, would have picked up their history at the Jordan River with Joshua because this was the beginning of the history of Israel's relationship to the land. They gave scant attention to what happened before that. They were concerned with the holy land as the place where God dwelt, for it gave them a position of privilege.

Stephen sweeps by that whole section of history in one short sentence and deals with the temple.

David . . . found favor in the sight of God and asked leave to find a habitation for the God of Jacob. But it was Solomon who built a house for him. Yet the Most High does not dwell in houses made with hands; as the prophet says, "Heaven is my throne, and earth my footstool. What house will you build for me, says the Lord, or what is the place of my rest? Did not my hand make all these things?" (7:45-50)

So much for the temple, rooted as it is to one particular locality and controlled by a privileged fragment of God's people. It cannot possibly contain God.

A Religious Lynch Mob

By this time the members of the Sanhedrin were very agitated. The Hellenists who had charged Stephen saw that they were losing the argument, and they became nervous and angry. They saw that they had brought in somebody who made the Palestinian Jews look foolish. Stephen, seeing that he had little time left, thrusts to the heart the sword of truth:

You stiff-necked people, uncircumcised in heart and ears, you always resist the Holy Spirit. As your fathers did, so do you. Which of the prophets did not your fathers persecute? And they killed those who announced beforehand the coming of the Righteous One, whom you have now betrayed and murdered, you who received the law as delivered by angels and did not keep it. (7:51-53)

That was as far as he got. "When they heard these things they were enraged, and they ground their teeth against him. But he, full of the Holy Spirit, gazed into heaven and saw the glory of God, and Jesus standing at the right hand of God" (7:54-55).

This same group of men had heard John and Peter defend the faith. And they had been a little upset about these Galilean Jews who to their minds were a little bit wrong. They punished them mildly and put them in jail for a while. But they had not been very upset because, as Gamaliel pointed out, every twenty years someone comes along claiming to be the Messiah and gathering a following. But it never amounts to much. "Let them alone; for if this plan . . . is of men, it will fail; but if it is of God, you will not be able to overthrow them" (5:38-39).

Stephen's message, however, so infuriated them that they immediately took him out to stone him to death (7:56-60). Stephen's explosive message made Judaism a universal faith. Anyone could come to God and be fully related to him without adopting an ethnocentric, Palestinian form of the religion. The Palestinian position of privilege, according to Stephen, was a sham.

I once thought of Stephen as a pious little angel who stood quietly while they stoned him. But now I see a man of faith, a man of prayer, a radical—not because he wanted to be, but because he had been driven up against the wall. He would not run; he was standing for truth. He was saying, "I'm in the hands of God. I've said my piece and now God can do with it what he wants."

Christians have got to stand for truth. We have got to realize that being meek does not mean being weak. This does not mean being aggressive either, but simply being willing to be steadfast for the truth, the truth of a universal gospel that is not bound by culture. That is what Stephen did.

7

Unified
but Not
Uniform:
Acts (Part Two)

▼▼▼▼▼▼▼▼▼▼▼▼▼▼

PAUL, OR SAUL—AS LUKE IDENTIFIES HIM IN ACTS 7—9, NOW ENTERS THE developing story of the early church. He had heard Stephen's powerful defense of God's world-embracing promise and plan, but went with the mob, out of the city, to the place of stoning. And how did he react to what he had heard and seen? With absolute rage.

He watched the coats of those who laid them aside to get better throws at Stephen, and thus he consented to his death (7:58; 8:1). He ravaged the church, "entering house after house, he dragged off men and women and committed them to prison" (8:3). Some time later he was "still breathing threats and murder against the disciples of the Lord" (9:1). Stephen's message had a profound impact on this bright young Pharisee. Luke's mention of Paul's presence at the trial and stoning indicates it to be an important turning point.

Though Stephen's basic message was the same as that of Peter and John (who had already been tried by the Sanhedrin and dismissed as not overly dangerous), Paul could see that Stephen carried the implications of this new message far beyond the provincial boundaries and concerns of Palestinian Judaism. This threatened the whole structure of Judaism as Paul and his fellow Pharisees understood it. This was something the message of John and Peter did not (yet) do. This kind of message had to be destroyed.

When the Holy Spirit begins to convict someone, the first response can be absolute anger—screaming, ranting and raving before final submission. That's what happened to Paul. He ranted and raved and persecuted the early church until Jesus finally got hold of him. But when Paul was converted, he says in Galatians, he did not go back to Jerusalem to learn from Peter and the other apostles (Gal 1:16-18). Instead he went out to the wilderness (presumably to restudy the Old Testament). He was already a scholar of the Scriptures, but he had heard Stephen dig some stuff out that he never knew was there. He went back through the Scriptures with a question in his mind. What does this teach me of Jesus Christ? He began to uncover all kinds of things. The letter to the Galatians provides one important summary of his findings. He says the gospel in its entirety was given to Abraham. The law which was given four hundred years later was only the schoolmaster to bring us to Jesus Christ. But the message given to Abraham (before the law, before circumcision) applies to anyone from any nation who has the same faith as Abraham. That is why he called himself an apostle to the Gentiles. Paul had been freed. His outline of the gospel in Galatians is almost the same outline that Stephen gave.

After Paul's third missionary journey he was arrested in the temple by Hellenists, as Stephen had been (21:27). They accused him of the same crime of speaking against the law and the temple (21:28). Paul evidently associated these events with Stephen's death, for when he addresses the people from the stairway, he dwells on his own persecution of the early church which arose out of Stephen's defense (22:4). Then he refers specifically to his witness and approval of Stephen's death (22:20). His next statement is that he received the commission from God to go to the Gentiles (22:21). Paul was arrested by the same kind of people, in the same city, for the same crime as Stephen, and in his message he associated Stephen with his call to the Gentiles. So even eighteen years later, Paul identified with Stephen greatly.

To the Gentiles Also
The apostles' provincialism, noted earlier, continued to the time recorded in Acts 8 where the church in Jerusalem could hardly believe what had hap-

pened in Samaria. The difficulty in overcoming their narrowness with non-Palestinian Jews could only be intensified with people who weren't any kind of Jews. Were even *they* candidates for God's saving message?

The opening of the fellowship of the children of God to uncircumcised, untaught, heathen (Gentiles) was a completely new concept for which there had been no precedent. The spreading of the gospel had moved from the purest Palestinian Jews to the Greek-influenced Hellenists to the Samaritans and the Ethiopian eunuch—all with the Holy Spirit's strong influence. Yet each of these come out of a Hebrew tradition. The ultimate test of the universality of the gospel was for a Palestinian Jew to go to a Gentile. Circumcision was the symbol that one accepted faith in God as expressed in Abraham. It also symbolized that you agreed to follow the law of a specific culture expressed in a particular language.

In the minds of every Jew, coming to God was a cultural process, a civilizing process manifest in a change of behavior. To accept God without learning that behavior was not possible because God had communicated himself through the behavior prescribed in the Old Testament. They had no way of conceptualizing how a heathen could believe in God through any other means—including Jesus Christ.

In Acts 10 God acts dramatically to correct this misunderstanding. The story of the meeting between Cornelius the Roman centurion and Peter the apostle begins on a rooftop in a Judean seaport called Joppa. Resting before lunch, Peter receives a vision of ritually unclean food being presented to him and a voice that says, "Eat!" Three times the vision occurs, and three times Peter argues with the Spirit (10:9-16). It is encouraging for me to see the fear and disbelief Peter expresses as he realizes in a dream what God is asking him to do. Peter is no superhuman missionary on a pedestal; he is the same weak Peter who followed Jesus. Today, like then, the gospel will not naturally cross cultural boundaries, but only with great sensitivity to the leading of the Spirit can we build bridges of communication.

The Spirit demonstrates the importance of Peter's vision by simultaneously giving Cornelius a vision thirty-five miles north in the town of Caesarea. The Spirit instructs Cornelius to send for Peter (10:1-8). The Spirit instructs Peter to go with the messengers (10:19-20). No other incident in Acts shows the Spirit so explicitly involving himself in human actions. Every detail is set down; there is no room for uncertainties.

The Spirit uses the natural bridge of selecting a Gentile who is favorable to the Jewish community, familiar with the Hebrew faith, and who worships God. Yet Cornelius has not been circumcised. Further, he has invited his relatives as well as his friends to be with him (10:24). It is quite clear to Peter that if this group joins the church, there will be no end to where this thing can go! When they meet, Peter tells Cornelius of his own perplexity. Yet he acts on what the Spirit told him to do (10:28-29).

The story is a clear case of a man who is beyond his understanding of cultural possibility, acting on knowledge that has been given to him from another source—God's revealed truth.

Cornelius explains that he wants to hear God's word from Peter, who willingly obliges. The houseful of Gentiles believes his message, and the Holy Spirit comes down on them all. Peter and the witnesses who came with him cannot deny that this is of the Holy Spirit (10:30-48).

Culture, I mentioned before, defines for us what is possible and what is not. What is not possible for you may be possible for someone in other cultural contexts. It is impossible for us to communicate with trees or rocks. But those in animistic cultures do it daily, or at least they believe they do. Christ blew down the cultural possibility-impossibility barriers and let Peter see that we have to live in the realms of the "impossible." The church today is not used to believing the impossible. Therefore when we see it written out in black and white, we reject it. We have been enclosed by cultural walls that are knocked flat when we see God at work in our lives.

Peter now had to explain this seeming impossibility to the people back home. "Now the apostles and the brethren who were in Judea heard that the Gentiles also had received the word of God. So when Peter went up to Jerusalem, the circumcision party criticized him, saying, 'Why did you go to uncircumcised men and eat with them?' " (11:1-3). The "apostles and the brethren who were in Judea" or certainly the "circumcision party," though Christians, still did not understand that Jesus had come to be far more than a Jewish Messiah; they still did not understand that he had come to reconcile everyone to God and to each other, breaking down all dividing walls such as the one dividing Jews and Gentiles. "But Peter began and explained to them in order" (11:4).

Luke considers this episode so important that he repeats the whole story of Peter and Cornelius through Peter's report in Acts 11:5-17. He does so because the conclusion to which this experience leads them and which is the culmination of much of what Luke records in the first eleven chapters of Acts is one of the most significant verses in the New Testament. "When they heard this [Peter's report] they were silenced. And they glorified God, saying, *'Then to the Gentiles also God has granted repentance unto life' "* (11:18).

What a giant step this is for this group of intensely religious, intensely nationalistic Jews who had followed Jesus for three years without ever quite seeing what he really was trying to do. Suddenly they are awakened to the fact that the gospel of Jesus Christ is for the whole world. For if a raw, heathen, uncircumcised Gentile may, without any purification process, be brought directly into the church, then certainly the gospel excludes no one.

Hundreds of years of hard-nosed prejudice was transformed—in an instant. The prejudice between Jews and Gentiles was as sharp and bitter as any we experience in the world today—Jew-Arab, rich-poor, Black-White. We know that this was not the end of the struggle within the church, but these early Christians responded to the Spirit's intervention by beginning to rid themselves of prejudice and all invidious distinctions based on notions of privilege and superiority.

Barnabas: The Bicultural Reconciler
Acts 11:18-20 is the cultural hinge of the book. Acts 11:18 marks the end of Luke's account of how the mind of the church grew to match God's plan. Acts 11:19-20 marks the beginning of how the church actively began to live out what they had learned and so become a truly multicultural church. This new part begins by referring to Stephen's death and the persecution that followed (see 8:1) which resulted in a geographic expansion of the people of God. These same verses, however, also indicate that the cultural issue was still to be worked out practically.

"Now those who were scattered because of the persecution that arose over Stephen traveled as far as Phoenicia and Cyprus and Antioch, speaking the word to none except Jews" (11:19). The Hellenistic Jewish Christians from Jerusalem went into Greek areas but only spoke to other Hellenistic Jews about Jesus. This was a perfectly normal process—people seek out their own kind in new areas.

When the Chinese come from Taiwan into San Francisco or New York, they seek out the Chinese community. If they are Christians, they find the Chinese church and identify with that. Some of them have been in such communities in this country for three generations and have never belonged to any other church. When African-Americans from Atlanta go to New York, they find certain churches that appeal to them which are different from the churches that appeal to those from Alabama. When you go into a Black church in New York City, it does not take long to find out where its roots go back, because they all have their roots either in the South, in the West Indies or somewhere in Africa. It is important to understand this in talking with such people. Our cities are filled with Korean, Chinese, Spanish, African-American and Anglo churches that have lines of communication that go back to a homeland.

When I went to Africa, I found the same tendency in myself. It was very easy for me to stay in the mission station and fellowship with the other American missionaries there. That is where I was comfortable. I had to force myself to get out of the mission station and down into the village to deal with people who spoke an unfamiliar language, ate unfamiliar food, held unfamiliar values and functioned in an unfamiliar culture. It was difficult to communicate the gospel in that setting. It took deliberate discipline to do that because naturally, of myself, I would have stayed on the mission station. I think this is precisely what many of these Hellenistic Jewish converts did. They went to the Jewish communities; they found their own kind of people; they felt comfortable there; and they began to share the gospel. That was wonderful, but it was not reaching the uttermost parts of the earth.

But not all these scattered Hellenists spoke only to Jews. "There were some of them, men of Cyprus and Cyrene, who on coming to Antioch spoke to the Greeks also, preaching the Lord Jesus" (11:20). So in the city of Antioch, some evangelized Jews only and some began to evangelize Gentiles as well. If Hellenistic Jewish Christians and Palestinian Jewish Christians had their problems (as we saw in Acts 6), what will happen when Gentiles start believing in Jesus? "The hand of the Lord was with them, and a great number that believed turned to the Lord. News of this came to the ears of the church in Jerusalem" (11:21-22). What news? News that for the first time large numbers of Gentiles were becoming Christians. Note that this comes in the context of the story of Cornelius and the truth that Jesus is Lord of all, that there is to be no division in the body of Christ. How would the potential conflict in Antioch between the two groups be dealt with? Jerusalem decided to send somebody. "They sent Barnabas to Antioch" (11:22). Why did they send him? "Joseph ... was surnamed by the apostles Barnabas (which means, Son of encouragement), a Levite, a native of Cyprus" (4:36). He was a reconciler; he brought people together. He consoled in the biblical sense of the word. He was also a Levite who spoke Hebrew, living in Jerusalem but born in Cyprus, who thus understood Greek and the Hellenistic peoples. He was a bicultural man whose gift was consolation, pulling people together. Now in Antioch there were Jewish and Gentile believers, some of them from Cyprus, and they needed to learn how to live together. Barnabas was the man to do the job.

Later, when Barnabas decided he needed help, he did not go back to Cyprus. He did not go back to Jerusalem. He went north to Tarsus to find another bicultural man—Paul, a Roman citizen who was also a Pharisee. Barnabas knew Paul's conversion as well as his background. He introduced Paul to the apostles shortly after his conversion. He had seen the effect on Paul of Stephen's message of a universal God as Paul argued with Hellenists in Jerusalem. The opposition this created caused Paul to retreat to his Hellenistic hometown of Tarsus where he no doubt also had a bicultural ministry (9:26-30).

A common misconception is that Paul received his name when he became a Christian. Rather, he used his original Jewish name, Saul, primarily when in a Jewish setting. Of course, once he began dealing more with Gentiles, he used his Roman name, Paul. The two names are therefore another reflection of how well suited he was for this special role at Antioch.

An important principle emerges from this episode: When there is potential for division, do not focus on it. Find someone who is able to be a consoler, who can bring people together. "When he [Barnabas] came and saw the grace of God, he was glad; and he exhorted them all to remain faithful to the Lord with steadfast purpose" (11:23). The centrality of Christ is the message for such a consoler. That is the only ground on which we can hope to build one church. If he had focused on which language they should use or on circumcision, they would have split down the middle. Instead, Barnabas preached Jesus Christ to both groups. He said, "Focus on Jesus Christ. That is where your unity lies. Come to understand *him*. You Jews, you've got to realize that these Greeks have a little different understanding of who Jesus is."

How do we know he succeeded in keeping them together? Because it says, "In Antioch the disciples were for the first time called Christians" (11:26). If you have peaches and pears and put them in the same bowl, you have to come up with a new word to describe them. If you have Jews and Gentiles and put them in the same place, you have to come up with a new word too. You have a phenomenon that has to have an identity. The name probably came from outsiders, but it highlights the believers' focus on Jesus Christ. When they considered what was their common ground, they could not find it anywhere except in the fact that they both cleaved to Jesus. This is a powerful message to our campuses and churches if we can see Blacks, Chinese, Hispanics, Anglos, northerners, southerners—whatever diversity we have—hang together on the name of the Lord Jesus Christ. They became one in Christ first in Antioch.

The last paragraph of Acts 11 cites the material aid the church of Antioch sends to the church of Jerusalem (11:27-30). This suggests first that the church in Antioch was able to unite on practical matters, that their oneness was not in name only. Second, it suggests a mature, coequal relationship between the two churches. Acts 12 continues this theme of the declining role of Jerusalem and the growing status of Antioch.

The death of James must have been a shocking experience to those in Jerusalem (12:1-2). Peter's arrest is turned around by an angelic visit (12:3-17), but the picture of a fearful group of disciples behind locked doors who prayed for Peter's release is a stark contrast to the early chapters of Acts. The final section gives some relief in the death of Herod (12:18-24). Nonetheless, the chapter ends with Paul, Barnabas and their fresh recruit, John Mark, heading back to Antioch (12:25).

Antioch: The Multicultural, Missionary-minded Church
Chapter 13 opens by illustrating the same principle we saw in Acts 6—splitting power multiplies the ministry.

> Now in the church at Antioch there were prophets and teachers, Barnabas, Simeon who was called Niger, Lucius of Cyrene, Manaen a member of the court of Herod the tetrarch, and Saul. While they were worshiping the Lord and fasting, the Holy Spirit said, "Set apart for me Barnabas and Saul for the work to which I have called them." Then after fasting and praying they laid their hands on them and sent them off. (13:1-3)

Note that each of the leaders (the prophets and teachers) is identified by his ethnic background (except for Barnabas and Paul who we already know about). Notice also that Barnabas and Paul are not listed together. They are not at the top of the heap, lording it over the other three. They are not at the bottom, as if to say in false humility that they do not have any influence. They are coequal leaders, and so Luke splits them, I think, purposely to show this. Again we see that the unity of the church in Antioch is more than superficial.

Each leader probably represented an ethnic contingent. Simeon was black. Lucius was Greek. Manaen was Jewish. An African. An Asian. A Palestinian.

These not only represented different ethnic and geographical areas, but almost certainly different language groups. Since people usually desire to pray in the language of their homeland, it is almost certain that Antioch followed the pattern of house churches started in Jerusalem. These house churches, however, would represent different languages as well—Aramaic likely in the Jewish sector and Greek (the trade language) for most of the others. It is probable that these three elders in Antioch were elected to represent smaller groups of believers.

This group were not leaders in name only. They had power to act on behalf of the church in setting aside two-fifths of their leadership, the entire outside representation, to go out. This once again demonstrates a considerable degree of unity and trust within the church in Antioch.

What would a powerful church in Atlanta look like? Bring together the leaders from the African-American and white communities to pray and act together regularly on behalf of the church of Atlanta, and you would see eyes being opened—much more so than one church developing a powerful ministry.

Commissioning Barnabas and Paul also indicates the kind of leadership these two were building in Antioch—strong, indigenous leadership. It was like saying, "You two have done your job. We're on our feet now. You don't have to stay. In fact, you should be out doing the same in places that need you more."

This multicultural church thus became the first missionary church. Peter preached to a mixed group at Pentecost by an accident of God. Disciples left Jerusalem after Stephen's death because of persecution. But people left Antioch because of a deliberate decision to send.

The Jerusalem Council

On Paul's first missionary journey, described in Acts 13—14, we see his pattern of going to the synagogue and preaching a message that appeals to both Jew and Gentile. Within these Hellenistic communities the core leadership of devout, establishment Jews, whose authority depended on their claim to *the* truth, tended to reject Paul because he introduced new ideas. Other fringe Jews who came to the synagogue for social reasons found him irrelevant. So Paul's greatest response was from those devout Jews who genuinely wanted to know God and from Gentile God-fearers. The God-fearers would likely be skeptical at first that they could be fully accepted by God without circumcision. But their excitement would grow as later they would tell more and more of their friends the implications of this incredible message.

When Paul arrives back in Antioch and reports to the people, his focus is on how God opened a way for the Gentiles to believe (14:26-27). This was exciting news in Antioch! It confirmed to the people that the nature of *their* church as a multicultural community was in God's will. They rejoiced that there were many other churches like theirs. The churches of Phoenicia and Samaria, where Paul gave the same report en route to Jerusalem (15:3), had the same reaction. This contrasts sharply with the circumcision party in the Jerusalem church who wanted the Gentiles circumcised. They were adamant. Paul and Barnabas argued fiercely with them but could not resolve the situation (15:1-2).

Although the church in Jerusalem accepted in principle that Gentiles were welcome (11:18), this did not guarantee that all the people would implement that principle. The token integration of Cornelius did not guarantee that every local fellowship would welcome Gentiles. The parties thus agreed to submit their dispute to the apostles and elders in Jerusalem (15:2).

The council at Jerusalem described in Acts 15 thus deals with two important issues lying just under the surface issue of circumcision. One is the right of every church to be independently responsible to God. The second is the responsibility of churches to relate to one another. These basic issues are still with us today. The first is broken when materially wealthy churches impose their will on less-developed ones. The second principle is broken when, for example, the African-American church stops communicating with other churches because of the real, previous rejection it has experienced, or when white American churches exclude people of other backgrounds because they do not think anyone can teach them anything. "We have the teaching that others need. What could we possibly learn from African churches?"

The council of Jerusalem soon becomes an extended debate between Paul and Barnabas on the one hand and some of the Pharisees in the church on the other. Peter again recounts the story of Cornelius, pointing out that the issue of circumcision has already been resolved by the Holy Spirit (15:10-11). Finally, everyone agrees to let Paul and Barnabas speak without interruption about what actually has happened (15:12). The apostles recognize that the question is not really one of circumcision, but of how Jewish Christians will relate to Gentile Christians. James's conclusion is that as far back as Amos God declared that *he* would restore his kingdom so that the Gentiles could come to him (15:16-18). The church of Antioch therefore has a right to decide its own affairs without consulting Jerusalem. "Therefore my judgment is that we should not trouble those of the Gentiles who turn to God" (15:19).

Circumcision is neither right nor wrong. But it is certainly not an essential part of the gospel.

On the other hand, James suggests that two thousand years of living under the law taught the Hebrews some important principles of God that should be passed on. If someone wants to reinvent the wheel, they are free to do so. However, it would be foolish. If the Gentiles want to painfully discover God's patterns for life, they also could do so. But it is unnecessary. James summarizes these principles as follows: the Gentiles should "abstain from the pollutions of idols and from unchastity and from what is strangled and from blood. For from early generations Moses has had in every city those who preach him, for he is read every sabbath in the synagogues" (15:20-21). These basics deal with God's impatience with putting anything before him. James's concern is to preserve the family and the health of his people.

James's first statement, better translated by the NIV as "abstain from food polluted by idols," sums up years of the Hebrews' seeking after other gods while trying to remain faithful to God. A great deal of the Old Testament account leads us to the conclusion that one cannot worship God and maintain other spiritual interests. The Gentile weakness at that point would come to a head over whether or not meat offered to idols could be eaten without showing respect to the idol. It is better, says James, to stay away from anything that even looks like a compromise.[1]

The second statement of James, "abstain from . . . unchastity," sums up the entire Old Testament teaching on the respect of people as people. It preserves the Old Testament teaching of the family which leads to both a healthy start for marriage (by avoiding fornication) and a healthy maintenance of a trust relationship in marriage (by avoiding adultery). Keeping sexual communication within marriage not only assures a stronger base for building the family but also prepares the larger base of love relationships on which the church itself is built. The close, personal and affectionate relationship between those who are married and the spouses of others, between married people and single people, and between singles is only possible when sexual fidelity is assured.

The third statement James makes regards the eating of strangled animals or blood. Even today we understand the importance of not eating raw meat. Modern technology and science has helped us to define more accurately the thin line between rare meat and raw meat. But in an ancient culture the best way to be sure meat has been cooked well enough to avoid disease is not to eat any meat with blood in it. Today we know that the blood spoils quicker than the meat. Every modern butcher slits the animal's throat with its hind legs suspended in the air immediately after it has been killed to allow the blood to drain out before it coagulates. Modern science has taught us the reason for this. In the Old Testament Levitical law God had not explained why but gave a long series of commandments regarding food preparation, and the nature of clean and unclean food. These laws were misused by the Pharisees and others. However, the Hebrews saw that the nations who were not as careful in their eating habits lacked the robust health of the Hebrews and often had shorter lives. The statements of James established the freedom of Antioch to do as they pleased but gave them some strong advice regarding their behavior.

Today we also should spend less time passing on our doctrinal and cultural idiosyncrasies, and give more careful thought to what basic principles can be distilled from the history of Christianity in our own culture. That could be beneficial to the church's vitality in other parts of the world, or within other communities in our society.

Both Prophet and Priest

Some have laid much weight on the apparent rift between the Palestinian church at Jerusalem and the missionary church at Antioch, and on the apparent conflict of Peter's more provincial gospel and Paul's more Gentile gospel. I feel we must see the church of Jerusalem and the church of Antioch as manifestations of a basic tension that is essential to God's revelation of himself.

This is represented in the Old Testament by the "prophetic" and "priestly" roles. The prophets explained that God's purposes included the Gentiles and therefore demanded responsible witness to the nations. On the other hand, the priests called people in to be faithful to Jerusalem and the temple.[2]

This split is reflected in the differing stands taken toward outsiders by the northern kingdom of Israel and the southern kingdom of Judah. Israel was involved with all the nations, and her sin was to deny the message by turning to Baal. Judah was more faithful to the message, but held Jerusalem in such high esteem that she disdained and avoided the other nations. The people in Judah could not believe that God would be angry because of such obvious faithfulness.

This dynamic is with us today in the Roman Catholic and Protestant churches. The Catholic church has tended to fulfill the priestly role by calling people into itself, while the Protestant church has tended to be prophetic by sending people out into the world. Yet the two roles are seen even within Protestantism. There are evangelicals who preserve the message and liberals who seek to change social structures.

The biblical message is that the people of God can err on both sides, either by becoming so involved with action that they lose the message or by becoming so concerned with the message that they fail to act. Faith without works is dead. Thus the church is only dynamic and powerful when both its priestly and prophetic gears are engaged.

It was in this way that the sensitive yet controlling hand of the Jerusalem church and the action-oriented hand of the Antioch church were essential to the vitality of the first-century church as a whole. Paul understood this. His missionary journey showed his compulsion to move on. Yet after each journey he insisted on returning to Jerusalem both to integrate what he had learned with the apostles' understanding of the church and to assure them that he was still faithful to the gospel. On his arrival in Jerusalem following his third missionary journey, the church expressed deep concern regarding his activities (21:17-21). Paul gives a full report in which he satisfies their concerns. His subsequent arrest is incidental to preventing a possible rift between Antioch in its concern for outreach and Jerusalem in its concern for purity.

Unity and Diversity

Culture is not the center of the Bible; Christ is. But when the Bible mentions culture, it is important. Likewise, we must take culture and cultural differences seriously—for the sake of the life of the church.

First, in regard to organization, when the first-century Christians took culture seriously and split the power structure, acknowledging the importance of different ethnic groups (Acts 6 and 13), the church expanded. We must follow their example. We need not waste our energies trying to integrate every Bible study, for example, with one African-American and one Hispanic for every eight whites. (In fact, this could insure that the minorities would always be outvoted eight to two.) Undoubtedly there were many house churches in the first century made up entirely of one ethnic group or another.

Rather it is far more crucial to integrate the leadership in national Christian circles. How many Christian radio stations, seminaries, publishing houses, service organizations or mission agencies are honestly giving Blacks, Hispanics or Asians the opportunity to share power effectively in their organizational structures? If we insist there is no unique African-American culture or Polish culture or Mexican culture, we will continue to cut them out of places of leadership. Let us recognize their importance, allow each part of the body to exercise its gifts and thus expand God's work.

Second, acknowledging the importance of culture strengthens the church by helping each individual grow in Christ. With my limitations of language and experience, I cannot fully comprehend the meditative nature of Eastern Christianity or the vibrant dynamism of Latin American evangelism or the spiritual freedom of the African mind, but by faith I can accept that Jesus Christ's manifestation of himself is far greater than I can comprehend on this earth, and I can accept all of these as brothers and sisters because our unity is found in the gospel of Jesus Christ. Why should young people have to look to Eastern pantheistic mystics for a meditative experience? Where are Eastern Christians to help us? We have failed to recognize their life as a valid Christian way. I do not have to be able to reproduce the emotion-oriented worship of many Black churches to accept them in Christ any more than I should demand that they endure my emotionless exercise in intellectual worship before they can be called Christians.

Where then is the unity of the church? We live in a world of rapid change that no Christian should fear. If we believe God to be unchanging and absolute, then the more rapidly life changes, the more visible are the unchangeables. As one culture contacts and interacts with another, we are better able to identify what unchanging universals are accepted by Christians everywhere. Today we are witnessing a worldwide council of Jerusalem in which the universals of the faith are being hammered out on the anvil of church-mission relationships. As in the book of Acts, there is much discussion, difference of opinion and direction from the Holy Spirit. We can face this "council" confidently, secure that differences will not divide us because God's revelation is complete in Christ.

The gospel incorporates all the nations and ethnic and social groups of the earth. That's what the early church discovered. Although they began with de facto segregation, the Holy Spirit began to open their eyes through miracles, through teaching, through all that they had seen Christ do. As the Holy Spirit began to open doors, they walked through them, one by one, until we find the church has changed from a sect of Judaism to a universal church that included Samaritans, Ethiopians, Greeks, Asians, Romans—anybody who would come into the faith. That's the story that Luke was telling Theophilus. That's the story we have to tell the world if ever the gospel is to reach the many pockets of social and ethnic groups walled up within their own worlds, all deprived of the reconciliation provided in Jesus Christ.

Part 2

▼▼▼▼▼▼▼▼▼▼▼▼▼

Communicating
Christ
Today

8
Rural
Christians
in an
Urban World
▼▼▼▼▼▼▼▼▼▼▼▼▼

IN PART ONE WE SAW THAT WHEN GOD'S PEOPLE TAKE CULTURE SERIOUSLY, God's work expands and is strengthened. While culture is not everything, it does play a crucial role—from Genesis all the way through the New Testament. If this is the biblical pattern, the obvious question then becomes, How should we be looking on culture today to expand and strengthen God's work in the world? This chapter and the next will seek to give practical answers to this question. To begin, however, we need to consider the two thousand years of church history between the New Testament era and the present.

Waves of History
When I was in California for a year of study at Fuller Theological Seminary, I became enamored with surfing. A great wave will loom over your head and you have to get on your board and ride the wave, or it will crush you. Once you are up, the ride is exhilarating until the wave carries you to shore. Then, if you are going to surf anymore, you need to get off the board and swim out to catch the next wave.

I have seen a relationship between these phases of surfing (catching the wave, riding it, getting off) and the history of Christianity. Kenneth Scott Latourette saw Christian history as a series of pulses—periods of expansion each followed by a period of retreat. Ralph Winter has found it instructive to place a four-hundred-year grid over the last two thousand years. Figure 1 summarizes how I see the three phases of a wave applying in each segment.

Figure 1   The Wave Theory of Christian History

Four-Hundred-Year Grid	Phase 1 Catching the Wave	Phase 2 Riding the Wave	Phase 3 Getting off the Wave
0-400	Early Church	Constantine	Barbaric Invasions
400-800	Barbaric Invasions	Carolingian Renaissance and	Moslem Advances
800-1200	Nordic Invasions	Alfred the Great Cluny Gregory VII	Crusades East-West Church Split
1200-1600	Mongol Invasions Friars	Plagues Corruption in Church "Babylonian Captivity" of Papacy	Early Reformers
1600-2000	Reformation	Colonialism	End of Colonialism
2000-	Urbanization Rise of Technology		

In the first phase, a hostile culture looms over the church and threatens to crush it. But in the second phase (with one notable exception) the church captures the cultural wave and rides it so that God's work is carried forward. As that cultural wave breaks up, the church must also get off the wave or relinquish the opportunity to expand in the next period.

Now dividing history into periods like this is somewhat arbitrary. It would also be simplistic to say, for example, that there were only positive trends in Christianity from A.D. 500 to 700 and no positive trends from 700 to 900. Then, too, the peak in each period is not reached at its exact center, nor is each peak as high as all the others. But the trends are there. Latourette expresses his own approach this way:

> After its origin, the course of Christianity is treated by what the author deems to have been its major epochs. These, as he conceives them, are best seen as pulsations in the life of Christianity as reflected in its vigour and its influence upon the ongoing history of the race. The criteria which he believes to be valid for discerning these pulsations are, in the main, three—the expansion or recession of the territory in which Christians are to be found, the new movements issuing from Christianity, and the effect of Christianity as judged from the perspective of mankind as a whole. Precise dates can seldom if ever be fixed for the pulsations. The lines between the eras are fuzzy. One age has a way of running over into its successor or of being foreshadowed before it is born. The eras are realities, but there are no sharp breaks between them which can be identified by particular years. Advance and retreat often begin at different times in the several areas in which Christians are found and the first indications of revival are frequently seen before decline has been halted. Terminal dates are, therefore, only approximations. Yet approximate dates can be named.[1]

The movements, the trends, the pulsations, the waves—however you put it—"the eras are realities," despite the difficulty in fixing dates. I will not expand on figure 1 in detail, but allow me to give a few examples.

At the time of Christ the dominant cultural wave that threatened to crush the early church was the Roman Empire itself. But with the conversion of Emperor Constantine, the church was able to use this wave for its own expansion. Not all the results of Constantine's turnaround were positive, but on the whole the church grew.

As the Empire disintegrated, the invading barbarian soldiers came into contact with Christianity. The church was, at this time, linked with Rome and could have been destroyed by its association. But two trends thwarted the possibility. First, "the majority of the pagan invaders were fairly quickly brought to an outward adoption of Christianity and their faith was even carried beyond what, in the year 500, had been its northern borders."[2] Second, "as the structure of the Roman Empire disintegrated, invasions multiplied, wars and disorder increased, and life and property became progressively unsafe. The Church stepped into the breach and took over some of the functions for which society had been accustomed to look to the state."[3] Again the full results of these trends were mixed, but the church turned a potentially disastrous movement to its own advantage which culminated in the Carolingian Renaissance. Unfortunately, the simultaneous advances of Islam during this period overshadowed this rebirth.

The period of 1200 to 1600, however, saw the church unable to let go of former waves and ride new ones. The crusades, which weakened the Eastern church and blocked the expansion of Christianity into Islam even to this day, were just ending as this period began.[4] After this bad start, conditions worsened as the corruption within the church hierarchy grew. There were a few bright spots. First, the church was able to stamp out a variety of heresies.[5] Second, two missionary orders of the Catholic Church (the Franciscans and Dominicans) took advantage of the Mongol invasion of Eurasia to plant missions from Russia to the China Sea.[6] And third, immense Christian energies were released to build the cathedrals and universities of Europe. On the whole, though, the church failed to ride the cultural wave.

The Retreat of the West

In reaction to this failure, the Reformers arose and were able to piggyback on the next wave of colonialism to spread the gospel even more. The ride on the top of that wave has been exhilarating, and we are still flushed with enthusiasm because of it. What many in the church do not appear to realize, however, is that the wave has come to shore. It has ended. We are in a period similar to the barbaric invasions of the shrinking Roman Empire. This is a period of withdrawal for the West and the rise of the Third World.

Ralph Winter has documented this incredible reversal, which he calls "the retreat of the West." In 1944, 99.5 percent of the population of the non-Western world was under the domination of the West. Just twenty-five years later only 0.5 percent was under Western control.[7] This was counterbalanced by heightened economic imperialism by the West,[8] but the control of the Third World over oil and other natural resources is reversing even this trend.

Despite the apparent end of colonialism, many still assume the Western church can and should continue to dominate the Third World church. Instead of letting go of a cultural wave that has come to shore and getting on the next wave, they continue to try to ride a wave that is no longer there. They are stuck in the sand and won't admit it. Others in the church simply do not know which way to go. They see the end of colonialism and the futility of trying to conserve colonial forms in the church. But they do not know where to look for alternatives.

What we need to ask now is, What is the next wave? What is the dynamic force that will be changing the world in the decades to come? What cultural movement looms overhead and threatens to crush the church which the church can catch and ride to its own advantage?

When you consider that missionaries have in the past been barbarian soldiers and Christian women taken captive by Vikings, you begin to see God's way with new eyes. Even "standard-type" missionaries like William Carey had to overcome great resistance from their own people and practically be stowaways on ships because the established church would not help them. The early part of any of these waves sees new, creative ways of getting the gospel out.

We have, for example, been used to asking governments to let in missionaries from mission agencies. But now many governments will not allow them in. Are we to forsake that country for years or possibly decades until the officials have a change of heart (or the country a change of government)?

For forty years Portugal was ruled by the facist dictator Antonio de Oliveira Salazar, who opposed both Protestantism and communism. When, a few years after his stroke in 1968, free elections were held, who was organized? The communists. By the end of 1977 they were able to topple moderate Premier Mario Soares after only seventeen months of democratic government.

Both communists and Protestants had been banned officially, and the Catholic Church was repressed. Despite this, the communists informally infiltrated every village. When the ban was lifted, it was a simple step to a formal organization. But where was the church? Because of the mindset that we can only work through governments, the church had little influence. There are other ways to communicate a message, as the communists showed. We need a new mindset and new, creative ways to communicate our eternal message.

The New Wave
We will find these new avenues in what I believe to be the overriding

movements that today are affecting people on every continent around the world: urbanization and technology. Figure 2 illustrates the rapid progress of urbanization since 1800.

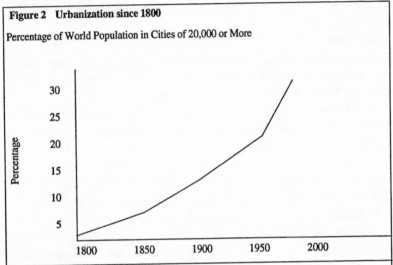

Figure 2   Urbanization since 1800

Percentage of World Population in Cities of 20,000 or More

Sources: Kingsley Davis, "The Orgin and Growth of Urbanization in the World," *The American Journal of Sociology,* March 1955; United Nations, *Statistical Yearbook* 1969; United Nations, *1990 Demographic Yearbook.*

Table 1 shows that while urbanization has progressed to different levels and proceeds at different rates, nonetheless, the trend exists in every region of the world.

Some might object that urbanization is not occurring, that people are in fact leaving the core cities for the suburbs. While this is so in some parts of the world, in most parts urban centers are simply expanding geographically. Suburbia is still sub-urban or is being absorbed into the total urban sprawl, and people find they actually need to move further out into the country to avoid a citylike environment. Nonetheless, the overall process is a movement away from rural living.

As you might expect when you begin throwing around sociological terms, there are a variety of definitions that scholars use and argue over. Kenneth Little distinguishes among three definitions.

The term "urbanization" has several different meanings. It frequently refers to living in towns as against living in rural settlements, and it is with

Table 1   Urbanization from 1950

	Percentage of Population in Urban Areas					Percentage Change from 1940-1990
	1950	*1960*	*1970*	*1980*	*1990*	
World	28	33	37	42	45	+17
Africa	14	18	22	27	34	+20
North America	64	70	74	74	75	+11
South America	40	48	56	64	72	+32
Asia	16	20	25	30	34	+18
Europe	52	57	63	68	73	+21
Oceania	62	66	68	70	72	+ 9
USSR	40	49	57	64	66	+26

Sources: United Nations, *Statistical Yearbook 1972*; United Nations, *1990 Demographic Yearbook*; John W. Wright, ed., *The Universal Almanac 1993*.

this meaning in mind that simple quantitative indices of urbanization are sometimes constructed. . . . Another type of definition holds that urbanization is a process of population concentration in which the ratio of urban people to the total population in a territory increases. . . . I prefer to regard urbanization as a cultural and social psychological process. By means of this process people acquire elements of material and non-material culture—including behavioral patterns, forms of organization, and ideas—that originate in or are distinctive of the city. A corollary of this is that country persons moving to the city, or visiting it, become urbanized to the extent that they acquire urban characteristics of behavior and thought, or material objects which through possession or use affect their conduct, ideas, and social relationships. Similarly, the farm or village resident may become urbanized as the culture of the city is conveyed to the rural community and there integrated into the ideational and behavioral patterns of the residents.[9]

I want to focus my attention on the last type of urbanization Little has described—a shift in behavior patterns and in values. A rural culture is one with *a geographical frame of reference.* In Africa, a people on a plateau bounded by a river on one side and a mountain range on another and a forest on another will develop a certain culture distinct from those who live in the mountains or those in the forest. Those on the plateau have long bows because they are moving around in a large open territory. They can see danger at great distances and can plan accordingly. Those in the forest will have short bows so they can run easily and at a moment's notice. Because of the vegetation, they can only see short distances, and danger is potentially close at all times. Their whole life, you see, takes shape around the geography they live in.

In America an east-west highway will be crossed by a main street, and stores and houses will grow around the intersection. If someone drives through that geographic area, he or she has intruded on the culture. "Who is it?" "What do they want?" "What are they up to?" The culture responds to all activity, natural or supernatural, that intrudes its space. There will be functional diversity but geographic limitation.

Urban culture, by contrast, has *a functional frame of reference.* People participate in activities or respond to events not on the basis of geography but on the basis of spheres of influence. Again in contrast to rural culture, there is geographic mobility. An American steel executive can travel around the world by jet, stay in Hilton Hotels and rent Hertz cars wherever he or she goes, discuss business in person or on the phone with Japanese, German and Nigerian steel executives—and never penetrate another culture. Such people operate in a sphere of influence and out of a value system that goes with them wherever they go.

The First National Bank of Chicago says, "In 1905, we decided to organize our loan departments on the basis of the businesses and industries we loaned *to,* rather than the geographical locations we loaned *at. We organized to serve the needs of our customers"* (emphasis theirs).[10] The bank saw seventy-five years ago that the city was not organized geographically but functionally. My hope, as will become clear in the pages to come, is that the church will begin to see the wisdom of doing the same.

From Notched Sticks to Computer Bits

Of course urbanization does have certain geographical characteristics. In New York, for example, you have the Hudson River on one side and the East River on the other side of Manhattan. Certain sections began to develop where the boats dock; the hotel district and the warehouses, and industries and retailing developed near there. All these functions are compressed geographically and stretch up fifty stories in skyscrapers for the sake of communication.

Communication is the key word. "Cities were evolved primarily for the facilitation of human communication,"[11] not because geography compelled people to move closer. I recognize, of course, that here again we find ourselves in the middle of a debate among sociologists and urban specialists on urban growth and structure, or on what makes cities tick. F. Stuart Chapin Jr. has highlighted no less than six main theories which emphasize, among others, economics, accessibility and communications as proposed keys to understanding urban activity.[12] While each theory has its merits and uses, I have found the communications approach the most adaptable to the needs of the church and the truest to my own experience. Paul Craven and Barry Wellman elaborate on this view, emphasizing the communication networks in the city and deemphasizing geography.

We have been careful not to define communities in spatial terms, as areas whose boundaries can be drawn on a map. In considering a community, we can just as easily be talking about a dense, bounded network of enthusiastic stamp collectors as of one of fellow residents in a particular locality. While many discussions have equated "community" with "neighborhood," we feel that it is intellectually more profitable to see the neighborhood as only a special case of community. Furthermore, *not all neighborhoods are necessarily communities;* there will be many residential localities in the city where there is little interpersonal network linkage among the inhabitants. The identification of neighborhood with community was probably more appropriate in the period before the development of widespread transportation and communication facilities; when mobility is low and communication difficult, much of one's interpersonal interaction will take place within a relatively confined geographical area.[13]

The consideration of widespread transportation and communication facilities leads us to the second major force active today—technology. Its combination with urbanization has been even more significant than it would be on its own. When cities first developed, "communication was restricted to face-to-face interaction but very quickly the need for records developed. Thus notched sticks, clay tablets, papyri, and smooth stone surfaces were marked with knives, styli, pens and chisels according to the local code, and communication became instrumented."[14] The next major development was the printing press. In the nineteenth century, steamships, railroads, telegraphs, telephones and photographs were introduced, and the wave of technology began to rise. Television, radio, air travel, trucking, satellites and computers have all added energy to the movement in this century.

The machinery of communication is merely a vast elaboration of the work of the scribe and the courier, two social roles that became important to the organization of large communities at the dawn of history. Face-to-face communications go back to the origins of language itself. Thus the proliferation of communications technique is a fundamental property of urbanism.[15]

While urban cultures tend to remain *functionally rigid* today as they did five thousand (or even five hundred) years ago, the chief difference is the far greater degree of *geographic mobility* made possible by the technological revolution.

I have a friend who was an executive in Borden's Milk Company. They used to buy milk from upstate New York and then process it right in New York City and sell it to the people in the area. They started trotting the milk out at five o'clock with horses and buggies; then they got trucks. That is all gone now, of course. Today they buy their milk from anywhere in the United States, because in twenty-four hours you can fly it in or move it through the night by refrigerated milk trucks and the like. Borden's has in fact moved out of New York almost entirely except for one of their major milk-processing plants. Their headquarters is in Ohio, and its major branches are located from one coast to the other. The executive officers use computers and telephones to keep track of their warehousing. It is not necessary to see face to face the people with whom they are dealing.

Another example comes from Kenya. Right after independence 1.5 million Africans were resettled onto the old European farms. They were each given seven acres. Traditional African culture would have demanded that they move their families onto those seven acres and plow them. But they did not. They organized into groups of farms with movable fences that were simple slats of wood tied together. Then they hired a tractor to plow all the fields. Next they arranged for a trucker with a fleet of Peugot station wagons to bring them seed from the city for the cash crop they grow, seed which the farmers purchased on credit. After putting their fences back up, they all planted. At harvest time the fences came back down and the families hired someone else to harvest the whole plot. Truckers then took the crop to market. Those who plowed, harvested and trucked the seed and the crop all took their cut from the cooperative. These families are 120 miles from Nairobi and have no education. But they are as urbanized as Borden's because their life is dominated by a functional frame of reference and not a geographical one.

I have another friend who raises cattle in Kansas. At first we might say he is rural since his nearest neighbor is eight miles away. But consider how he does business. He buys thousands of head at one time from breeders in Texas when the cattle are three months old. He then fattens them for a few months and sells them. That's all he does. It is his whole business. If he is forced to sell them three days too late, his whole profit is lost. How does he know when to buy and when to sell?

First, he is in constant contact with the big breeders in Texas. Then he has an agent in Chicago buying grain for him. By checking *The Chicago Tribune* every day he can figure the cost of grain per pound of meat and calculate the date of sale. Finally he keeps in touch with buyers in Iowa who will complete the fattening process before slaughter. He is on the phone constantly. He even has a small airplane so he can be in Texas and Chicago regularly.

Is this rural America? He does not know his neighbors. Why? His neighbor raises poultry. My friend's whole life is beef. His entire social, economic and political relationships revolve around the beef industry. The people he goes to dinner with, the people he socializes with, the people he goes to the theater with are all connected to the beef industry in Chicago or in Texas or in Kansas.

I asked him if he went to church. "Well, I've been to church in Wichita, about twenty-five miles away." He is not too interested in the people in Kansas, however—other than those in the beef industry. So how is the church going to function effectively in that kind of context?

Consider the people who live in high-rise apartments. They are as difficult to reach as those in the ghetto. It is pointless to suggest one do door-to-door evangelism in a high-rise because the people who live there are buying protection from any stranger who might knock on their door. If you do knock, you are their enemy. The first thing they will do is call the guard and say, "How did this creep get in here? Get him out!" They have locks on their doors; they have guards; they have phone systems; they have two-way radios that communicate up and down. You ring the buzzer and the buzzer says, "Who is it?" They do not want you in and they pay big money to keep you out. They did not choose a high-rise so they could be close to lots of other people, but so they could be separated.

The kind of housing you select in the city is determined by the kind of values you have already selected, unless you are one of the oppressed. To come into a ghetto and start talking about building a neighborhood church will achieve little since there is no neighborhood. If people are not functioning on geographical lines, the church is not going to function on geographical lines either.

Even in suburbia, how many people know everyone on their block? How many have best friends whom they got to know because they lived in their neighborhood? Communication is possible over a much wider geographic area with those whose values are more similar than those who live next door. So we do not talk to our neighbors but to those in our profession, in our family, in our volunteer groups who may be scattered across the city or state or nation.

The rise of urbanism has profound implications for us in the church in the West and especially in America, because, for the most part, we in the church have a rural, geographic mindset. Foreign missions to most of us means ministry thousands of miles away, not ten miles away in the Puerto Rican district. Door-to-door evangelism dominates the witness of many groups. The changes in the church in the coming years will necessarily be substantial. I do not know precisely what forms the church will use to spread the Christian message in an urbanized world, but I hope in the next chapters to draw the broad outlines within which I believe we should work.

In Two Worlds

Let me close this chapter with the story of Bill, a Christian business executive with Amoco in Chicago. His work took him around the world, including Kenya, where I met him. One time he was playing golf in Kenya alone and decided to pair up with another man who was also alone. They teed off and began to chat. In the middle of the game Bill asked his partner what he did for a living. "I'm a missionary," came the reply. Bill stopped suddenly and stared in shock. Moments later he began to weep.

His home church had sent two missionaries to Kenya. Bill had been to Nairobi three times. It had never occurred to him that he was on the mission field. He traveled to Saudi Arabia and to Kenya and back home and never left his culture. His mind functioned entirely along business channels. Yet fifteen miles from where he stood on that golf course was a missionary his church supported named Maria. For the first time in thirty-five years of being a "rural" Christian and twenty-five years of being an "urban" businessman, his two worlds crashed together, and Bill could not cope.

The two of them did not finish the golf game. They picked up their balls and went to visit the missionary his church supported. When he met Maria, Bill got so excited and was in such culture shock that he bought her $250 in gifts. For a day and a half all he could say was how funny it was that he was on the mission field.

We in the church in the West are like Bill. We are simultaneously in two worlds. We can pretend that one world is not waning and strain to hold on to it; or we can be suddenly shocked into an awareness of the new coming era. We can be paralyzed by fear of the wave of urbanization and technology that is coming upon us. Or we can seek out creative new means of dealing with these movements as Christians throughout the centuries have done. I do not know exactly what these new ideas will look like, but I believe they are there to be found by courageous Christians willing to try. We can, we must take advantage of those forces that threaten to destroy us and use them to expand and strengthen God's church.

9
Networks of Communication
▼▼▼▼▼▼▼▼▼▼▼▼▼▼

URBANISM IS A DYNAMIC MULTIDIMENSIONAL ARRAY OF HUMAN COMMUNI-
cation networks. But our rural mindset blinds us to the importance of these.
Rather, our orientation is toward impersonal power structures and institutions. These are really what matter, aren't they?

Russell Hitt, author and former editor of *Eternity* magazine, provides us
with a striking illustration of this kind of thinking in an article entitled "New
York City: Spiritual Power Failure."[1] This was part of "Evangelicals in
America," a series of articles in *Eternity* focusing on different sections of the
country. I respect Hitt and believe he did a remarkable job, considering his
limited sources and the deadlines involved in putting out a magazine. But his
article betrays a one-dimensional perspective.

Power Structures and Human Networks
He begins with people, but his choice is telling. "The Big Apple . . . is
worm-ridden on the inside with muggers and dope peddlers, Mafia capos,
and slimy politicians." As soon as he introduces power structures, the change
is startling.

With all its filth and crime and political corruption, it still remains the most powerful city in the world. It is the capital of the U.S. world of finance, communication, book and magazine publishing, and the garment industry. It's the nation's richest port. There is only one Wall Street, one Broadway, one Fifth Avenue lined with smart shops like Tiffany and Cartier. Not far away from Central Park and the Plaza Hotel is Bloomingdales, mecca of ecstatic shoppers. Gleaming skyscrapers house the offices of the conglomerates and multi-national corporations.

The positiveness with which he approaches these institutions, all in the heart of the downtown area, is apparent. But when he talks about people and the human networks of communication, he mentions only those in another part of the city, not in the downtown area. These he sees negatively. This underlying value system places worth in the power structures. The communication networks among the people are secondary at best.

Then he switches from power structures back to people.

The ethnic and religious complexity of New York is staggering. It is, for example, the largest Jewish city in the world.... Of the 1.7 million Puerto Ricans living on the U.S. mainland, half live in New York, especially in East Harlem, the South Bronx and enclaves of Brooklyn. Here is found the largest black population of any city of the United States, congregated largely in Harlem and the Bedford-Stuyvesant section of Brooklyn and Newark. Blacks make up 25% of the population in Manhattan, the Bronx and Brooklyn which compares to 11% of the general U.S. population.

It is not Hitt's fault that negative images jump into the minds of most Americans when they hear about 1.7 million Puerto Ricans and African-Americans in the Bronx and Brooklyn. But he goes on to give his perspective on this situation which reveals his own myopia. "One has to search for vital Christianity," because we don't expect it among 1.7 million Puerto Ricans. "And yet it can be found—in unlikely places." Again, value and worth, according to a rural mindset, should be found in the institutions, not among the people.

He returns to power structures when he mentions the Billy Graham Crusade in Madison Square Garden. He institutionalizes Billy Graham—and not Billy Graham in Manhattan, but Billy Graham in the institution of Madison Square Garden. "The next time Billy Graham conducts a crusade in Madison Square Garden, he'll probably have to speak in Spanish. Besides its huge Puerto Rican population, other Hispanic groups are pouring into New York, legally and illegally."

Unfortunately, Russell Hitt is mistaken. Billy Graham will never speak in Spanish in New York because Billy Graham has been there three times in the last fifteen years, and few who are Spanish come because most do not know he is there. The auditorium will be filled with twenty thousand suburbanites who drive into the city. They are the ones who know Graham is there, and they come to see him. There is this vast difference between the structural approach to the city, which is a top-down approach, and the people approach. Hitt is vaguely aware that this difference exists, but he has not seen the degree to which the structural approach misses the people of the city.

He continues to consider the church from a structural perspective.

The once great Protestant churches of Manhattan and Brooklyn gradually are disappearing. . . . Yet there are some surprising bright spots. . . . There are still some strong conservative churches like the Fifth Avenue and Madison Avenue Presbyterian Churches and near Columbia University Broadway Presbyterian that ministers to the academic community.

It is difficult to relate that paragraph to people. He has not mentioned the name of the pastor; he rarely mentions what kind of people attend there. He has simply mentioned that these are the going churches. The city is such a spiritually dark quarter, however, that even establishment churches with a little life are called "surprising bright spots."

The sentences which follow in the article focus on more institutions: Norman Vincent Peale's Marble Collegiate Church (another institutionalized person), Calvary Baptist Church on 57th Street, New York Theological Seminary, "the huge Protestant center at 475 Riverside Drive, headquarters for the National Council of Churches and many major Protestant denominations. Nearby is theologically liberal Union Theological Seminary." In doing this, Hitt is communicating a whole way of viewing life and what is important. The overall picture is a dreary one because the institutions of the church, its power structures, have come on hard times and are on the way out.

The picture changes, as does the whole tone of the article, when Hitt begins to focus on the unexpected human networks that are on the way up.

The sovereign grace of God is not thwarted by the migration of believers to the suburbs. In the Puerto Rican and Hispanic barrios of East Harlem and the Bronx, there are literally scores of storefront churches led by obscure but faithful men of God who are preaching the gospel of love. . . . There is a quality to the Spanish-language churches that is light miles above traditional Protestantism. The ebullient Hispanic people not only preach the gospel, they demonstrate their love for fellow members to those outside that recalls the infant church of Acts. . . . They share their possessions. . . . Many of these little churches surround new immigrants with a love that is matched by their obedience to the law. . . . There are many eloquent black preachers. Dr. Gardner C. Taylor, leader of the Progressive Baptists, who serves a flock of 12,000 at Concord Baptist Church in Brooklyn, is an outstanding illustration. . . . The stones cry out in another unexpected quarter—the number of Jews who are acclaiming Jesus Christ as their true Messiah.

The tone is suddenly bright and alive—*quality, ebullient, demonstrate their love, share their possessions, eloquent black preachers, serves a flock, outstanding.* He does not emphasize buildings or streets. He speaks of powerful leadership and faithful men.

In this article, I believe Hitt has viewed the city and the church in the city the way most in the middle class do—as institutions. When he discovers that there is a vital church out among the people, it amazes him. Even so, it is clear that he has not understood that some of the institutional churches he names are doing little that affects the city. They are two-thirds empty; the people who do attend are elderly; and even their money is drying up. Because he is not plugged into the human communication networks but deals primarily with establishment power structures, he has completely missed a five-thousand-member church whose leadership has started a two-thousand-member subchurch and is now planning five other new churches.

Bishop Brown started an independent Pentecostal church in the Bronx with a membership of twelve hundred and set up Bible-school training for all of his people, six nights a week. Out of that has developed a leadership class that runs the church and a group of young preachers. They have planted eleven churches in New York—all of them with a membership of more than two hundred. They have $1.6 million of property under their control. They have 480 people registered in their school which has grown from a one-year basic course for all new Christians to a three-year curriculum of Bible study. They also offer a one-year advanced Bible-training course and a doctrinal course for those who want to become pastoral ministers. A five-year Bible school that meets six nights a week is not unusual. There are at least ten similar schools in the African-American community alone in New York.

Where is the church in the city? We do not see it, because we are oriented toward the power structures and see only emptiness and decay, and conclude the church is dead. When we are among the people and begin to see their experience and the strength in their leadership, we see that there is vitality. The church is alive and growing and dynamic in the city.

In chapter eight I briefly mentioned the main lines of communication that run through our urban world. I like to think of these as cultural stripes which cut across broad geographic areas. In the remainder of this chapter we will look at four primary categories of these networks (government, professions, kinship and volunteer associations), and in chapter ten we will explore one more—ethnicity. Through these cultural stripes we will be better able to see the nature of human relationships today.

Government: More Than Bureaucracy

One of the basic ways we understand the city is as a political unit. From a communications perspective, we can see the city as a group of administrative responsibilities, as Amos Hawley does in *Urban Society: An Ecological Approach*.[2] Administration is simply one way to communicate. When you see a plow outside in the snow, you know somebody told the driver in the plow to get out and clear the streets. The driver's boss told him to get the plow out, and so on until you come to the person who has final administrative responsibility. In other words, nothing happens by accident.

We would be misled, however, if we thought that the only communication in government comes down from the top of the administrative pyramid and occasionally goes back up. American cities, especially, were not planned. They were formed haphazardly. Often, therefore, administrations will not respond to their own system but will react to other influences such as interest groups.

For instance, I found two Christian teachers in a public school system in Newark. Assuming that there were also some Christian children in the system, we turned loose two summer volunteers in our urban outreach ministry to canvass the neighborhood to find out where the children went to church. In that canvass we uncovered eight or ten Christian homes that were concerned with the school. They represented three or four churches who had an impact on another thirty or forty children in their Sunday schools. So we began with fifty schoolchildren, eight parents, two teachers and three churches.

Next we got the parents together in a small prayer group with the teachers.

As a result, they developed a child-evangelism type of program, but with neighborhood parents and neighborhood teachers working together in the neighborhoods.

Later, we recruited another Christian from outside the system to apply for a job at that school. We also encouraged two of the parents to get into the PTA and extended our influence there.

The fifty children, of course, reported to their parents about what was happening in school. So we were able as a group to keep close tabs on problems as they developed and respond effectively to them. For instance, we discovered that two Muslims in the school were pushing their theology on the kids. Of course when we raised some questions about this, they in turn raised some questions about our prayer group. Eventually, however, the Muslims got uncomfortable. They saw that they were not going to accomplish anything in that school system; so they left.

After this two other Christian teachers who had been hiding in the woodwork began to identify with the prayer group. Then we were joined by two other teachers, one African-American and one white, who were not religious conservatives but who were concerned for the good of the children. They recognized that this was the body of people that was doing the most for the school. So they got on the bandwagon.

Quite unexpectedly, we then had a change in the administration. A new principal was brought in from the outside, and nobody knew who she was. As it turned out, she was a Christian who was excited about working in the system and was very supportive of the prayer group. Now we had a neighborhood school that was beginning to provide solid education. It was not the best education; it was still part of the Newark school system. It was full of all kinds of problems. But you see that here was a government system we could affect positively by ignoring the board of education and looking to the lines of communication that naturally existed in the city.

Professions: Opening Closed Circles

Another functional culture is the professions. The medical, legal, ministerial, military, governmental, academic and entertainment professions are all cultural stripes that transcend geographic limitations. On the other hand, professional people are not so mobile that they can walk into a ghetto. They are functionally restricted.

In fact, it is easier for one doctor to communicate with another doctor than it is for the doctor to communicate with a schoolteacher. That is what you see when you attend a PTA meeting. Parents cannot communicate because union workers do not know how to communicate to doctors about the school system. Union workers can go to doctors for checkups. But they cannot talk about the local school system together because their value bases are being isolated more and more from each other.

William Goode of Columbia University highlights the following eight characteristics of a professional community.

(1) Its members are bound by a sense of identity. (2) Once in it, few leave, so that it is a terminal or continuing status for the most part. (3) Its members share values in common. (4) Its role definitions *vis-à-vis* both members and non-members are agreed upon and are the same for all members. (5) Within the areas of communal action there is a common language, which is understood only partially by outsiders. (6) The Community has power over its members. (7) Its limits are reasonably clear, though they are not physical and geographical but social. (8) Though it does not produce the next generation biologically, it does so socially through its control over the selection of professional trainees, and through its training processes it sends these recruits through an adult socialization process. Of course, professions vary in the degree to which they are communities, and it is not novel to view them as such.[3]

If you want to be a doctor today, you have to determine it before you get into high school, because you have to take college preparatory courses in high school that will get you into an elite premedical school. Then, once in medical school, you have to agree to be a part of that system. I have probed this with medical students in InterVarsity Christian Fellowship. They are essentially being told what kind of car they can buy, what kind of games they can play, what kind of neighborhood they can live in. They have to demonstrate through their style of living a willingness to sell themselves to the system. If they don't, it will be very difficult for them to get their degree. The social pressures to conform, though often subtle, are tremendous. Social ostracism and harassment in schoolwork or internships are real, if unconsciously used, weapons which aim to push renegades out or make them toe the line. Some can withstand the pressures. Others cannot. It is the same in the legal profession.

Professional sports are the same. If you are going to be a professional athlete, you will know it when you are in the eighth grade because you will be the superhero. You will be the quarterback on the high-school football team because you will be the best. When you get to college, you are going to make the first string in your first or second year. If you inherently have the quality that is going to make you a professional, it will be obvious back in the seventh or eighth grade. So all through high school and college you will develop a superior attitude that says, "Everybody worships me." This is then fostered by the profession itself with its pomp, grandeur and hero worship. If you refuse that style of life and those values, just as if you refuse to drive a Mercedes (and all the values that go with it) in the medical profession, you will be ostracized.

This is precisely what happened to Roger Maris after he broke Babe Ruth's record for home runs in one season. He decided he did not want to go along with the hero-worship system; he just wanted to play baseball. Maris himself said,

All I was trying to do was my job. I played from 1961 to 1968 with people on my ass in every ball park in the country. I don't know how it got started. I'd look in the paper and see myself described as "sullen" and "arrogant" and "surly." I mean, take this whole temperament thing. The fans and writers wanted me to be Babe Ruth all over again. Well, I never wanted to be Babe Ruth in the first place. What did they want from me? . . . To go down Broadway with 10 dames on my arm and stand on street corners eating hot dogs by the dozen? No, it was never any fun after I hit those 61 homers. . . . I know what happened back there. I know how the system used me; that's what I know, and nothing will ever change it. You can call it bitterness if you want. I don't think so.

Maris quit baseball early, just after turning thirty-four, a drained and broken man because he would not abide by the rules of his profession. He refused to be a superhero, and it destroyed what was left of his career.

Our concern as Christians should also go beyond the issues of individual lifestyle to larger issues. Who will be deciding when old people will be allowed to die? Who will be making recommendations on abortion? The doctors. Who will be ruling on issues of freedom of religion? The judges. One of the main channels of power in our urbanized world are the professions.

How do we infiltrate these lines of communication for Christ? We do what missionaries have been doing for years. We learn the language. We get to know key individuals who can then communicate even more effectively to their peers, and suddenly we have a church.

We could be misled if we viewed the task solely from a structural perspective. There is more to the medical profession than the AMA, more to the legal profession than the American Bar Association. We should focus on the communication networks rather than on the organizational structures.

There was a time when conservative Christians said, "You can't be a professional baseball player and a Christian because they play on Sunday." So for years those in baseball and other sports did not hear the gospel. Then the Fellowship of Christian Athletes (FCA) organized to penetrate that cultural system for Christ. They brought the church to the people instead of making the people come to the church. When the gospel was communicated to the athletes in a language and a context that they could understand, they responded. The result? Most teams have Sunday chapel in the locker room. Many have even hired chaplains. It is not uncommon to hear a quarterback give God credit for his gifts on nationally televised interviews. FCA probably has more to do in helping these athletes relate to the Christian church at large, but FCA certainly has begun by moving in the right direction.

My question now is, Who will penetrate rodeos, opera, the circus? Why are these groups so patently unchristian? Because the Christians are not there. Who will be the missionaries who will penetrate not unreached lands but unreached value systems? People are already doing it in the world of professional skiing.[4]

Government circles are also starting to be reached. Many prayer fellowships have developed in Washington, D.C. And now they are starting to pop up all over the world. Why? Because Ethiopian leaders can communicate more easily to American Congressional representatives than to Ethiopian peasants just outside Addis Ababa. Why? The concerns and priorities of government leaders are the same around the world. How do you spend this money? How do you solve that transportation problem? How do you resolve that international conflict?

As important as the local church is, we must not forget that it is a human network of communication. The church is not ultimately an organization or an institution or a building or a ministry. It is the fellowship of all believers wherever they may be. Let us, therefore, bring the professions into the church.

Kinship: Family and the Family of God
The third major communication network is kinship. This is distinguished from ethnicity, which I take up in the next chapter, in that kinship concerns

one's extended family (cousins, uncles, grandparents and so on) while ethnicity concerns larger racial groupings (Poles, Hispanics, Chinese and so on). They are, of course, related in that kinship is the backbone of communication in any ethnic community. While we generally acknowledge that the white, middle-class family is deteriorating, our stereotype of Black families is an even bleaker one: the father never home, the children on the streets all night. But if you measure family strength by the extended family rather than the nuclear family, by the ability of a wide range of relatives to live harmoniously under one roof, then the African-American family is stronger than the white family. Kinship, therefore, remains a strong force in areas where ethnicity is strong.

Kinship is, in fact, one of the key funnels in the movement to the city. Most people do not go to a city in which they know no one and start looking for a house. Rather, they go to the city of a brother, a cousin or a distant uncle who can put them up for a while and help them find housing. Often, then, you will find Black churches in Philadelphia relating regularly with people in Mississippi or Georgia but not with Black Christians in Pittsburgh. The kinship lines go south. The need to survive in the city can, therefore, draw family connections even tighter.

I used a slogan during my four years of ministry in Newark: Every person is a doorway to a family, and every family is a gateway to a community. I would start all kinds of ministries by simply saying to the staff that worked under me, "Go into the streets and find any way you can to build trust with an individual. That becomes your program. Once you have developed trust with that individual, look for opportunities to communicate the gospel, but do not get all hung up on that. Try to get beyond that individual into their family relationships. In other words, if you are playing basketball in the afternoon with a young guy, and he takes to you and you like him, offer to drive him home. Find out if you can get an opportunity to stop by and visit him in his house and meet his parents."

I have found out that in an amazing way this counteracts what has evidently been one of the greatest problems in the communication of the gospel in the city. Untold Christian organizations, including local churches, will involve themselves in the lives of young people and never take time to communicate with their families. Pretty soon families are refusing to allow their children to be involved with Christian groups. I have come across good Christian parents who are doing this simply because they do not know or understand who their kids are hanging out with.

Young Life has developed a training program for urban workers that stresses this. If you go to a high school and meet a student, spend a few weeks hanging out with him or her in various places. By the third time you meet him, make sure you meet the parents. Otherwise the parents are going to develop a block against you. The same is true for those reaching out to urban commuter campuses. You cannot form a group that is independent of family ties. You must trace the kinship lines back to have an effective campus ministry.

In an urban, commuter college setting, students maintain strong ties to the community they come from—for example, to their jobs or their families. This contrasts to the residential campus in which college is a student's whole life. Therefore, it is relatively easy to reach these students through a campus organization. But if one is to successfully influence urban, commuter students, one must be willing to follow their lines of communication back to their community base.

It is easy to initiate contact with an individual in an urban setting. But moving from the individual to the family is a difficult process. Much of it has to do with our built-in stereotypes, our built-in racism and our inherent reluctance to get involved with the problems of the city. I would suggest that if you want to get involved in an urban ministry, getting involved with an urban family is a process you need to go through yourself before you start giving direction to anyone else.

As you approach a family, it is helpful to see that most families have at least three communities in the city which influence them. Sometimes these may be geographical communities, but often they are not. First is the community of the parents' work. Second is the social community with which the family will be involved. It may be a volunteer association or the corner bar. Third is a church community. It may take a theological stance that you are not comfortable with, but you have to take it into consideration because urban families are often deeply rooted in their churches.

Because one cannot deal with a family or an individual in isolation from the other forces that are at work on them, you need to know who and what are influencing them. I would even suggest getting involved with their church community. In other words, if you want to disagree publicly with the teaching of their present church community, you had better do it from a basis of trust. You have to know the family well enough to say, "Having visited your church, I want to raise some questions about what they are teaching." But if you stand off on the outside and begin to condemn the church, you are rejecting the community of which this person is a part. Their conclusion will be that you are rejecting them too.

Some people criticize urban churches for being too social. But many middle-class whites are also wrapped up in the church because it is their social life. People use the church as a volunteer association. In many urban (and suburban) churches, people attend for years and never get any Bible teaching. That does not necessarily mean they must leave that church. It may mean we will have to work in it.

In Newark, when I would start teaching a neighborhood Bible study on Tuesday or Thursday night, we would get all kinds of people. Sometimes they would be involved for a year before they really understood the gospel. After coming to know the Lord, they would stay involved for another year or two before suddenly raising the question, "You know, maybe this church that I'm going to isn't the one where I belong." Then they would say, "But if I pull out, where am I going to go to socialize? All my friends are at church." The church in the city can replace both kinship and volunteer associations. Because the city is an impersonal place, people need a home ground that they can come to. They will find it in a bingo hall or on a baseball team or in a church. We should, therefore, be careful about calling people out of a church.

The responsibility for in-depth follow-through is seen vividly in the story of Walter, a fourteen-year-old with whom we got involved in Newark. We found that he was staying with his aunt for the summer though his home was Mississippi. His aunt was not satisfied with the church she attended but was impressed with what happened to her nephew through our program. So she came to adult Bible study and began to appreciate what our church was doing. She even encouraged Walter to go to our Sunday school. She returned to her own church because of established social relationships, but was also able to help start a Bible study during the week.

By the end of the summer Walter's older sister Barbara came up from Mississippi to visit. After being with her younger brother for a few hours, she turned to her aunt and said, "What happened to this kid? His whole life has changed." So the aunt said, "There's a group of kids in this neighborhood that introduced him to some new thinking, and now he's a Christian." Barbara had to find out who these people were. Soon she was having a long talk with one of the girls on our team, a student from Massachusetts, who told Barbara,

"I want to keep in touch with you. Give me your name and address."
We had contacts in Mississippi. So we wrote to ask a friend to just give this girl a call. He called up Barbara, and it nearly blew her off the earth. Somebody in Mississippi called her up and said, "This girl you met in Newark was concerned enough to tell me about you and I want to be in touch." This so impressed Barbara that she spent a whole weekend in Massachusetts and came to know the Lord. She went back and led her whole family in Mississippi to the Lord.

Our ministry was partly in Mississippi that summer because that is the way communications flow in the African-American community. And on that block, the only one we were able to touch was Walter, a visitor from Mississippi. Following through on that network opened a ministry that was for the Lord's glory that summer.

Volunteer Associations: Pizza Parlor Evangelism
While the movement to the city is often along kinship lines, it can also be a movement away from the family. In other words, some people come to the city because they have decided to break with their primary family. If they are successful, they will also tend to move away from kinship contacts in general. The communication network that replaces the family will often be volunteer associations.

A volunteer association is a group that is born and organized around an activity that people participate in because they want to. It can be social; it can be political; it can be economic. I am using the term more broadly than in the sense of "a Red Cross volunteer." Ethnicity is not voluntary, though there are many clubs created around ethnicity. Neither is age nor sex. The YWCA, Lions Club, Union Hall, a hospital volunteer association, country clubs, athletic clubs, the Masons, business clubs, senior citizen's groups—all of these are volunteer associations. In the city of Reading, Pennsylvania (population 80,000), I have identified over three hundred such groups.

Many of these groups were established by rural-minded people who came to the city, felt uncomfortable there and developed associations that would help them to adjust. Many downtown churches have performed the same function. They have become protective groups of people with little outreach because the very need out of which they have been created thwarts outreach.

Other volunteer associations are organized either for economic benefit, for developing a power base, or to get a job done. Their concern is to organize against outside forces. Unions, street gangs, burial associations, neighborhood coalitions or cooperatives fall into this category.

Understanding volunteer associations is very important to the body of Christ because these are the groups of people with whom we are often in competition. When we call people to Jesus Christ, we may also be calling them out of the bowling league. We need to be able to provide them with more than the bowling league does.

Yet as Christians over the centuries used forces which threatened to destroy the church to expand its influence, we too can use volunteer associations to spread the gospel. We can join such groups and communicate the gospel there. Many people who are open to the gospel do not have time to talk anywhere else, but would have time to talk in a bingo hall or a bowling alley.

Joining just a few groups will make our time most effective. We can make our selection by doing two things: first, keep our own interests in mind; and second, look for the strategic centers of communication. If you like politics, join one of the major parties or a citizens' group. If you are an athletic person, join a tennis club or a handball league.

I personally happen to like food, so I joined an Italian pizza club, Victor Emmanuel II in Reading. I paid five dollars to get in, and I had to wait four weeks for my membership to clear. My last name is Hopler, you see. They finally cleared it, mainly because I'm white. (I have never seen a black face in the whole organization.) I was aware of that. But I got into it just to see how it operates. Every Sunday afternoon a group of Italians get together for terrific Italian food. You can buy a pizza for ninety cents if you belong to the club. You have to show your card at the door, then they let you through. There's a second door which has a two-way mirror, and you stand out there while the guy inside looks you over. He then unlocks the second door, and you come into a lobby where you are grilled with all sorts of questions. Finally they let you come in and buy your pizza. That's culture. That's a private association—a channel for fellowship.

One day I got a concerned phone call saying that nobody should come next Sunday because they found a bomb in the kitchen (seven sticks of dynamite). The Mafia must be in there somewhere. I'm just a member, but it's interesting to get even that close to the internal operation. The next Sunday afternoon Anthony's Bar and Grill on 8th Street (which is just a block from my home) blew up. The Sunday after that four buildings on Cotton

Street owned by another Italian were blown off the map. Now it was apparent that something was going on in the Italian community in Reading. There was nothing in the newspaper except mention of a fire here and a burning there. But I knew something was happening in the Italian community because I belonged to Victor Emmanuel II, where I could buy my pizza cheaper than anywhere else.[5]

10
Dynamic Ethnicity

▼▼▼▼▼▼▼▼▼▼▼▼▼▼

I HAVE A FRIEND WHO IS A PROFESSOR IN UCLA'S GRADUATE PROGRAM IN education, working with doctoral candidates. His students go on to train teachers at a variety of schools. One day his daughter came home from school and reported what her teacher had taught that day.

"Well, I'm sorry, dear," came his response, "but I'm afraid your teacher is wrong about that."

"What do you mean, my teacher's wrong?" And she proceeded to argue the matter with her father.

Finally he stopped her and said, "Daughter, don't you realize that I'm the person who teaches the people who teach your teachers? So how in the world can I be wrong and your teacher be right?"

"Well," came her answer, "I don't know. I'll have to ask my teacher about that."

I have had similar experiences with my own children. They latch onto something they hear at school and reject my authority or opinion. Part of the thrust of American education has been to forget one's past and become part of the new America. There continues to be great pressure, or heat, to melt us into a uniform culture in America. Those in power have purposefully (I do not say consciously) attempted to keep the country from fragmenting into its many component parts. If the country is to survive, so the argument goes, it has to have some basis for unity.

The United States is unique in the world in this regard. While Canada has been influenced primarily by the British and French, and South Africa by the British, Dutch and Indians, no other country has absorbed so many from such a variety of countries. Ethnicity, then, represents the fifth and final major category of lines of communication that cut across geographic borders, the first four being government, professions, kinship and volunteer associations.

Americans have come to regard their ethnic origins with increasing respect. Much of this increase is, I believe, related to the retreat of the West and the rise of the Third World out of colonialism. It is apparently becoming less of a problem not to be Anglo-Saxon. Yet even the way I phrased that last sentence betrays a breakdown in the melting-pot myth. All our races and cultures and values and ideas do not melt into a smooth, even, well-balanced mixture. The taste of Northern European Protestantism dominates the soup. How did this come about?

The Making of America

America's value system was formed in a dynamic relationship with the waves of immigrants that came to this country. Some groups have had greater impact on the culture than others. The impact of each group, in my view, has been determined by a combination of at least five factors.

1. *Chronology.* The earlier a group came to the country, the greater its impact on the value system is likely to have been since fewer values were already fixed. The English came first and so had the greatest impact. (This is reflected in table 2.) Any groups which followed were first required to interact with an already established culture. Other Northern European Protestant groups, notably the Germans, came in great numbers after the English. That leads to the second factor.

2. *Number.* Although a group may have been represented early in the history of the United States, if a significant number did not immigrate, its impact would be small.

3. *Length of Peak.* Not only did Northern European Catholics arrive after their Protestant counterparts, their peak in immigration lasted almost fifty years; compare this to Eastern Europeans, whose peak period was about 1915-1935.

Table 2   Distribution of White Population in the United States in 1790

Nationality	Number	Per Cent
English	2,605,699	82.1
Scotch	221,562	7.0
German	176,407	5.6
Dutch	78,959	2.5
Irish	61,534	1.9
French	17,619	.6
Others	10,664	.3
TOTAL	3,172,444	100.0

Source: Samuel P. Orth, *Our Foreigners* (New Haven: Yale University Press, 1920).

4. *Shock.* Riots and unionization are examples of highly visible events which raised the country's awareness of different groups and forced it to take their concerns into account.

5. *Push/Pull.* Generally it is held that the greater the pull a group has felt toward America (a promise of quick wealth, for example), the easier it is for that group to integrate. If the push of a group out of their homeland dominates their decision to move (famine or religious persecution, for example), they will integrate less easily. On the whole, the easier the integration process is for a people, the greater will be their impact on the culture as a whole.

Figure 3 shows that Northern Protestant Europe has (until just recently) always dominated immigration to the United States, primarily by the English and the Germans. They came first; they came in the largest numbers; their peak lasted the longest. The next large group was the Northern European Catholics which included the Dutch and the French. But the main representative of this group was the Irish. Over three million Irish came in the years 1841-1890, almost a million between 1851-1860.[1] Irish riots also broke out in both New York and Boston. Their Catholicism was suspect, but they made their mark and became part of the value system. Today Irish policemen and politicians are still highly visible in New York, Boston and Chicago. Nonetheless, Catholicism has had such negative connotations in the country as a whole that only twice has a major party nominated a Catholic for president.

Beginning in the 1880s the next two groups came—the Southern Europeans and the Eastern Europeans, including Russians. Although the latter group was larger, the former seems to have made a greater impact. The Eastern Europeans were split among many national groups while the immigration of Southern Europeans was dominated by Italians who came in greater numbers

Figure 3   Foreign-Born Population of the United States: 1850-1970
(figures in millions)

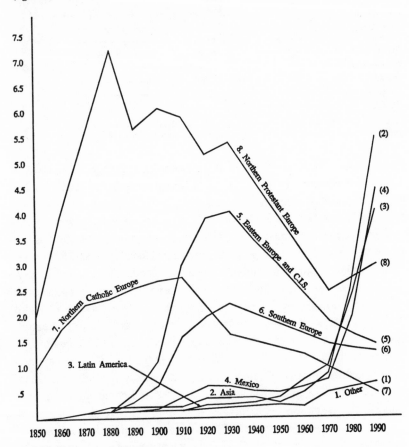

Source: U.S. Bureau of Cesus. *Historical Statistics of the United States: Colonial Times to 1970.*
Bicentennial Edition, Part I, Washington D.C., 1975; John W. Wright, ed., *The Universal Almanac 1993.*

Note: No figures available for 1940. For 1950 figures available only for Mexico, Asia and Other.
Key: 8 = *Northern Protestant Europe*—England, Scotland, Wales, Northern Ireland (1930-70 only), Norway, Sweden,
         Denmark, Iceland, Netherlands, Luxembourg, Switzerland, Germany, British Canada (estimated for 1850-80 and
         1960-70).
         7 = *Northern Catholic Europe*—Ireland, Belgium, France, Austria, French Canada (estimated for 1850-80
         and 1960-70.
         6 = *Southern Europe*—Albania, Greece, Italy, Portugal, Spain.
         5 = *Eastern Europe and C.I.S.*—Poland, Czechoslovakia, Hungary, Yugoslavia, C.I.S., Latvia, Estonia,
         Lithuania, Finland, Romania, Bulgaria, Turkey in Europe.
         4 = *Mexico.*
         3 = *Latin America*—Cuba, West Indies, Central America, South America.
         2 = *Asia*—Armenia, Palestine, Syria, Turkey in Asia, China, Japan, India, Korea, Philippines. Other Asia.
         1 = *Other*—Africa,Australia, Azores, Other Atlantic Islands, Pacific Islands, Country not Specified. Born at Sea.

than either Russians or Poles. In fact, over three million Italians came between 1901 and 1920.[2] Today we still hear a lot of Italian and Polish jokes, more in the North than in the South. These arise out of a need to keep people in their places, to indicate that we each have our station in society.

What I find even more interesting is that Italians are the ones who often laugh the hardest at Italian jokes. It expresses their rejection of Italianness and acceptance of the melting pot. Those who do not reject their Italianness stay outside the melting pot. Some remnants of Italian values, nonetheless, come through those who melt. Spaghetti is now American. So is pizza. The Italians also reinforce the place of Catholicism in American life.

A similar process occurred through Polish jokes. We lumped together all Slavic people (Russians, Czechs and so on) and called them Poles because the Poles were most visible, coming the fastest to the new world. This allowed us again to establish a place in society for such people which was negatively reinforced by jokes.

Mexicans have had the next greatest influence on the country as a whole, though in the Southwest their impact is far greater than some European groups. After World War II people from other Latin countries came in large numbers, especially from Cuba. In the last two decades we have seen a huge influx of Mexicans and other Latin Americans. Altogether, the Hispanic population of the United States increased 53% between 1980 and 1990 to over 22 million people.[3] (Is it any wonder salsa is now more popular than ketchup in the U.S.?) This made up 9 percent of the population, up from 6.4 percent ten years before.[4] This figure includes an estimated 6 million legal and 2 million undocumented immigrants who came to the U.S. in the 1980s. By the year 2000, their numbers are expected to reach 30 million.[5]

The difficulty of using one term (*Hispanic*) to describe this whole community is apparent when you look at their ethnic composition. Mexico accounts for 52 percent (13.5 million). Twenty-four percent (6.2 million) are of Puerto Rican descent (both on the island and on the mainland, and to be discussed below). Twenty percent or approximately 5 million are, to use the language of the U.S. Census Bureau, "other" Hispanics. Four percent or approximately 1 million are of Cuban descent.[6]

U.S. Hispanics are predominantly urban. Miami follows Havana as the second largest Cuban city in the world. New York is the second largest Puerto Rican city after San Juan. Los Angeles is the second largest Salvadoran city.

It is, in fact, the large cities that continue to attract the Spanish-speaking newcomers.[7]

The last group, Asians, have been represented in the United States since the middle 1800s, notably by the Chinese who helped build the railroads of the West. California, of course, received most of these. But Asians never came in great numbers until recently. Also, the Chinese who did come tended to remain a closed community. In the 1970s the Vietnamese and other Indochinese refugees became highly visible. With them in the last two decades have come large numbers of Koreans, Indians, Filipinos and Chinese.

Between 1970 and 1990, almost 12 million people immigrated into the United States—more than in the previous five decades combined.[8] As a result, for the first time in our history, those from Northern Protestant Europe do not make up the largest foreign-born group in the United States. In fact, they have fallen to fourth place. Not only are foreign-born Asians a larger group, but so are Mexicans and other Latin Americans (see figure 3). This is a major shift which will have a significant impact on this country for decades to come.

Figure 4 is an attempt to visually represent the proportionate impact all these ethnic groups have had on the Middle-American value system. This is not a statistical chart of any kind but a weighted scale indicating who has affected the melting pot most and least based on the five factors I mentioned earlier: chronology, number, length of peak, shock and push/pull.

The circle represents all those in America. The areas outside the circle are the host cultures from which the immigrants came. The shaded areas represent the proportion of those within each group who have not melted from their heritage. These ethnic holding grounds within geographic America are often termed *exocultures*. The unshaded area in the circle represents those who have melted. Because the British and other Northern European Protestants dominate the melting pot, I have (arbitrarily) assigned them the number eight. The Northern European Catholics have contributed to the value system a little less, so they are seven, and so on.

An Unbalanced Mixture
The melting pot is real; it is just not what we normally think it is. It is not an even mixture of all peoples and ideas. It is unbalanced, biased. Those who want to melt will have to accept a culture dominated by Northern Euro-

Figure 4   Model of American Dynamic Ethnicity Based on Value Impact

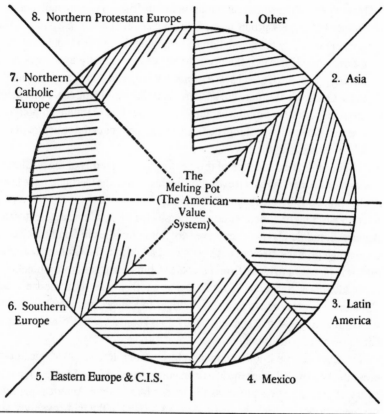

Key: ○ circle represents geographic America

/ / / / shaded area represents exoculture in America (immigrant holding grounds)

unshaded area represents the melting pot

1-8   areas beyond the circle represent host cultures from which immigrants came to the United States

pean Protestants. The further down the scale they are, the harder and longer it will be to melt.

Immigrants from England, for example, could, if they chose, lose their Englishness in about six months. Some may retain their distinctives, as do those in the small British community that exists in New York City. But most will melt.

The Germans are another example.

In terms of size or the achievements of its members, the Germans ought certainly to be included among the principal ethnic groups of the city [of New York]. If never quite as numerous as the Irish, they were indisputably the second largest group in the late nineteenth century, accounting for perhaps a third of the population and enjoying the highest reputation. But today, while German influence is to be seen in virtually every aspect of the city's life, the Germans *as a group* are vanished. No appeals are made to the German vote, there are no German politicians in the sense that there are Irish or Italian politicians, there are in fact few Germans in political life and, generally speaking, no German component in the structure of the ethnic interests of the city.

The logical explanation of this development, in terms of the presumed course of American social evolution, is simply that the Germans have been "assimilated" by the Anglo-Saxon center.[9]

In contrast, it takes almost three generations for many Chinese to enter the American middle class—if they ever do. Some families in San Francisco's Chinatown go back five or six generations, all within the Chinese community. It is far easier to move from Taiwan to Chinatown than from Chinatown to middle-class San Francisco. To put it another way, if someone from Chinatown marries an American and moves to Kansas, and they have a son who moves to Iowa, that son will have far less contact with Chinatown than Chinatown has with Taiwan.

The same is true in other communities, though less so. A Mexican can cross the border and enter the Mexican community in Los Angeles in a few hours. It may take years to cross the border into Middle America, perhaps two generations. During the revolution in Portugal in the mid-seventies, six thousand newspapers were flown daily from Lisbon to Newark. Why? Because the Portuguese community in Newark was far more interested in what was going on in Portugal than in New York. Their values drew their attention there. Ethnicity is another aspect of our urbanized culture that is a far greater barrier to cross than geography.

The system illustrated in figure 4 also reinforces itself. The longer it takes to immigrate to the center of the pot, the more likely it is that an exoculture will develop as a means of mutual support and protection. The lower the number in figure 4, the stronger the exoculture. The stronger the exoculture, the more difficult it is to step over the line into Middle America.

Glazer and Moynihan conclude their book *Beyond the Melting Pot* by indicating how ethnicity is woven together with the other lines of communication:

We have tried to show how deeply the pattern of ethnicity is impressed on the life of the city. Ethnicity is more than an influence on events; it is commonly the source of events. Social and political institutions do not merely respond to ethnic interests; a great number of institutions exist for the specific purpose of serving ethnic interests. This in turn tends to perpetuate them. In many ways, the atmosphere of New York City is hospitable to ethnic groupings: it recognizes them and rewards them, and to that extent encourages them.[10]

The Nonvolunteer Immigrants

By this time the careful reader will have noticed that there are three major groups which are not represented at all in figure 4. These are the three nonvolunteer immigrant groups. The three are not on the chart because they represent a zero or a negative factor in regard to the melting pot. Their values are essentially unmeltable. This negative factor is even expressed in the way we talk about them: the Indian problem, the Puerto Rican problem and the Black problem.

The first, the Indians (Native Americans), are not technically immigrants since they were already on the continent before the English arrived. But they were forced to become part of the United States; so I include them here. In the process of coercing them into the United States, we rejected Indian values. There is almost no Indian value that I can find that is a significant part of the mainstream American value system. We have adopted barbecuing, archery and other things, but we seldom credit these as being part of Indian culture. When Indians are visible, they are negative. If we have games of cowboys and Indians, the Indians always lose. The broken treaties and inhumane treatment of the Indians have been ignored in our history texts. Because the Indians still only number approximately one million we have been able to keep that problem hidden and pretend that the Indians are not there.

The second nonvolunteer immigrant group is the Puerto Ricans. They are nonvolunteer in that the island came into the hands of the United States after the Spanish-American War of 1898. The people then became citizens of the United States. All other nations, once they began to come in too quickly, were put on a quota system. But we cannot stop the Puerto Ricans. They keep coming. Between 1950 and 1965 one-third of the population of Puerto Rico moved to the United States, half of whom live in the New York area. It just finally got to the point where we could not handle it anymore, and we began to ignore the Puerto Ricans. Irrational fear of Puerto Ricans developed because there was no control on how many could come in. They are citizens and can move as they please. To replace this kind of control another was substituted—Puerto Rican values became negative.

The negative value of Puerto Rican culture is muted somewhat because it is part of the larger U.S. Hispanic population which arose as a result of voluntary immigration. Figure 4 shows the Mexican and Latin American groups having some impact on American values, though significantly less than the European groups.

The third nonvolunteer group is African-Americans. They are here because they were forced to come as slaves. In 1860 4.5 million slaves were freed. They were given citizenship, but they were not given land, jobs or training. They were not given any means by which they could be incorporated into the cultural value system. The result was that almost any Black value became negative. About a half million did manage to immigrate into the mainstream in the fifteen years following the Civil War. But soon the country could take no more, and reconstruction ended. The history of African-Americans shows that about every twenty years the system opens up and absorbs several hundred thousand Blacks who give up their values and accept those of Middle America. Then the system again closes and won't allow any more in.

Absorption is a terribly hard process because it is difficult to give up Blackness when one's skin remains the same color. But Blacks have wrestled with that for a hundred years. Some have worked through it successfully. Not all of these are Uncle Toms. Some have sold themselves to get into the system, but some have found creative ways to get in.

Some African-Americans, of course, argue that it is pointless even to try to get into the mainstream. If you are going to be an American, you are going to have to reject your Blackness. This was the fight of the sixties, the attempt to get Blackness accepted as American. There are varying opinions of whether that was successful or not.

I am personally more concerned about the regression that has taken place in the late seventies. Virtually all of the gains that took place in the years between 1959 and 1974 have been withdrawn. Just as in years past, after a period when Blacks have been accepted, the system cannot accept any more, and it closes the Blacks off. While perhaps half the Black population has achieved some degree of assimilation, the rest are again locked in the holding grounds of the rural sharecropper South and the urban ghettos. Those two holding grounds contain a population of over fifteen million people whom the system ignores.

After the Vietnam War ended in 1975, a massive national effort was made to accommodate a quarter million Vietnamese refugees. Spurred on by a sense of moral responsibility and guilt, groups all over the country tried to find them jobs and housing. If it took a year to get them all out of Air Force camps and two years to find a permanent place for them in society when the country was so highly motivated, how long will it take to absorb fifteen million African-Americans the country does not want? But the extent of the problem is just not seen. To most, it does not exist.

I have conducted an informal survey with various groups. I hand out a piece of paper and ask people to account for all African-Americans by the occupation of the head of the house. Thus the figure for high professionals would not only include doctors, lawyers and the like but their families as well. The other categories range from medium and lower professionals to skilled and unskilled labor, unemployed and illegal professions. When the average white suburbanite totals these figures, the result is about three million African-Americans. Rarely have I seen it higher than eight million. Actually, there are over thirty million African-Americans. Thus, when whites say we have a housing problem for Blacks, and the Blacks agree, the whites are thinking, say, two hundred thousand, and the Blacks are thinking two million.

Institutional racism is coming back into our culture, and it frightens me. I saw a simple manifestation of this just recently when I was in a bookstore. In one section I counted twenty-seven cheap paperbacks that dealt with the subject of black-white slavery-sex relationships, all sort of interwoven and tied together. On the front cover was the old theme of a Black slave in the South being caught out in the woods with his mistress or of the white lady going down into the slave quarters or the Black male raping a white woman. These themes are part of a mythology that was developed in order to put across the idea that African-American males are to be feared and controlled. If you give them a certain amount of freedom, we say, certain results will follow.

Where does this literature come from? From somebody who is clever enough to recognize that this is a theme that the American people want to believe again. So they capitalize. They package it in a slightly new format: pseudohistory of the South. And it sells because somebody wants to buy it. The end result is to reinforce all the myths that the sixties attempted to debunk. There was a whole body of literature written in the sixties that discredits those myths and shows that they were created for the purpose of destroying the African-American male image. But it is ignored.

In William Pannell's *The Coming Race Wars?* he quotes Sergeant Stacey Koon: "In society there's the sexual prowess of blacks on the old plantations of the South and intercourse between blacks and whites on the plantation, and that's where the fear comes in."[11] Pannell goes on, then, to consider

Rodney King as "Mandingo." So the female cop, gun in hand, was fearful of this menacing black man, armed with a handful of buttocks. Thus Sgt. Koon begins the legitimating of the atrocity recorded on videotape on March 3, 1991, by George Holliday. Eighty-one seconds of hell.

Koon was acquitted of any responsibility in the beating, although he was the senior officer in charge. . . . One juror expressed puzzlement over all the fury because, after all, "not much damage was done."

But the reference to black sex is straight out of Dixie and a thousand lynch-crazed mobs. According to Koon, this beating was in the defense of white womanhood: not just that of the female officer at the time but, by extension, all white women in society.[12]

The July 1977 blackout in New York City is another indication of the turnaround that has occurred recently. Sociologists are still trying to understand why only Blacks and Puerto Ricans responded to the power failure by getting into the streets to take whatever they could get. Many consider it a simple issue of robbery. But if we understand the degree to which the American system rejects Blackness and Puerto Ricanness, we can understand the response of total disrespect for the system that cut them off.

In 1973 *Time* ran a brief article called "The Irregular Economy" which further illustrates how African-Americans and Puerto Ricans are cut off from the system. It begins,

For many have-not blacks, Puerto Ricans and other ghettoized minorities, the exemplar of business success is the jaunty dude in a wide-brimmed hat and high-heeled shoes who has made good—as a pimp. A few highly enterprising procurers pocket $100,000 a year. Indeed, crimes like narcotics peddling, prostitution and gambling are major moneymaking activities in the ghettos. They constitute a kind of irregular economy. . . .

Though figures are imprecise the turnover in the ghetto from narcotics, numbers, prostitution and other rackets amounts to at least $5 billion a year. According to one study, the black population of Brooklyn's Bedford-Stuyvesant section spent $88 million on drugs and policy gambling in 1970—about $11 million more than it collected in welfare. . . . The numbers operation alone had an annual payroll of $15 million, making it the biggest private employer in the area. . . . Some criminal entrepreneurs plow back a part of their earnings into legitimate ventures like dry-cleaning shops, real estate developments, bars, nonlicensed gypsy-cab fleets. . . . "There is community support for such crimes because it delivers vital services," says [Columbia University Professor Francis] Lanni. . . . Opinions differ on how Government should deal with the irregular economy. The Lasswell-McKenna report on Bedford-Stuyvesant calls for legalized gambling as a means of taking the play away from criminals. . . . Poor blacks tend to be against such a change because they distrust government, and they figure that the proceeds from gambling would be taken away from the black numbers runners and other local operatives.

The middle class gets uptight because they feel the government gives too many handouts. The poor distrust the government because they see where the handouts go. All the welfare money that comes into the city, by order of the government, must be used immediately. You cannot buy a house with it. You cannot save it in the bank. You cannot invest it in any way. You can pay as much as $800 per month in rent, but you will not be allowed to pick up a mortgage for $350 per month. Therefore, most of the money that comes from welfare goes into the hands of people in Bedford-Stuyvesant and Harlem, stays there for one cycle and then flips back out to Middle America. Welfare is a major route by which money is poured from government back into the suburbs, because that is where most of the landlords live. The poor have the money in their pocket for a week and then hand it on. Food stamps work the same way. The money comes in, it goes into a big grocery chain and in one hop it is back in suburban banks.

This is why *Time* says, "Poor blacks tend to be against [legalized gambling] because they distrust government, and they figure that the proceeds from gambling would be taken away from the black numbers runners and other local operatives." They want the gambling to stay in the hands of the Mafia and others who run it because the Mafia will reinvest that in legal businesses like taxi cabs, restaurants and dry-cleaning establishments. It is one of the main ways the ghetto gets any improvements. The *Time* article continues:

> Lisle C. Carter, a Cornell University sociologist, notes that ghetto crime "is a source of investment resources, of both equity and debt capital." Some criminal kingpins, for example, lend money to people who want to go in honest business. Carter warns against moving too fast in rooting out crime in the ghetto lest this capital source dry up, leaving the inhabitants worse off than ever.

Time's conclusion is a stark one. "Until more blacks are given greater economic opportunity, the brutalizing irregular economy may be the only crack at the free enterprise system.[13]

In Harlem about one-third of the population is on welfare. Another third—social workers, teachers, police officers and the like—is hired by the local and federal governments to supervise those on welfare. So well over half of Harlem is directly or indirectly controlled by the government which is itself, to a great extent, the handmaid of the suburban value system. The sixties did not change the negative perception we have of such people. They are a people to be controlled, not accommodated.

If this seems extreme, consider also that in 1978 over one-third of the people arrested in the United States were Black, but Blacks are only 11 percent of the total population of the country. In Maryland, for example, twelve African-Americans are imprisoned for every white.[14]

William Pannell says that in the long run

> probably the greatest single threat to the black community is the white community's diminished commitment to a society under law. Law has become the province of vested interests. It is no longer informed by a relationship with religion. As a result, law has become the handmaid of order rather than justice. And order is defined by the ruling class, by people who can afford the best judges money can buy.[15]

Certainly most are in prison because they committed crimes, but the value system left them almost no alternative. It has refused to accept African-American values as positive.

A Third Way

What alternative is there? The people of the ghetto are not going to go to the federal government. It has perpetuated the negative value the melting pot places on African-Americans and Puerto Ricans. The alternative is for the church to establish a third system that provides people with the same kind of real help that the Mafia does. We, as Christians, if our commitment is to people, must understand what every kid in the ghetto understood long before Lisle C. Carter came down from Cornell University. If we can provide genuine economic relief, people will pour into the church. The Black Muslims (now called the American Muslim Mission) have demonstrated that. Our call to salvation must include more than salvation from sin. It must include salvation to Christian community that pays the rent, puts clothes on my back, and gives me people that I can fellowship with and trust. I'll join that. But just freedom from sin, that's meaningless. If the church can become a living, visible, demonstrative community in the city, we can start any kind of evangelism.

That is a very large *if*. We in the church must change our thinking before that *if* can come to pass. Let me highlight three issues we must consider seriously: first, how the lines of communication in ethnicity affect our Christian witness; second, how ethnicity affects our approach to missions; and third, how ethnicity affects our own value system.

First, the lines of communication. Rarely is the communication system of Middle America hooked up with that of ethnic exocultures. They run parallel and never intersect. In Philadelphia, for example, Dr. Lee, a pastor of a Korean church, is an adjunct professor in a Bible school in the Korean community of Los Angeles and also in Seoul, Korea. You do not find him teaching the Word of God anywhere else in Philadelphia except in the Korean community. Yet he is a highly qualified man. In fact, churches five blocks away from his know less about what he is doing than churches in Los Angeles or in Seoul because his communication follows the lines of least resistance.

In Philadelphia two dozen churches meet and preach in the Korean language. And because of this they have little fellowship outside their community. They are Korean Christians serving Koreans. (An interesting sidelight is that graduates of Westminster Theological Seminary went to Korea as missionaries fifty years ago to develop a church. Their crosscultural sensitivity led to Korean leaders migrating to Philadelphia and now comprising one-third of the student body.)

Because of cultural barriers, many do not know that there is a federation of over five hundred evangelical, Spanish-speaking churches in New York—and that does not cover all Spanish-speaking churches. There are also Puerto Rican churches in New York that send their young people back to Puerto

Rico to study the Bible. Chinese churches as well often send their young people to Taiwan to study the Bible. A recent congress of the Chinese Christian community met in Hong Kong with some three thousand representatives. One of the main topics of discussion was the evangelization of the Chinese in North America. The Chinese communities in New York, Philadelphia, Chicago and San Francisco knew about that conference and its implications for them. Hardly any of the rest of us got the word. That kind of communication is important to the ongoing existence of the Chinese churches in America, but it is not on their agenda to communicate with other American churches.

A tremendous drive is necessary to get out of an urban ethnic community and to begin communicating with Middle America. Should we require ethnic churches to make all the effort to come to us to communicate? I think not. There is a cost to be paid on both sides if communication is to take place, but the cost for ethnic groups is greater than for those of us in Middle America. Their cost is possible rejection by their exoculture, their ethnic community, if they become too closely identified with white America. The lower the number as seen in figure 4, the greater is the pull to stay in the exoculture and the greater the cost to those who communicate on our terms. Such an identification could destroy them or their ministry. The cost for us is giving up the notion that Christians have to look alike. It means acknowledging the validity of other cultures and the richness they have to offer our cultural form of Christianity.

Admittedly, I am suggesting something foreign to our way of thinking. The flow is toward the center of the circle in figure 4. We speak of integrating the Vietnamese or the Cubans or the African-Americans *into* white society. We never speak of reversing the flow, of integrating into African-American society. This one-way communication is the cause of great tensions in the nation.

The Black-White confrontation is like a twelve-volt resistor attached to a six-volt wire. By the time you get enough voltage to jump the resistor, the wire is burned out. Likewise, by the time Blacks lift their voices loud enough so they can be heard, there is a riot. Then we reject that form of communication, saying it is extreme.

It is up to us in the white community to go to them. We should not attempt to cross the cultural barrier to the non-Christian African-American community. We should first go to the Christian African-American community which is one step closer to our value system, though their Christian expression will still be different from what white Christians expect evangelicalism to look like. Then we should attempt to build a trust relationship with an individual in that Christian community. After discovering through that person what God is already doing in that setting, you can ask, "How can my particular gifts be of service to you?" Then together you can walk into the non-Christian community with a bond of trust between you.

Of course this same principle holds between ethnic groups. Again, because the flow is toward the center, it is difficult to cross over from Korean to Puerto Rican or Italian to Chinese. Cultural diversity, as I argued in my cultural survey of the Bible in part one, is an essential element in Christianity because God wants to save all nations and because his nature is reflected in the diversity of peoples he has made. He also showed the legitimacy of entering into different cultures on their own terms through Joseph in Egypt, Daniel in Babylon and Barnabas in Antioch. Can we do any less?

The Credible Missionary
The second major area urban ethnicity affects is our view of missions. As we have seen, the exocultures within America are in vigorous communication with their host cultures around the world. Africans are well informed of race relations in the United States. Therefore, more and more new missionaries are being asked on their arrival in Africa, "What do you think of the Black issue in America?" Africans are not as concerned with the missionaries' solutions as with how much they are aware of the problem and what their attitudes are toward the problem. Africans realize that their attitudes are a good barometer of what their attitudes will be toward the church in Africa. If missionaries can show a deep understanding and concern for the Black problem of America, their acceptance with the church of Africa is going to be much more rapid and smooth.

I remember one day being in the company of three missionaries when an African asked, "What are the trees of America like?" Almost simultaneously, the three missionaries began to speak. One missionary said, "When you stand on a hill and look out over the vast rolling tops of dark evergreens, it's a thrilling picture to see trees as far as the eye can see." Another was saying in the meantime, "Why, in America we hardly have any trees at all." A third was saying, "The trees in America are as big around as twelve men's arms can reach and stand more than one hundred feet tall." You see, the one had come from the evergreen forest of Maine, another had come from the deserts of Arizona and the third from the redwood forest of California. Each was speaking about America, but each was speaking about the America that he knew, and none was truly representing the picture of America. Let us realize that virtually every missionary is speaking of a white, middle-class, Protestant America and not of America as the home of thirty million Blacks. What does this mean to the Black people of Africa? It means our statement of concern for Black Africa is a sham when we have not shown concern for Black America.

One solution would be for every foreign mission agency to link up with an established urban ministry in the United States paralleling the area of its overseas concerns. This would be used both as a training ground for missionary candidates and as a learning ground for the agency as a whole for what the overseas operation should be like. In the 1980s some mission agencies oriented their candidates to crosscultural ministry by providing an experience in the urban context in America before going to, say, a European city to serve.

Individuals considering missions in, say Peru, should first involve themselves with an indigenous Spanish-speaking ministry or church here at home. The experience would be invaluable.

Another possibility would be for agencies to seek more Black candidates to work in Africa, more Hispanics to work in Latin America and more Chinese to work in Singapore. First, their background often gives them a rapport overseas that may take years for a white to develop. They would also help broaden the agency's own horizons culturally.

Second, hiring American ethnics aids credibility. In the 1990s Black candidates in our missions help the witness of the mission in African countries. The American Embassy in Nairobi has deliberately gone out of its way to make almost one-third of its staff African-Americans. Under the Carter administration, the U.S. ambassador to the U.N. (dominated by Third World countries) was Black. These steps are political, but they are appreciated by the governments of Africa, and I think that missions would do well to learn from our government's example.

Third, ethnic missionaries, especially if they are mature, could become a third force in church-mission communications. Because of their color they can affiliate closer with the church than white missionaries can. Yet, because they are Americans and have been exposed to the American culture, they would have some understanding of the white missionary. The white missionary could speak more freely to the African-American missionary, and the African church member could more freely speak to the African-American missionary. In pursuing this last possibility, however, we must be careful not to pull the rug out from under indigenous Black ministries in the United States by "stealing" their best people. Today we see Blacks called and pursuing ministry. Let us welcome them openly.

Among the realities of the present are African-American, Asian and other ethnic-centered mission agencies that send out people to the Two-Thirds World. One such is Ambassadors Fellowship in California. I saw that what goes around comes around when on InterVarsity Staff at Temple University I was able to encourage some African-Americans to go on a summer missions trip to Kenya. My students served with the people in the churches I had served. They paired with African-American missionaries from AF in Nairobi whom I had met at the National Black Evangelical Association's convention! The students also served some of the family we had bonded with in Nakuru, whose youngest member attended U.S. graduate schools, supported by the large extended African family, and has begun a mission agency called PACE.

The Failure of Rural Christianity

Lastly, ethnicity—and the entire wave of urbanization flooding our world—affects our own value system. In this chapter I have highlighted the priority we have put on conformity to a culture dominated by Northern European Protestantism. While some melting has indeed occurred, my conclusion is the same as that of Glazer and Moynihan.

The point about the melting pot is that it did not happen. . . . We may argue whether it was "nature" that returned to frustrate continually the imminent creation of a single American nationality. The fact is that in every generation, throughout the history of the American republic, the merging of the varying streams of population differentiated from one another by origin, religion, outlook has seemed to lie just ahead—a generation, perhaps, in the future. . . . It is striking that in 1963, almost forty years after mass immigration from Europe to this country ended, the ethnic pattern is still so strong in New York City.[16]

This is still true nearly thirty years after Glazer and Moynihan's study. This failure to be "One Nation Under God" should alone cause us to ask if we should continue to embrace this dream. The added failure of the church to substantially Christianize the city would seem to make the view even more untenable. We have assumed that if everyone would accept Middle-American values, we could all be "One Nation Under God." This has not happened, and the failure is most visible in the city.

Consider who is in the city: Asians, Latinos, Mexicans, Slavs, Italians. These are usually Muslim or Catholic cultures. And even much of the Catholicism in the city is laced with overt or more subtle forms of superstition. In such a setting the mayor of Newark can be reelected while sitting in prison, and no one blinks. In rural-minded America, however, one small misstep by a president and the country is bellowing for his resignation. Why the double standard? Because Northern European Protestantism dominates the culture as a whole. But it has not touched the city.

Such a failure in the city is magnified if the wave to come is urbanization. To be effective in such a world, the church must throw off its cultural blinders. We must ask ourselves, "Are we committed first to the melting pot or to Christ?" If we are committed to the former, our attitude will be, "The city is a hopeless pit. There is nothing we can do for it. Let us use our gifts where we will see fruit." If we are committed first to Christ, our attitude will be, "Our values have failed in the city. Because we are committed to reach it for Christ's sake, let us let go of these values and adopt new ones that will fulfill the Great Commission." I am not suggesting that the "new values" merely be what works to get the job done. Rather I am suggesting we go back to the Bible to see what values transcend all cultures and can therefore be applied to any culture. This is the thrust of part four.

I still remember the day I was in a stadium of fifty thousand Africans watching a soccer match. The game was lousy. No one was excited about it. So at halftime some politician decided he was going to say a few words to an apathetic crowd. But he could not rouse them either. Therefore he got onto his favorite subject—nasty white people, the bad colonialists, the awful English and what should have been done to them when they were in power. I think I was the only white in the whole stadium.

Finally, he got them going enough that they were ready to lynch somebody. I was about eighteen rows from the exit. Some very angry faces began turning and recognizing that I was there. It was an uncomfortable moment. A mob was about to develop.

I was with ten members of the church, some young people and some couples. But they turned to the crowd with the focus of their eyes on the people closest to them and just said, "He's with us." To the twenty or thirty people sitting nearby, that meant nothing would happen, so that section quieted down. You could then see the quiet move through the crowd like wind across a wheat field. As each group realized that nothing was going to happen, they lost interest and turned away.

We are different, but we can still be one. Indeed, despite the real differences that exist, we in the church can be a source of protection for each other and a source of peace to the world.

Part 3

▼▼▼▼▼▼▼▼▼▼▼

Bridging Gaps

Marcia Hopler

11
Urbanization: Bane or Blessing?

▼▼▼▼▼▼▼▼▼▼▼▼▼▼

UNQUESTIONABLY THE WORLD IS INCREASINGLY URBANIZED. THE ISSUE Christians face is whether we will see this as a problem to be overcome or an opportunity to take advantage of.

The bell rang one cold winter night about 11:00 p.m. I was alone. When I answered I found a woman without a coat and with only one shoe who wanted to use my phone. Quickly I called out to the Lord to help me balance truth and love. It took quite a while to get a telephone number I could call for her. She was weeping and I was tense. I took my coat, a blanket and tea and sat with her on my porch. She seemed disoriented and perhaps drunk. I hugged her, prayed and sang about the blood of Jesus. She would not tell me her name. That evening I did what I could.

Eventually her father and son came for her. Her father, a gentle, older Black man, was stunned. He wasn't sure how to react to a white woman helping in such circumstances. He repeated over and over, "I don't care what they say about Whitey! I believe all nationalities are good. I don't care what they say about Whitey!"

I simply explained that I was a Christian.

This is a partial picture of our urban world—poverty, drugs, crime and racial tension. But people who only see the dirt and corruption and evil do not see what God sees, do not see with God's heart. This setting provides a garden for Christ's love to blossom. His church (Black, Korean, Chinese, Puerto Rican and others) has actually flourished in the crises of the city because he was the only way when there was no way.

Much of what happens in our urban world is no blessing. Intense concentrations of people can also mean unemployment, housing shortages and hunger. But such a situation provides an opportunity for a variety of God's people with a variety of gifts to meet those needs. In our weakness Christ's power is made real.

The Ad Man Cometh

As explained in previous chapters, there is much more to our urban world than a geographic concentration of people. Urbanization can be defined as "that process whereby people acquire material and material elements of culture, behavior patterns and ideas that originate in, or are distinctive of the city."[1] Lewis Mumford, an anthropologist, saw an urban setting as a potential place for positive human development.[2] He also described the birth of a town as a "mutation," a sudden, major advance for humanity. Aylward Shorter feels Mumford's optimism with the city and says, "It certainly does represent a leap forward in the history of human collaborative effort."[3]

These collaborative efforts have been maximized in recent years by the stunning advances in the uses of technology, communication and transportation. Geographic barriers are virtually eliminated as impediments to collaboration in business, government or entertainment. Rap music is worldwide. Fashion comes from Tokyo, Paris and New York. Communication runs in cultural stripes now more than ever.

William Ecenbarger wrote recently, "Over the last several years it has been my good fortune to travel through much of the world, and two things have become inescapably clear to me: First, the global village forecast just 30 years ago by Canadian philosopher Marshall McLuhan is already here, and second, the vehicle that brought it here is the United States of America."[4]

Ecenbarger describes the impact of American culture on faraway places through television, MTV, fast food operations, CNN, movies, VCRs and advertising—all in the universal language of English. He writes, "In the years ahead, global advertising—using the same message in South Africa and South Dakota—is expected to become commonplace. *Such advertising doesn't merely sell a product—it transmits a system of values and homogenizes cultures"* (my emphasis).[5]

Ecenbarger goes on to quote Stuart Ewen, a professor at the City University of New York who specializes in the history of advertising: "Advertisers are playing a role very similar to the role of church in the past. . . . Rather than being perceived as having another way of life, people in other countries, especially less industrialized societies, are seen as people wanting to be ushered into the church. It's very much a missionary thing."[6] Ewen makes the point that there is a kind of fellowship of mutual experiences gained through the unlimited connections of communication. This new world sees its role clearly—to unify the world in common values, a role the church had taken on in years past.

Media: The Twentieth-Century Roman Road
What a challenge and an opportunity this presents us! Os Guinness says, "The most significant change of the last thirty years is the developing speed of 'modernity.' People are living in a wrap-around environment drastically different from any environment humanity has experienced before."[7]

Are there elements of modernity that Christians can use for the church's benefit? It is definitely a two-edged sword. Sometimes Christians forget the pluses involved with the rapid changes taking place in our world. Consider the advances in health care, transportation and telecommunications. They are providing us the greatest opportunity to reach the world for Christ since the age of the apostles.

Guinness goes on to say, "Media may be twentieth-century equivalent of the first-century Roman roads and Greek language. They make the task of spreading the gospel message easier, faster, and more efficient than ever before."[8]

The role of the media, whether in TV, videos, computers, films or newspapers, is a crucial one in urbanization because reality is furnished and believed by it. Whoever controls the gateway of the media makes all the difference in how reality is understood. Truth is taught in large doses this way. Truth has always been the concern of the believer in Christ. Our main intent is to communicate to others about God.

In 1966 the Black clergy were responding to the concept of Black power in race relations in the U.S. during the civil rights movement. They addressed the mass media in a statement entitled "Power and Truth," which had great foresight concerning the power of those who control the channels of communicating truth.

The ability or inability of all people in America to understand the upheaval of our day depends greatly on the way power and truth operate in the mass media. . . . During the Southern demonstrations for civil rights you men of the communications industry performed an invaluable service for the entire country by revealing plainly to our ears and eyes, the ugly truth of a brutalizing system of overt discrimination and segregation.

Many of you were mauled and injured, and it took courage for you to stick to the task. You were instruments of change and not merely purveyors of unrelated facts. . . .

The truth that needs revealing today is not so clear-cut in its outlines, nor is there a national consensus. *Nothing is now so important than that you look for a variety of sources of truth in order that the limited perspectives of all of us might be corrected.*

The final word to the media from the Black clergy in 1966? "The fate of this country is, to no small extent dependant on how you interpret the crisis upon us, so that human truth is disclosed and human needs met."[9]

Perhaps we live in a continuing jet lag because we can be in New York in the morning, Mississippi at noon and Miami at night. Add to that the visual pictures of hunger, war, killing and other strong stimuli that flow from a box in our secluded yet secularized living rooms. We can see someone walking on the moon, getting a heart transplant or engaged in graphic intimacy in color in an hour and a half.

This is the context of the people we disciple for Jesus. It all presents a psychological and emotional, to say nothing of spiritual, influence on reeds already blowing in the wind. How do people absorb and treat all this?

TV: Creator of Reality

In a recent *Leadership Journal* article entitled "Target the Trends," Leonard Sweet writes, "Today the T.V. screen is as powerful as the printed page. . . . The impact of visual communication is so profound that there ought to be a screen in every worship service. Part of today's culture is technology. If we open our eyes to the new communications technology, the potential for enhancing worship and enabling community to be formed is tremendous. . . . Through the automatic dialing feature of computers we can reach anyone we want, as many as we want, providing a way to make house calls without entering the house."[10]

This is one of seven responses of seven leaders who are reading the culture and know how to respond in ministry. The seven are dramatically different. Yet they agree on the immense power of the television in the culture.

James Boice said, "The most significant thing that has happened to the Western world is television. We are an entertainment-oriented, feeling-oriented age. I spent last fall preaching Romans 12:1-2 about being transformed by the renewing of your mind. I analyzed our culture in terms of secularism, humanism, relativism, and materialism. I also talked about television."[11]

In addition, Eugene Peterson commented, "We just moved to Vancouver from Maryland. In Maryland the movers spent all day gathering up our stuff, and at the end of the day, one of the workers said, 'You know something? I just realized I didn't take a single TV set out of the house. That's never happened to me before.' I don't own a TV set anymore. I don't want to spend time drinking that poison."[12]

Whatever perspective these leaders come from, all agree that television is powerful. How we use or abuse it has much to do with our clarity of Christ and lifting him up. We have to consider that *our* audience for the gospel for the most part lives in the context of not only television but global media. Is it, like music, an amoral channel? Christians disagree about this. We should remember that evil comes out of our own heart and we cannot legislate holy living. It is a fruit of the Holy Spirit. Perhaps how we as Christians develop that fruit will always mean a certain creative tension. The Holy Spirit works in different individuals in specific ways. Christian liberty, but not license.

Television with all its many parts opens up a stage for extensive drama. A Black man seeking confirmation for the United States Supreme Court was confronted by a Black woman who had accused him of sexual harassment. I was one of the millions watching Judge Clarence Thomas and Ms. Anita Hill on television. I also saw the men on the Senate Judiciary Committee. I viewed a large part of the discussions because I was in an auto body shop for car repairs. As soon as I left the garage I switched on the radio and was glued to it for a couple of days. I knew that wherever things came down, it was a major drama in America. What might have been hidden in some courtroom years ago was now public soap opera material.

William Pannell in *The Coming Race Wars?* states: "The results of the confirmation debacle are not all in, but already a major trend is clearly in view. Clarence Thomas and the White Republicans won the battle, but women may be well on their way to winning the war. By the time elections came around in 1992 the stage had been set for a far reaching political revolt of sorts among women. In primaries across the nation women won significant support for key offices at the state and national levels."[13] Pannell goes on to give examples of the increase in power for women in the political arena directly related to the debate.

Whatever your personal view, it seems a fact that the media's presentation before the public eye and ear was the major factor in the perception of the truth people had and their action afterwards. I myself felt I had gained much insight into some of the senators who would never hand out political fliers door to door or make speeches in someone's Germantown parlor. The drama allowed me the opportunity to know in a new transparent way the men who asked and replied to Anita Hill. It definitely influenced my voting and thinking.

The following interview with Anita Hill appeared in *Essence* magazine, an African-American publication for women, in March 1992.

E: Were you shocked when the story broke?

A: Well, I knew on a Saturday that it was going to be aired the next day, on Sunday morning. But I was shocked at the response. I had no idea the media would come so quickly. I had no idea there would be television cameras camped out in my neighbor's yard. I had no idea there would be such an eager reaction to the story. The Gary Hart situation did not receive this much attention. And remember, Gary Hart was a presidential candidate. This was really an unprecedented reaction [by the media].

E: How did that make you feel?

A: It made me a little frightened at first, and certainly confused. I couldn't quite figure out what the media wanted, because they never seemed satisfied. When a press release was issued, they came and stayed out in my yard. When I spoke at a press conference, they were still there. It was baffling to figure out what they wanted from me. Did they want me to give my testimony to them, prior to the hearing? Had I not been a lawyer, perhaps that would have happened. Perhaps that's why the media reacted the way they did. They thought I would tell everything I was going to say at the hearings to the media.[14]

Another recent example of the impact of the media on all of us is the recent trials of the police officers who beat Rodney King and the Los Angeles riots which we saw on television. Although in the past thousands of Black men have been stopped by police, it became an issue of public empathy through the vehicle of the media. One of the prime pieces of evidence in the Rodney King case was the video. This not only greatly affected the public but was key for the jury as well. After the first verdict a juror related how they spent a lot of time viewing the video of the beating, viewing it frame by frame and talking about it.

It was not that long ago that knowledge of such an incident or such a trial would be much less and spread more slowly, making a tremendous difference in how it would be viewed. But as with the Gulf War, there was an "entering in" experience for the reader and viewer with constant, immediate coverage. The mode of communication predisposes certain methods and biases. Since American viewers are highly stimulated, they want to be entertained—even with the news. There is a great difference in news coming over an American station or over the BBC, which is much less flashy and more information oriented.

The media communicate the "truth" to us. People and information can travel fast! Kenneth Little says, "Urbanization is a form of social consciousness."[15] It is how people perceive their reality.

Traveling to college with my eighteen-year-old son and his college friends could have been a lonely experience. In five and a half hours their focus was on the radio, music and their experience of it. I knew the conversation was in my language, English, but could not grasp any of the meaning. They were able to communicate for hours at a meaningful level because they had a common pool of knowledge. Their values and understanding of themselves were defined in the media framework. I could not enter because it was outside my experience.

Rural Urbanization

Speaking at rural churches has given me the privilege to be in some of the most beautiful Pennsylvania countryside. Recently I drove down a country road which ribboned through hills, past neat farmhouses and shining silos. I noted three "For Sale" signs on them as I drove past.

When I approached the rustic church I saw satellite dishes on homes as prime decor. The media theme continued in the Sunday school, which featured a large television and VCR in the middle of the room.

What a delight it was to fellowship with the young pastor, his wife, two-year-old son Billy and the new baby! Real country cookin' too! Their little cottage was nestled in three acres of green grass and trees. A robin's nest outside the door was occupied by featherless babies stretching their new necks. Inside, the parents turned on the VCR and proudly showed Billy's skills at singing along to the bright, garrulous video of Christian songs.

The setting of the farms, the church and the homes may have seemed rural, but the values were urban since they came through the media. This is what it means for urbanization to be a process and not a place.

In the *Daily Item* of Sunbury, Pennsylvania, the August 12, 1992, edition ran an article entitled, "A Miracle City Unhappy with Its Status." It told how Rudy White hit rock bottom after fifteen years as a heroin addict. After a week in detox, he was given new clothes and a one-way ticket to Williamsport, Pennsylvania. Today he has been clean for five years, has a job, is married and owns his own home. He is working on a graduate degree.

Williamsport, a pastoral setting in north central Pennsylvania in the Susquehanna Valley, is known for motherhood and apple pie, and is the home of Little League World Series. It is also called "The Miracle City" by addicts coming from the drug-plagued inner cities of New York, New Jersey and Pennsylvania because of the high success rate in turning addicts around. The results come from a combination of a strong state-funded community network of services that offers counseling, "sobriety homes" and a hedged environment.

But the indigenous residents now struggle with the changes in their lives. Higher crime rates and overcrowding seem to have come with urbanization to their formerly bucolic region. Mobility provides the flow to other places so that divisions are not geographical any more. Worldwide there are likely very few places that are not urbanized.

The Computer Network
"In science as in many other realms," writes William Broad, "computer networks are having a revolutionary influence. Worldwide, up to four million scientists are thought to be wired into the rapidly expanding maze of interconnected networks, which now number 11252 and are known as the Internet or sometimes just the net. . . . In the 1970's the main users of packet-switched networks were the military and its contractors. The 1980's saw an explosion of civilian spinoffs, often physically based on fiber-optic

lines leased from phone companies.... Today electronic mail with an address in the regular Internet format . . . can zip through an electronic labyrinth around the globe to reach its destination almost instantly. *Remarkably, the labyrinth has no overlord. It is an alliance of technical republics.*"[16]

Larry Smarr of the University of Illinois speaks of the shift in science communication from paper to computer as the one "unifying technology that can help us rise above the epidemic of tribal animosities we're seeing worldwide. One wants a unifying fabric for the human race. The Internet is pointing in that direction. It promotes a very egalitarian culture at a time the world is fragmenting at a dizzying pace."[17] This fragmentation is one of the major results of technology in society. We are made more and more independent of each other. We can shop, buy airplane tickets, do our banking, work, pay our credit cards and access the library, and never leave our home or talk to another person.

Eugene Nida, an anthropologist missionary, said in 1981 that pluralism in the society may make the body of Christ (the church throughout the world) ghettoize—restrict itself to a monastic mentality. *Christians, in fear, may respond by withdrawing and polarizing.*[18]

This is the challenge that urbanization and technology offer the church. Will it imitate society by being just one more fragment in a mosaic of millions of disconnected pieces? Or will it offer a model of unity, reconciliation and community in a desperately disjointed and lonely world?

Recently InterVarsity has seen many urban mission projects spring up in the United States. Students live together in various cities for a summer under the direction of InterVarsity staff. Their goal is to demonstrate the gospel as a loving community. The success of their visible witness is even seen in the questions asked by neighborhood children who observe the behavior of the students and become curious. "How do Black, Hispanic, Asian and Anglos all live together as friends?" And, "Why don't the students have sex with each other, and why don't the single women have babies?" And, "Why do the students invite children into their homes and spend time with them?" Here is relational, incarnational evangelism in action!

Breaking Down Walls

Barbara Brown, InterVarsity's multiethnic development coordinator in Philadelphia, and I teach about reconciliation to students. Barbara is an African-American who grew up in a white culture. There are some things I can teach about racism, but Barbara can teach even more. But the example of the two of us and our love for each other expresses more yet.

If we remember who God is and what he has done in the past, we catch the vision—a vision of a stage prepared for reconciliation among Christians worldwide. Churches or groups of Christians are sometimes separated because of ethnic hostility or past history. As each group acknowledges the richness of the other's history, each can learn what the other can contribute and receive.

Biblical reconciliation can occur when we count the experiences of the other group or person as completely valid. They have a real history with heroes too. They are not, as the media will have us believe, as a secular society will have us believe, negative experiences. God is not partial, and he has made all men and women in his image. That is not just a written creed, but an actuality.

Reconciliation between Christians means that both sides give and take. The powerful does not merely give to the powerless. If we cannot learn from everyone, we will miss God's voice.

Barbara Benjamin (Archilla) wrote *The Impossible Community,* a book about a group of InterVarsity collegians at Brooklyn College during the upheaval of the sixties and seventies. There was struggle and tension within the group especially as Blacks sorted out what it meant to be Black and Christian on campus. The overall unity they achieved, with some pain and cost, was a vital witness to Christ in the university's life. Their motivation to stick together came only from a love of Christ.

Much of the church's anemia comes from disunity in the body of Christ. When the impossible community is vibrant with love, the witness of the gospel will be strong and loud. If racism is confronted and eradicated it will be a sweet smell to God. And we will be more human by calling others human. We will fulfill the first and greatest commandment and the second one which Jesus said is like it—to love our neighbor as ourselves.

What the world looks like can excite us or depress us. As Christians seeing God working out his sovereign plan, we can begin to see that with all the nations present in the United States, with a global stance developing, it is a special time—perhaps a fullness of time—to ride the new wave of urbanization.

Living in an urban context in the U.S., one can build the church of Jesus Christ. God has allowed Cuban, Vietnamese (five hundred at Philadelphia

Community College alone), Polish and many other people to populate many places. Advances in transportation have collapsed geographical distances and boundaries like the Berlin Wall. Jesus broke down the dividing wall between Jew and Gentile (Eph 2:14-15). The cultural and functional barriers can come down too if we are willing to be humble and listen to those who are different. The division comes from within our own hearts telling us that some group is less than us. When there is spirit-led reconciliation among diverse Christians, this vision and power of grace will be unleashed to the world such as has never been seen before. How we can work toward this type of reconciliation is the topic of the next four chapters.

12
The
Key of
Community
▼▼▼▼▼▼▼▼▼▼▼▼▼

THE WORST PUNISHMENT HAS OFTEN BEEN TO PUT SOMEONE IN SOLITARY confinement. The practice began in an unexpected way.

The penitentiary was the brainchild of the Philadelphia Society for Alleviating the Miseries of Public Prisons, which practically made a separate religion out of prison reform. Benjamin Franklin himself was an early member. In their idealistic fervor, the members of the society concluded that since their own faith was rooted in silent meditation and soul-searching, the best treatment for criminals would be solitary confinement. . . . It was a well-intentioned, dreadful error.[1]

Sometimes our image of the city is of an impersonal place of isolated people, locked up in their homes, afraid of each other. Actually community often happens and has more depth in the city than in some suburban areas. Community can be a healthy response to urban stress.

Help in Times of Stress
When we began our ministry in the city of Newark, New Jersey, one of the resources we had was the Christian Africans in our circle. Tabitha and Joseph

moved into the city with their three young sons. Highly educated and motivated as students, they were an attractive couple. But I did think it a piece of madness when Thom introduced Carl and Donna, a white suburban couple new to the city and a month past their wedding, into our ministry and our living environs!

After some time had passed Donna told us that the arrangement had been a lifesaver. She felt lonely and anchorless giving up her elementary school teaching; Tabitha and Joseph's three sons were a real boon, as were their parents, to this newly married urban mission couple.

One day Mrs. Green, a neighbor, rang my bell. She talked excitedly, "Bring Jason right in; there is a weird man walking around the neighborhood and I know he's bad. I clean over at the hotel and he is there. Jason will be safer inside!" In our neighborhood a real sense of community was operating.

Often women in mission or in the city survive absentee husbands who are not there when you make your best coffee or when the house begins to burn. That seemed to be true for me. Joseph, who was Thom's right-hand man first in Kenya, had come to do some chores in Thom's absence. After finishing, he turned to go out the gate and looked back over our garden. Bright red flames were eating the house eaves, so he hurried back. I assigned him the children and moved Thom's camera to a safe place.

After calling the Nakuru Fire Department—that I wasn't sure existed or would come in time—I began yelling for my neighbors to start a bucket brigade as I had seen in the movies. It was a friendly neighborhood with many shops and a brothel. Soon there were about two hundred people. I called Julia, a plain lady with the power of the Holy Spirit, to defend us in prayer. Shortly the garden was quiet. The Nakuru Fire Brigade was not only completely existent but completely efficient.

I told Joseph that when he returned to his home he should be low-key in describing the incident at the Hoplers'. He agreed. Later that evening I was impressed with the communication grapevine when a taxi roared into our driveway. Two doors opened, and a church elder ejected out one side and a dear friend out the other. Their faces expressed it all. Joseph had not been as low-key as I had hoped.

"I expected to find you and the children sitting in a heap of ashes," the elder said.

This same elder came with another businessman from Kenya in 1978 to comfort us at Thom's death. They brought a gift of money from the African

Inland Church and an offer for participation in the dry fish fly business which was doing very well in England. They offered my family the franchise in the States! This is our community helping in times of stress.

A Center for Ministry

Community creates an atmosphere of our common humanity where God's love can be experienced.

Once Thom said, "The best thing we did in these last four years [in Nakuru, Kenya] was to raise chickens." When we went back to Kenya for our second term we went to the African church in an urban center to ask the pastor and some of the elders where we should live. At the time, missionaries lived up on the hill in a nice neighborhood. We all drove around looking. They finally settled on a cement block house for us that had three acres of land. It was near the roundabout where you departed the city, and was a virtual thorough-fare. Our home became known as Hopler's Hotel, and for four years, through hospitality of different hues, our ministry developed out of the home.

Our large living area was used for Bible studies, tea and raising day-old chicks which were sent up by train from Nairobi. They were kept in the corner of the sitting room in a tall cardboard box with overhanging lights for heat. (When they were old enough we kept them outside.) As you might imagine, this made a wonderful conversation piece and point of contact which only deepened our bond with our African Christian friends.

There was constant discussion over the immunizations, method of care and the rooster. People questioned us as to why our chickens escaped disease and why they were so tender. We relied on Jeci, an African Christian, for the shots. All this community and more in the urban context!

Our social life centered in the African church in Nakuru. One of the fullest blessings was the young marrieds Bible study which began at our home. Some people were neither young nor married. When their children from their common-law marriages asked why they could not take Communion, a series of weddings occurred—renewal weddings with all the trimmings: dress, cake, gifts and new white sneakers. God is a God of redemption, and as his Word is alive and took root, the marriages were redeemed while the nurture began in a community.

Our African couples were clever in making the most of community as well. When a new couple attended a Bible study, they were told the next meeting would be at their home! With the high value on hospitality found in the African culture, the new couple would be pleased and honored—and, of course, they would definitely be attending the next time and have more opportunity to hear the gospel.

Many Patterns

One pattern that has gained broad-based support in recent years is called holistic ministry, in which people seek to meet the emotional, physical and spiritual needs of the whole person. There can be many patterns of community in the city.

Ruth is a friend in an urban church who has a broad vision. She leads the women of her church in a ministry to women who have incarcerated husbands. "I think," says Ruth, "that getting hunks of cheese at church doesn't cut it with these women. Are we just patronizing them? Do we want our contact with them to remind them of their poverty?" Her goal, instead, is to create "an aura of specialness" around them.

So what does this truth of the gospel look like in Ruth's hands? She invites a hair stylist from the church to demonstrate some skills for the women, and gives away one free cut. As a result, they feel loved and special. On another occasion she distributed an invitation. "Has anyone sent you flowers lately? Come and make your own corsage. Materials, coffee, donuts and loving child care will be provided."

The church wants folks to know that Jesus loves them and gave his life for them. His life looks and feels like this, I think. There is a real walking demonstration of that in this "aura of specialness."

The activities opened the way for counseling (another gift of the church community). Four or five women have taken advantage of this. The goal is that they would join a support group.

As a result of these efforts, gifts of church members were used, Christians were encouraged to serve, heart needs were met, and the possibility of a long-term relationship was opened with the body of Christ on a city corner.

Moving into the City

Although one size does not fit all when it comes to community in the city, some good general guidelines in relocating to the city were recently found in *Urban Family* magazine:

1) Do not move to the city to get cheap housing. You may be shifting the poor out of their home.

2) Do not go in alone. You need a support community.

3) Give yourself time to adjust. It may take a couple years to deal with "culture shock."

4) One family can't change an entire community. Join a voluntary association to build together.

5) Don't come on a shining horse thinking you have all the answers. Build relationships with your neighbors. Listen to them. Be dependent on them.

6) Network with people who share your passion for inner-city development.[2]

To these I would add the following. To any place we can only bring who we are. Just like in a marriage, we bring all our quirks and weaknesses as well as our spiritual gifts and other strengths. Under the cultural stress and anger of the city, things will come out that we never thought were in us. That is why we need the Christian community and dependency on God. Sensitivity and humility are vital.

When we fail, how will we handle it? Will we want to get out and say it was an awful mistake? Will we be critical of others, full of anger? Or will we persevere and learn from God who leads us?

Viv Grigg identified with the poor in a Manila slum by living in a shack of indigenous people. In his book, *Companion to the Poor,* he said that because he had an education he would never be able to fully identify with the poor. He had certain cultural limitations. He had to have clean water and a typewriter, and once a month he went into a hotel for a day to regroup.

After a long time of living in African and American cities, I look back with awe at how God kept us. In Kenya I stayed alone with a baby, with no car or telephone for a time. Later in Nakuru I was alone again (with three preschoolers and a husky dog) while Thom traveled doing youth ministry. So I asked Hulda, another missionary, to stay with me.

In the night I roused Hulda saying, "Let's go! They are stealing the chickens!" Hulda heard the dog barking and knew it was true but refused to go out. I was able to salvage most of the chickens, and they did not get the rooster. Hulda was reasonable and British. I was counting my chickens so they could hatch.

On our busy street in the city schoolchildren passed by twice a day, eyeing our grape arbor. What message did we want to give them? Should we shoo them away and protect our possessions, or should we send a message about the gospel? Were we owners or stewards of the grapes?

We asked the children to bring their bags, and we would provide help (my children) and a ladder so they could gather the grapes carefully. This became a great way for us to become known and for us to get to know the youth—which was good protection for us and, in Philadelphia, good gospel too.

In crosscultural ministry the only thing to guard is our attitude. Not our time, not our possessions, not even our absolutes, but our attitude.

Some people will not relocate, some will stay for a time, and some will make it a life's call. God is not so much concerned with the place as with the process he is performing in our lives. Some people can be prideful about living in the city and look down on the suburbanites. God never looks down on a person in that way. He looks only at the hearts.

Moving out of the City

Community happens in a variety of ways. One pattern that makes a lot of sense but is not often considered is to assist able people in a less-advantaged area to move, with Christian support, to another place. Migration can take place in both directions.

Let us say that instead of a church body in a suburban or rural context sending a family to the city to present Christ, they enable a mother to move into a place with advantages for her family. Three groups share and are involved: the church's people, the woman and family, and a mediator who can function in both arenas and is trusted in both.

The money, physical and spiritual support which would be forthcoming to the urban missionaries is used for this chosen family to help make up the gap; it would enable them to reach long-range goals that could not be reached otherwise. Instead of improving housing, Christians build a family. The mother might go under without help. With the help certain mothers enhance themselves, their children and those around them—their extended family.

It has long been known in international development that aid given to the woman is to the betterment of the whole family. It is a different form of relocation and redistribution. Wisely monitored, it can be effective. Compassion International helps families in many countries with a financial boost. A person can support a child with clothing, education and books in a Christian setting.

A local church can truly make a ripple effect that continues in one family. I know this from experience when a church did that for me, allowing me to remain in my home, grieve and regain stability after my husband's death. They faithfully supplemented the social security payments with some extra money each month.

Changing Character, not Circumstances

Families move to the city to be salt and light, but often find it difficult to remain when they have school-age children. Yet with even a single-parent home children can experience a solid, biblical lifestyle at home. They begin to integrate their faith early when they see so much of life daily, not hidden behind tall fences, manicured lawns and manufactured goods. Life is all of one piece. They learn to express love and make decisions in the context of worldly values.

The tendency is to change our circumstances. God wants to change our character in the midst of evil. It is like an infusion—tea leaves become tea when put into hot water!

God's perspective can be seen in the young boy Samuel who was born to a pious Old Testament family (1 Sam 1—3). His story really begins with his father Elkanah who, as was the custom of the time, had two wives. He loved his barren wife Hannah very much, but she was upset because Elkanah's other wife, Penniah (who had Elkanah's children but not his love), constantly ridiculed her.

At the temple, Hannah had only one thing to give the Lord—"her asking." God had everything to give and in his mercy took Hannah's prayer for a child and her vow to give him back to the Lord. She soon gave birth to Samuel who became a great priest and prophet of Israel. In all of Scripture, nothing negative is said about Samuel—his character was sterling.

No more than a toddler, Samuel was brought to Shiloh to the elderly, passive priest, Eli, as Hannah had promised. Eli was the chief caretaker of the newly weaned boy in an atmosphere that was immoral and decadent. Hopni and Phineas, his sons, were sexually promiscuous. Eli himself is described as lying or sitting. The three were gluttons and large. God tells Eli that he has honored his sons more than he honored God! Hannah was giving her son, tender and weak, into a corrupt temple system. This was not, from our perspective, a likely place for a youth to develop godliness. But God has the last word as Samuel became one of the heroes of the Bible and eventually anointed Israel's first two kings—Saul and David.

God is a creative God. He knows the nature of the world we live in, whether city or suburb or farm. Since all places are marred by sin and selfishness, he is more concerned about who we become than about where we live.

13

The Controversy
of Black
Culture

▼▼▼▼▼▼▼▼▼▼▼▼▼▼▼

W. E. B. DUBOIS'S DESCRIPTION OF THE AFRICAN-AMERICAN IS AS TRUE TODAY
as it was the day it was written:

> The Negro is a sort of a seventh son, born with a veil, and gifted with
> second-sight in this American world—a world which yields him no true
> self-consciousness, but only lets him see himself through the revelation
> of the other world. . . .
>
> One ever feels his two-ness—an American, a Negro; two souls, two
> thoughts, two unreconciled strivings; two warring ideals in one dark body,
> whose dogged strength alone keeps it from being torn asunder.[1]

The tension that DuBois refers to arises in the context of a broad, controversial question. Do Blacks have a dual heritage (one from Africa and one from
America) creating a distinct Black culture, or was their uprooting from Africa
so traumatic and complete that their culture has virtually no continuity with
their home continent? This may sound a bit academic (and it is hotly debated
in some circles), but it nonetheless has profound implications for issues of
racism in America.

To me it is amazing that the question of whether a people has a culture of its own is so widely argued. Isn't it interesting that there is no similar debate about any other group in America? When we want a group of people to disclaim where they came from or who they are, we need to ask why this is occurring. Usually if a group goes back in their history, it is considered healthy. It is considered good. Why is that not always the case in this situation?

Similar Cultures

From my study and experience, I see continuity between Africa and America. Melville Herskovits observes a number of cultural elements that are not traceable to Euro-American culture. One trait he points to is the widespread existence of close-knit extended families in the New World which are still part of African culture today, especially in West Africa where most of the Africans were captured for enslavement.[2]

When Paul and Bilhah Kihika married in Kenya, we were involved in the festivities. We had not been married long ourselves. When they returned from their Mombasa honeymoon, I was amazed to find that Kihika's twin brothers had moved into their minuscule apartment in order to attend school. Bilhah was feeding three men! Many years have passed; now all Paul's brothers have married and have families. As the eldest he is responsible for the extended family. From time to time he will visit his sisters-in-law to see how they are faring. Do the wives have any complaint, especially in their relationship to their husbands? He is there to sustain and mediate. It is for the good of all the family.

I was told by Simon, one of the brothers of this large Christian family, that each Sunday the entire extended family meets in one of the homes for fellowship. Simon, a prosperous businessman, emphasized that no other social engagement can take precedence over this family gathering. There is a time to eat, the devotional is brought by another family, and there is a time to pray. One of the brothers, Wachira, was studying in the States, and his needs were carefully rehearsed and prayed about with some of the younger children who had not really known him. Cousins play and learn together, and so the next generation begins to fuse at the Sunday meetings.

The strong extended family is demonstrated in the same way in my Black neighbors in Germantown. Everyone contributes, even in a non-Christian family structure. The home provides the emotional and economic base to help family members make it. Then they are expected to give back to the matriarch. The grandbabies are dropped off every morning. The older children go there after school; no daycare for them. There are some family members who have overflowed into the apartments next door, and there is a steady flow of goods and communication in this extended Black family.

Having lived in Kenya for ten years and having made a return trip in the last twenty, I have intuitively sensed other similarities even when I was unaware of what I was observing. Sometimes after returning to the States to live in a predominantly African-American area, I would catch myself thinking, "Am I in Kenya?" The dress and body language of the people around me made it seem like I was in Africa. Women had the same type of head coverings as well as the same poise and carriage as the people walking by our home in Nakuru!

There is political continuity as well. Tom Mboya was one of Africa's most vigorous younger statesmen. Between 1952 and 1960 Mboya's major contribution consisted in explaining African aspirations to foreign audiences. He was one of the chief architects of Kenya's independence in 1963. The following are excerpts from an article he wrote for the *New York Times,* the outgrowth of a visit to the United States shortly before his death at 38. He was assassinated in Nairobi on July 5, 1969.

Black Americans today are more concerned with their relationship to Africa than at any point in recent memory. . . . Our struggle and goal are the same, and we need a common understanding on strategy so as not to cancel each other out.

In a fundamental way, Africans and Afro-Americans find themselves in remarkably similar political and economic situations. Our slogan during the independence struggle was, "Uhuru Sasa," and I do not think it is a coincidence that its English translation, "Freedom Now" was the slogan for the civil rights movement. For the black American struggle in the 1950s and early 60s was very similar to our own. The objective of both was political liberty for black people. . . . Like their African cousins who must meet the challenge of development, they now confront the more difficult task of achieving economic equality.[3]

Tom Mboya felt that the independence movement in Africa posed many important questions for white America in regard to the race problem in the United States. The U.S. government understood very well that it would have trouble making friends in Africa so long as the Black American remained subjugated. He said, "Africans are highly conscious of the plight of Black America, and they will be suspicious of the intentions of American foreign policy until they are convinced that the goal of American domestic policy is social justice for all."[4]

Mboya also noted the remarkable transformation in the Black American's attitude toward Africa from his first visit in 1956 to his last. He saw it due to the independence that the different African countries gained. As stereotypes were broken, the shame of the Americans in their African heritage was transformed into great pride; they began to identify with Africa.

He speaks of how African interests extend beyond their own borders, saying that it is the basis of the bond between African nationalists and Black leaders from other lands. "Africa is the birthplace of the Black man, but his home is the world. To us, this is the meaning of total independence. We refuse to think of being free in Africa but treated as inferiors the moment we step out of the Continent."[5]

Similar Spiritualities
Dean Trulear speaks of continuing similarities in the Black church between Africa and contemporary American practice. For example, Africans and African-Americans do not distinguish between secular and sacred (as the white, largely European-American population does) but between sacred and profane. In addition it is common for Africans and African-Americans to actively believe that God's presence never leaves us, but there are evil spirits we must contend with, while white Americans are less likely to hold this.[6]

Like Trulear, I have also observed similarities in spirituality. When I first attended a Kenyan church I observed the simplicity in the prayer. The Africans dealt so much with the basics and even thanked God "for getting us up this morning"! I was surprised when pastors thanked God for the breath in their mouths, for strength to stand up and for getting us on our way. Why did they deal so much with the obvious? What about the attributes and majesty of Almighty God? I wondered if it was due to a lack of education.

But God was patient in teaching me. One day I stopped by the bookstore in Nakuru where our friend Samuel worked. His baby had been hospitalized for an illness, and I wanted to know how she was. He told me in heartbroken tones that she had died. I was shocked because she had had diarrhea and was not an infant. She had been under care in the hospital receiving intravenous fluids. I couldn't understand what had gone wrong.

I began to realize then that I came out of a scientific, Western worldview that depended on a materialistic perspective of reality. I looked to science for answers. But in the African mindset this was "shauri la Mungu"—the work, the business of God. No one could be sure if God would give breath or strength. So when he did, one was thankful.

When we returned to the States we ministered in the city of Newark, New Jersey, among African-American churches that we attended in storefronts on Sundays. What a comfort to my ears and heart when the deacon began to pray, "Thank you, Lord, for getting us up this morning, standing us on our feet, and giving us strength to move!" It was the same nation of people with the same worldview.

Positive or Negative?

While there have been attempts to disprove the existence of a distinctively African culture among Blacks, there have also been efforts (or at least a widespread belief) that we should view Black culture as it exists negatively. The message that "Black is beautiful" is a debatable one to whites in a different culture. I remember teaching a crosscultural course to raise the level of consciousness among white students. Pictures were presented on the depth and richness of ancient African kingdoms. Afterwards, in their evaluation forms, some said it was a waste of time.

Even some African-Americans wonder about their validity. Is it because much of what is being said offers a negative view of them and their worth? Why, if a people who were denied citizen's rights in America can still produce strong leaders like Martin Luther King Jr., Malcolm X, Mary McLeod Bethune, W. E. B. DuBois, Frederick Douglass, Phyliss Wheatley and many others—why must this group always prove that they are decent humans? Why do we look so negatively on African-American young men in particular? Aren't young white men also criminals and thieves? Doesn't evil infect all humans? At every level in our country we have acted corruptly— from judges to baseball heroes. Why, then, is the fear and focus on Black youth?

In the chapter on dynamic ethnicity we saw that American values were first designated in the Euro-centric frame and especially the German and English root. The immigrants that came to the United States tried to conform to that rule. And different factors such as when they came, how many and why made a difference as to how they "melted." The educational system was the filter through which the next generation moved to make them true Americans.

But with the Blacks we have a group of people who were compelled to come, torn from their own place and time through slavery, whose memories were forcibly erased so they could survive, and who were afforded neither dignity nor human worth nor family life nor land nor education nor history. Thomas Jefferson, more liberal than most of his contemporaries, was nevertheless certain that "the two races, equally free, cannot live in the same government."[7]

Since the educational system is so important to Americans, we need to ask why both test scores and classroom performance show a tremendous disparity between African-American and white students. This is at all levels. The National Alliance of Black School Educators tells us that in 1984 nearly 28 percent of African-American high school students dropped out before graduation. In addition, "African Americans represent about 13.5% of the college age population (18-24). But African American students represented only 9.1% of the Associate Degrees, 6.5% of the Bachelors, 6.4% of the Masters, and 3.9% of the Doctorates, and 4.1% of the first professional degrees in 1980."[8]

Other explanations are possible besides Black inferiority. Educator Janet E. Hale-Benson writes:

Even though the term "cultural difference" was introduced in the 1970's, it has remained essentially a cliché. "Cultural difference" has been a superficial acknowledgement of Black Culture but it has never been developed as a construct.[9]

Culture difference occurs when children have not had experiences that provide them with the kind of information that is usable in school. A child might have a storehouse of information, but it is not the background that is required for the school curriculum.[10]

Martha was a six-year-old with American parents. She had been born in Kenya, East Africa, however, and as a first grader was tested at the local American school. She did very poorly in the visual test. I remember one question on the test. A woman with a small cap and a tray was to be identified. The correct answer was "waitress." Martha identified her as a nurse. She had no concept of "waitress" at all. In her experience in East Africa, "waiters" were tall Black men wearing a fez and caftan. She had quite a vast experience and knowledge beyond that of a typical six-year-old. But most of it would not be tested in her American classroom. The same is often true for African-Americans.

It is important to us as Christians and important to the gospel to ask about the negativism toward African-Americans. Why particularly are Black males viewed as violent and dangerous whether they be in three-piece suits or leather jackets? Does it have to do with attitudes practiced in an economy that demanded slavery and later sharecropping? And later in the cities and wars that required manpower to do the work needed for us? The Black person was tolerated as long as he would take his place.

That is one key issue in *The Color Purple.* In the movie, the character played by Oprah Winfrey was to be a white woman's maid—but she could not drive a car or be aggressive. Similarly, Coalhouse Walker in another film, *Ragtime,* could not proudly drive around a fancy car; it was not his place.

One time sitting with my "African son," John, at a Bible college dinner I found the same attitude. When John got up to go to the smorgasbord, the president of the college (who had been sitting with us) asked me if John wasn't rather arrogant. I reviewed as best I could the preceding conversation and could not think of any arrogance I had heard. John, an African, had simply expressed his opinions. Was that arrogant? Was the man really asking why John did not take his place, but gave opinions as a man?

God has already determined each human's place. "Let us make man in our image," he said (Gen 1:26). "Thou hast made him little less than God, and dost crown him with glory and honor. Thou hast given him dominion over the works of they hands" (Ps 8:5-6). We in the church are his "chosen race, a royal priesthood, a holy nation, God's own people" (1 Pet 2:9). We are to struggle while we live to *take our place together* under his lordship.

14
Black
Church
Power

▼▼▼▼▼▼▼▼▼▼▼▼▼

AFTER WE WENT TO AFRICA AS MISSIONARIES, WE FOUND OURSELVES BACK on the doorstep of the American Black church. It was to get answers to the questions we were asked. "How are our Black brothers and sisters in America? What is the Black church doing there?" they would ask us. We had to admit that we didn't know. So we returned to find out.

The Black church grew out of the loins of the Negro church which died in the "Savage Sixties" as many African-Americans struggled with whether they could be both Christian and Black in America. It is difficult for outsiders to comprehend all the layers of definition that have been part of the Black person following Christ. For some whites observing this struggle, it may also be hard to comprehend that the present Black church is out of both the white church and the Negro church.

The Black Church: Two Parents
The institution of the Negro church was a marriage of the "invisible institution" born in slavery and the visible church of free Negroes started before

the Civil War. The invisible Black church existed among the slaves unofficially, although it had its origins in the preaching of the gospel that came through white Christians, sometimes white slave owners. So it was hard, for both African-Americans and white Americans, to separate the two sides of the coin—biblical mutual submission and slavery.

At the same time, the free Negroes in the north developed their own churches. Generally, the beginnings of the Negro church in the north are dated from 1787 when Richard Allen and Absalom Jones left St. George's Methodist Church because they were interrupted in prayer "to take their right place." The Blacks had become rather numerous and so were relegated to separate seating. In April 1787, therefore, Richard Allen began the Free African Society, which later developed into the African Methodist Episcopal Church which currently has a membership of over two million.[1]

After Emancipation and the Civil War, the freed slaves found themselves in a vacuum. There were no officially ordained ministers to marry them or to baptize their children. So it was that the invisible institution came together with African Methodist Episcopal churches and with other Black denominations.

Filling the Gap

The Negro church, and later the Black church, gave stability, dignity and hope to African-Americans in the United States. Leaders for the community were called from within the church. The gospel was contextualized in the Black church in a wholistic manner. Black people were outside the American community; although they might have worked there, they did not reap the full benefits of that society. Cornel West wrote in *Prophecy Deliverance* that it was in the Black church that the two needs of the Black person as an individual and Black people as a group were fulfilled: those of self-identity and self-determination.

I once heard Alice Walker, the author of *The Color Purple* and one of the spokespersons for African-American women, speak to a very large group at Temple University. She was telling about her own pilgrimage in a unique and ingenious way. She said she respected the creation and the creatures but that the church was not relevant. Nonetheless, she carefully clarified that she did not mean the Black church. Even though she did not cast her lot with the Black church, she believed that it has been important in the lives—the total lives—of African-Americans.

A front-page article in the October 6, 1992, issue of *The Chronicle of Philanthropy,* "Helping Black Churches Heal Cities," with a picture of a Black pastor in Brooklyn, said in part:

When Los Angeles erupted in riots last spring, members of the First African Methodist Episcopal Church, along with its activist Pastor, the Rev. Cecil Murray, quickly hit the streets to calm rioters, distribute relief assistance, and lead the crusade for community healing.

Identified by civic leaders as the most effective spiritual and social institutions in the strife-torn area, the black church and its social-services arms were flooded with $800,000 in contributions from individuals, foundations, and corporations—many of which had never supported a church before.[2]

The African-American church has in numerous ways demonstrated its viability to the general public and to the African-American community.

Black churches have two powerful allies in the foundation world: the $3.8 billion Lilly Endowment in Indianapolis and the $6.6 billion Ford Foundation in New York, both of which make grants to study the social role of the Black churches and to enhance their capacity to deliver services. Some observers say it is no coincidence that these two foundations have put a focus on Black churches. The staff members responsible are daughters of Black ministers!

The Piton Foundation in Denver has begun to be involved with Black churches and hopes to provide grants for the area's 150 Black churches. The first-year budget is in the $150,000 to $200,000 range. Grant Jones, the program officer, said, "Whenever we see a flare-up like in Los Angeles, the church is always at the center of resolution of that crisis."[3]

Still Invisible

While some within the public sphere have appreciated and recognized the role of the Black church in America, significant portions of the white church world have rendered the Black church invisible. Such noted African-American scholars on religion as C. Eric Lincoln, Charles Long and the late William H. Bentley have argued that the African-American religious experience is still not taken seriously by most white Christians. In the March 8, 1993, letters to the editor section of *Christianity Today* magazine, one letter reads:

I eagerly began to read the chart in the News section for December 14, "The 1992 Vote, Evangelical Style." Then I noticed the (first category),

"Percentage of voters identifying themselves as white evangelicals." Are there any black evangelicals in the U.S? Were their votes and opinions not worth surveying?

Mrs. Winsome Davis
Plevna, Ont.

Answer from CT: We, too, would be interested in the voting patterns of African-American evangelicals. Unfortunately, our source did not provide such statistics.—EDS[4]

Actually, there are millions of Black evangelicals in America—most of the 23 million Black churchgoers who belong to conservative, evangelical, Baptist or Pentecostal denominations.[5] But most whites are ignorant of their existence.

In his book *The Coming Race Wars?* Pannell tells of his own frustration and pain as an African-American in the white institutional system. I know the author to be a mild man, gentle and kind, and yet he expresses some long and hard truths for white Christians. Vernon Grounds, in his comment at the beginning of the book, defines himself as "white, middle-class American of the older evangelical establishment who greatly respects the author." He says about the book:

I cannot shrug it off. I cannot simply point out its exaggerations, its reactive lopsidedness, its lack of balance as through my ideological grid I perceive such faults in this formidable indictment against my kind of Christianity....

I can only pray for grace to let its message painfully penetrate my defenses, my rationalizations, my prejudices. If I can—if I do—and if many others like me also can and do! perhaps a saving change will be slowly effected in our schizophrenic society. Perhaps instead of interracial destructiveness, there will be war-preventing reconciliation.[6]

What does Pannell say about the Black church? He describes the African Methodist Episcopal in terms of that old European marque BMW: Black Men Working. "Older men are fashioning new relationships with black youth, serving them as mentors, and equipping them to find work and advancement in the city."[7]

He says the churches have two things in common: they are evangelical in the sense of being unfailingly faithful to the Word of God and to the conviction that salvation comes through faith in Jesus Christ alone. Second, these nonwhite Protestant and growing churches are urban to the core.

Throughout Los Angeles not only is there a vital Black church but vital churches in the Hispanic and Korean communities as well. Fervent, committed to the Scriptures and to mission, these are thriving oases in the city.[8]

Because the Black church has an identity outside the mainstream of society, its origin, characteristics, mode of operation, its very perspective is different from the white church in America. The major forces shaping the Black church were its African heritage and its history of oppression. Therefore, the results were different from the white church. Its message (its core, Jesus, was the same, but its form was different), music, spirit and organization—all resulting from a different historical experience—are all different. So instead of saying, "The Lord Jesus Christ arose!" the same glorious truth might sound like, "Ain't no grave gonna hold my body down!"[9]

Different cultures have different values. It is not surprising that the Black church also expresses values that differ from those of the dominant culture. For example, it is *event-oriented* (concerned more about what happens rather than when it happens), *noncrisis-oriented* (leaves options open rather than locking into one course of action), *person-oriented* (gives higher priority to people than to tasks) and *holistic* (withholds approval or disapproval, being tentative to condemn but also suspicious of those who appear faultless).[10]

A Model and Force for Change
The Reverend Clarence L. James, president of Youth Leadership Development Programs in Atlanta, in addressing the making of African-American men (with an emphasis on growing from a boy to a man), says, "We need a system of producing men that touches the masses of our males, rather than a favored few. The Church is undeniably the most powerful institution in the African-American community."[11]

He goes on to describe the duration and expanse of the church, which he says sways with power the lives of all of the people in the community. This is whether they are members of individual churches or not.

James goes on to say: "The contemporary Black Church is a sleeping giant. It is a vast repository of underdeveloped resources in the form of people, talents, and monies. It remains our only self-standing, self-certified, inner-directed institution that has no dependency upon foreign sources for its existence, authority, and finance."[12]

In his book *Malcolm, the Man Behind the X* Carl Ellis, a Black theologian from Westminster Seminary, says: "Thus far, the historic African American church has produced the only unified soul dynamic in the African American community. In fact, history shows that no Black movement has survived for long apart from the Black theological dynamic. The secular and Islamic Black intellectuals failed to produce it, and no African American cultural identity has been possible without it."[13] Even in a secular magazine such as *Ebony*, it is acknowledged as a phenomenon of hope.

Several years ago Anglican church leaders in Oxford, England, were concerned because the churches in their cities were empty. So they did research to find where in the world such urban churches were thriving and growing. They discovered that Black churches in America were doing just this. So they issued an invitation to several Black church leaders to come to England for three weeks to give lectures on their experiences so those in England could learn from them. Those invited included William Pannell (who headed the team), Brenda Salter-McNeil, J. Derek McNeil, Don Thomas, La Voughn Thomas and Richard Farmer.

Brenda Salter-McNeil was startled at the realization of what she had in her church tradition. She was amazed, with her brothers and sisters, at the Cambridge professors taking copious notes. Later she was struck by the global significance of the Black church.

The Black church has brought the gospel to urban centers in ways that fit that setting and presented many wholistic models. But it is often invisible to the larger church, which could miss the intent of God on a people who have suffered much and rose up as strong believers in Jesus. It is responsible for a spiritual witness to the scientific-oriented world in a day when we need that voice.

As any human institution has weaknesses and faults, so it is in the Black church. That is no reason to be ignorant of it. It has had a tremendous impact on society and has the potential for even more. Perhaps most American Christians will come to understand something that most Black believers have always understood. God has sent the Black church for such a time as this.

15
Keys to Reconciliation

▼▼▼▼▼▼▼▼▼▼▼▼▼

THE TENSIONS BETWEEN THE RACES ARE ALL TOO REAL IN THE UNITED States. After so many years, can they be resolved? Can there be healing and reconciliation? I am convinced of the power of the gospel to do just that. Still we are faced with the question, Where do we begin?

Learning *About* Each Other

One basic starting point is learning each other's history and culture. When we do not know one another's culture, there is likely to be suspicion as to what the other person or group is doing and why, which can grow into fear and hate. These are often reinforced by cultural stereotypes which still have strong negative perceptions of Blacks.

The next step is to get up close and personal. Sometimes churches will have an exchange of choirs or a pulpit exchange. This is certainly fine, but it is not deep. More individuals on both sides have to get to know one another. This will call into question commonly held myths. Unless we sit with someone, eat with them and stay in their homes, we will not get past the masks.

The first step does not have to be huge. It just needs to be taken from where we are. Returning to inner-city ministry under the same mission which had sent us to Kenya, East Africa, we began to ask some questions of ourselves. Had we known any Black students during our Bible-college days? We got out the yearbook. Sure enough, we had. We remembered several Black friends with nostalgia. We remembered the fun in the dorm, in the snack bar, on campus.

But then we realized that although several of our Black classmates were from New Jersey, like us, we had never asked them to ride home with us. Thom used to fill his car for the trip between Rhode Island and New Jersey at $5 a head. (His girlfriend introduced me as a possible paying customer and that's how we met!) But it never entered our minds to ask our Black classmates.

Several years ago at an InterVarsity student camp I met with a student leadership team which included Tina, a Black woman. They were doing well on campus and wanted go a step further by beginning to deal with racism. How could they make an impact—especially with Tina's involvement with them? I asked them how they had served Tina. Had they visited her home or her church? No, they replied, that hadn't come up.

Sometimes a simple step is the place to begin. Often we lack the insight of someone else's context even though we may be fairly involved with them.

There are ways to go further, however. James Baldwin once made a pact with his friend Budd Shulberg, a fellow writer.

I think you owe it to me, as my friend, to fight me, to let me get away with nothing, to force me to be clear, to force me to be honest, to allow me to take no refuge in rage or in despair . . . and of course I owe you the same. This means that we are certainly going to hurt each other's feelings from time to time. But that's one of the ways in which people learn from each other.[1]

This sounds like 1 Corinthians 13 to me: Love rejoices in the truth. It sounds like Romans 12: Love that which is sincere (genuine); hate that which is evil. But this sort of relationship is rare.

People find it hard to confront in this way even within their own culture or in their own marriage or their own church. It is very costly and painful. Yet it is also cleansing, energizing and makes grace flow in abundance. The only motive that will carry off this kind of friendship is love. It means forgiving and being forgiven. That is an experience that is at the heart of the gospel of Jesus.

You can invite people into your home and still fail to build bridges, however. In Luke 7 we join a dinner party Jesus attended at the invitation of the host, Simon, a Pharisee. A woman devoted (in Simon's eyes) to sin anointed Jesus' feet, first with her tears and hair, then with her kisses, and lastly with expensive perfume—and all this in full view of everyone as Jesus was seated at the dinner table. This woman treated Jesus as someone significant and worthy of great honor.

Simon was upset that Jesus let such a sinful woman fawn over him in this way. Yet in Jesus' eyes, she was treating him much better than Simon had. The Pharisee failed to offer Jesus the common courtesies so basic in the Middle Eastern hospitality—no washing of feet, no kiss of greeting, no anointing with oil. He had depersonalized Jesus, judged him to be uneducated and to have little to offer Simon except perhaps some notoriety. And by so characterizing Jesus in this way, Simon missed the chance of his life!

Learning *from* Each Other
If the first step is learning *about* each other, the next step is learning *from* each other. This can be risky and threatening to us because sometimes the so-called truths that we hold dear can be shaken and challenged when we meet up with someone from a different culture or mindset.

Marv Mayers tells a story about his own experience in a Latin country as a missionary. He called some of the church elders together because his daughter's tricycle had been stolen. There followed a discussion of all the details surrounding the theft: the time of day, description of the toy and finally just where it had last been seen. It was determined then that the tricycle had been on the path just in front of the Mayeres' home.

"Oh," said the elders, "we see. We understand! This is not a theft."

"Why not?" Marv asked. It seemed to him that it was. Someone must have taken it away; it was no longer there. That seemed like a theft to him.

"Well," they answered, "yes, we could see how you might perceive it that way. But here anything on a public path is considered public property. If an object is left in that area, it is not considered to be private property but up for grabs."

So what seemed like a clear-cut truth (stealing is stealing) is not so absolute in another culture. A similar example can be found right on the streets of Philadelphia where I live. On garbage day in the city before the actual trucks arrive, there is quite a bit of "gleaning." All steel, aluminum and good furniture is culled out of the piles. No one would ever accuse the gleaners of stealing before the garbage trucks arrived even though they were taking things that didn't belong to them!

What frees us to hear things that are different from our cultural absolutes? It is that Jesus is the same yesterday, today and forever. When Black Christians tell us their stories, we can accept them without fear. If we happen to see things differently, we know (as James Baldwin knew) that it is an act of love for us to ask questions.

Sometimes we discount what a child says to us because we consider the source: "Oh, this is just a child talking." What we don't realize is that the same thing can happen when listening to a Black person. Subconsciously we believe more what the society says about them than what God says—that they are made in his image.

I believe a current example of our inability to listen is exhibited in some who say that affirmative action produces reverse racism. In the March 1993 issue of *Ebony* one of the letters to the editor said this:

As a White woman, I have never read *Ebony* before, but have long admired the work of Denzel Washington that I read in this month's issue. I found Mr. Washington to be very intelligent and well-spoken until I saw his remarks about White people defending themselves about slavery and racism. What many of us say is true; it was my great grandfather. I do not know why, in 1992, this issue is so controversial.

. . . I wonder what would happen to me if I arrived at my school (70 per cent Black, 30 per cent White) one day wearing a T shirt that said, "It's a White thing—you wouldn't understand."

. . . Please remember that I am not responsible for something that happened over 400 years ago, and I refuse to take the blame for it.[2]

This is a teacher in a predominantly Black school. Her remarks show that although she considers Denzel Washington an intelligent man (until he disagrees with her data), she does wonder why many of the Blacks, even intelligent ones, keep harking back to slavery and racism.

She is right that she does not know why the issue is controversial. She is not listening. She doesn't want to see the problem through the eyes of the victims. She has a fear of being rejected by them. She discounts, from her opinion, what a whole group is saying is their experience.

No, she says, even though you are Black and know how you have experienced racism, I am telling you that you are wrong. In 1992 you should get over it.

I would say she is not in touch with her own culture enough to know that it is the hegemonic one—the ruling group. Whites need to understand that since they have power, they do not need either affirmative action or T-shirts to achieve equal status or visibility. Affirmative action with its problems was developed because injustice had occurred. There may be some over-compensation in correcting an injustice, but it does not invalidate the basic premise.

When I was widowed I was suddenly without that "power group" and felt it as I stood in line a lot. I looked around and saw the elderly, the handicapped and the minorities in line with me.

Being white I still assumed power, and when social security people treated me poorly, I would speak up, argue, call and write letters. Everyone did not take that attitude, however.

Maybe we can point out other examples of how we have been discriminated against because of our religion or our accent or our gender or our ethnic heritage or our looks. The problem is that we are talking, not listening. We hear about racial problems through our own data, which may be great for us but does not match another's experience.

We may say we are sick to death of hearing about race. Yet we never tire of hearing about it if an injustice was done to us. All of us could give complete, vivid details of the time we were robbed or mugged or someone scraped our new car in the parking lot . . . five months ago, five years ago, fifteen years ago.

Although we deny the history of others, we do not feel that way about our own history. In my church we have a very beautiful stained glass window that I love. It is part of my tradition and history. It seems rather "cultural," but it means a lot to me. It says "Scotland" in big letters, and I warm up inside every time I see it.

Perhaps we do not realize that what happened in our country to African-Americans, free or slave, happened to all of us. Our attitudes have been shaped by historical events and how they have been presented to us. Although no one group is superior or has a premium on the truth, we need to examine our attitudes toward other Christians. Do our attitudes come from the Bible? Do they come from our cultural history? When our values conflict, which should have preeminence? If another group of people define a conflict in terms of Scripture and we are terribly uncomfortable, do we deny their truth?

Recognizing My Truth and God's Truth

Can we trust the Holy Spirit in another group of believers, the church? They have the same truth of God, but the questions from their lives need different answers than ours do. So when one cultural lifestyle is different from another, how is that truth applied in the body of Christ? Is love contradictory to truth—are they on opposite ends of a line? Or is it a circle which surrounds and encompasses both strokes of the essence of God?

In Kenya, when we were robbed of wedding gifts, I tried like Marv Mayers to define *right* in my new setting using what I understood to be an absolute. One of the Ten Commandments is surely that we should not steal. If someone stole from me, taking my possessions, in any cultural setting they were wrong.

I was very excited one Sunday morning when I saw my Montgomery Ward shoes walk down the aisle at church. At long last all the thieving injustices perpetuated against me would be avenged, because I knew those feet! I knew that family. So I told Thom that I demanded that the stolen goods be returned.

Thom talked to several people, and one happy day a person arrived with a basket of my goods! It was a small basket and contained only raggedy symbols of cloth, stained and shredded. It was a pitiful collection. I went inside without a word.

Later I shared some strong words with Thom. I wanted to pursue these thieves to a final solution. Thom quietly told me that I could. As my feverish brain began to make plans, I heard him speaking off in the distance and tried to tune him in. But quietly and gently he was saying, "Yes, you can get justice [he did not say *revenge*], but it may just split the church." Truth may be truth, but when do you apply it and how much and to whom? Truth without love is not God's way.

I visited an elderly British couple for tea with the children one Sunday afternoon. Returning home I felt quite righteous, having informed the grandmotherly hostess that she was indeed far off the mark by criticizing African children for poor manners at a wedding. I had been to quite a few African weddings and had never seen one child out of order—mainly because their parents would kill them. I knew this woman was exhibiting a colonial attitude.

Afterward I told Thom about our conversation. He replied with a sentence that has stayed with me over the years. "Marcia, there is a difference in speaking the truth and having a cup of tea with an elderly lady." So I ask myself frequently, Do I want others to know my truth or my love or both?

Recently I heard a minister tell about his international church in the Middle East. He described the reconciliation and love among Iraqi, Iranian and American Christians during the Gulf War. I thought it sounded like something from the book of Revelation!

As Christians we have a supraculture that transcends political and cultural barriers. It is an answer to the hostilities expressed throughout the world, nation against nation and brother against sister. The Bible states the common state of all. Rich and poor alike die. All are under God's eye. All sin.

When you are stopped for speeding you are under the law, that is, the truth. There is a standard that you have fallen short of—and it is no use arguing with the police. They are applying the truth—twenty-five miles per hour in this zone and no more. Now you can bribe the officer, ask for mercy or ask your dad to pay the fine. Other than that your only option is to pay the fine because you did not abide by the truth.

Most police who have stopped me did not have mercy. Once I was stopped in a small town where I was to speak. Later, I told the congregation that I was glad that in the spiritual realm I was under mercy. Someone else was paying my fine and all I got was love, not truth.

In Christ Jesus mercy and truth have kissed. Forgiveness because of the cross opens up options for those who clutch at their own way. The resurrection of Jesus gives us the power to jump over our hearts' evil sometimes expressed in our cultural barriers.

Failing to Do the Truth

The Pharisees and the experts of the law definitely had the truth. The scribes told Herod where the Messiah was to be born—and they were right. They just did not consider going to see for themselves.

On the other hand, the tax collectors, the "sinners" and the soldiers were repentant and were baptized by John the Baptist (Lk 3:11-14). They asked how to work this out in their lives. John the Baptist didn't tell them to perform religious acts like praying or going to the temple. He told them to do social things like sharing clothes and food, and collecting taxes honestly.

We see how the way for the Lord was prepared in Luke 7. Following public baptism their hearts were softened to Jesus' words of truth when the time came. "When they heard this all the people and the tax collectors justified God, *having been baptized with the baptism of John;* but the Pharisees and the lawyers rejected the purpose of God for themselves, *not having been baptized by him"* (Lk 7:29-30, my emphasis).

The attitude of pride, a hard heart, kept the experts of the Law from seeing or hearing Jesus when he was there before them. It was a woman of the street who was drawn to him; it was women who had been cured who traveled in a group with him from one town and village supporting him with their means.

Once Jesus' mother and brothers tried to see him when he was teaching. Who does he say is his real mother and brothers, his closest family members? "Those who hear the word of God and do it" (Lk 8:19-21).

We can have the truth, even the truth from God's word. But we may, like experts of the law, fail to practice it. We may fail to reckon on our own needy reality. We are in great debt. When we grasp that we will love much. Perfect love will cast out fear.

One in Christ

Sometimes we have the hardest time learning from one another when it comes to religion. Even our Christian "truths" divide us. What kept Peter from eating with or staying with the Gentiles (Acts 10)? Was it his perception of reality as a Jew (a devout Jew) who sought the Messiah, who followed the Christ, leaving everything? "No, Lord; for I have never eaten anything that is common or unclean" (10:14).

Peter said to himself, "This is not what I learned in Hebrew school. Clean is clean, already!" But God was teaching, the Holy Spirit was showing that cultural limitations can be broken down and through. Peter had walked with that reality as he walked with Jesus for three years and had breakfast with him on the shore following the crucifixion and resurrection. Times were changing for Peter.

If we are unable to bridge our differences, we could be invalidating the gospel of Jesus Christ which says that "we, though many, are one body in Christ, and individually members one of another" (Rom 12:5). In Ephesians we read that God's eternal plan is to make one body (3:6). In Jesus Christ the walls have gone down (Eph 2:14). The Holy Spirit can overcome barriers of all kinds as the realness of Jesus is experienced in relationships together as one body. The question is, Since the wall is down, who is going to carry away the bricks?

An Overgrown Tree

Jesus' cross is central and it means death. No one can be Jesus' disciple unless she or he gives up everything. The call is to biblical values and not our own cultural values. Where there is conflict, the cultural values need to die. In Jesus' prayer before his death, he asked for obedience and unity from his church. The sin of disunity among Christians in the United States is obvious. From different communities many have cried out against racism in the church.

I have a large poplar tree in my minute backyard. When the former owners bought the tree, they carried the young sapling home in their car. Today this tree presents a big problem to me. It is very tall, towering over the house. Just a few years ago Jason, my son, climbed into its bottom boughs. Now that is not possible. Quietly in the night, secretly in the noon, they have both grown—one due to soil and sun, and the other due to hormones.

The tree man says it will cost $800 to cut it down, leaving the stump in the ground. The roots have taken over the entire backyard. From the size of the tree one knows that the root system is invading the cellar and patio, although it is silent and invisible.

Twelve years ago I could have transplanted the tree to another area. But I didn't. I did not know that poplars grow so big and strong. I thought it was like the dogwood in the front that spreads out but remains small.

I have to navigate the large roots anchored in the grass when hanging out the wash. They remind me of the Los Angeles riots—a visible eruption of a deeper, more complex set of roots underneath, growing silently toward destruction.

Racism is rooted in our history and could have been managed in small areas in the beginning. After the Civil War a mule and forty acres might have made all the difference.

George Caywood once asked a historian, a Ph.D from the University of Southern California, what might have happened if in the 1840s American Christians, just because the Bible says to in the New Testament, had repented for the sins of the nation and sought to integrate African-American slaves into the mainstream of American social, economic, spiritual and political life. Suppose they had incorporated them into positions of power and spiritual leadership over a twenty-year period and fully made these people a valued part of the society. What difference, he asked, would it have made in American history?

"Well," the historian friend said, "it sure would have prevented the Civil War, and one of the most difficult periods in American history, Reconstruction." And then he said, "And it probably would have prevented World War I."

And Caywood said, "What?!"

The historian answered, "Yes, repentance at that level would have changed the history of the world."[3]

We cannot go back. We have to go forward. Now our urban centers are blights in the land and our most precious heritage—our children of all colors—are losing. They are being destroyed in every way. Partiality toward certain people is not the way of the Bible's God. He wants a variegated people for his own. Each people bear his image in a special way.

I think I have to get a tree surgeon. It is going to be very costly. I should not have waited. The beautiful tree will have to be cut down. The stump will have to be dug out. And the roots in the yard eradicated. Otherwise the whole yard and the foundation of the house will be destroyed.

Part 4
▼▼▼▼▼▼▼▼▼▼▼▼▼
Christ
Beyond
Culture

16
One in
Christ in Truth
and Love

▼▼▼▼▼▼▼▼▼▼▼▼▼

I CAN STILL REMEMBER WHEN I FIRST TRIED TO COMMUNICATE THE GOSPEL
to a Maasai tribesman sitting under a tree in his red blanket. He had never
been far from his home. But I could see in my conversation with him that he
valued three things: that he could walk fifty miles a day; that he knew all that
there was to know about his cows; that he was one of the Maasai, the most
important people on the earth. He could see that I was not a Maasai, that I
did not know a thing about cows and that I could hardly walk ten miles. So
to him I was completely valueless. He had an air of superiority that began to
get to me. I asked myself, "How can I communicate my very important
message when he can't care less about anything I have to offer?"

As a result I gave up talking about Jesus Christ and started talking about
my travels, my education and my car. Of course we were not communicating,
but I persisted. In fact, I decided to try to sell him my Volkswagen. It started
as a joke, but it became quite serious. In the bartering process one can always
back out, but I found that with all my bartering and pushing I could not get
him to trade one of his cows (which I could have bought on the open market

for about $15) for my Volkswagen (which was worth $3000 in Nairobi at that moment). Cows were the important things in his life, and anybody who did not know everything about cows was, in his view, an idiot. I knew nothing about cows; therefore, I was an idiot. Then how could I convince him to listen to me about Christianity?

I tried to convince him that I knew something about cars and that I knew something about philosophy and Plato. But that meant about as much to him as the man in the moon, whom he hadn't heard of either. I began to realize that we had to have some common values before we could begin to communicate.

This is true whenever two people encounter each other. Recall Beth, who was mentioned in chapter two. She was living with a man because she needed protection. I had to examine how I viewed her and the decisions she was making. Likewise, as I work on college campuses I need to reconsider the Greek system of logic that has so influenced Western Christianity. Or if I am looking for a church, I need to ask myself whether the vibrant preaching of a Black pastor ought to become a part of my worship. As I come into contact with different cultures, different sets of priorities, even different expressions of values similar to mine, I need a biblical value system by which to judge them all. Truth and love, I believe, are at the core of this system.

Who Is God?

John Perkins in *A Quiet Revolution* writes, "If you take all the verses in the Bible and organize them under themes, the two major themes with the most individual verses supporting them are God's hate for idolatry and God's concern for the poor and the oppressed."[1] You could also turn those two themes into positive statements. God's concern is truth, and God's concern is love.

These themes are prominent from Genesis through Revelation. There are dozens of places in the Bible in which those two themes are even put into one verse.[2]

When Abraham, for example, sent his servant to look for a wife for Isaac, the servant introduced himself to Rebekah by saying, "Blessed be the LORD, the God of my master Abraham, who has not forsaken his steadfast love and his faithfulness toward my master" (Gen 24:27). In other words, he identified himself as a servant of Abraham who followed the God of mercy and truth. God was just beginning to introduce himself to Abraham, but these two themes were already impressed on him.

Later, when Jacob was on the verge of his confrontation with Esau and in need of God's help, he prayed, "I am not worthy of the least of all the steadfast love and all the faithfulness which thou hast shown to thy servant" (Gen 32:10). On Mount Sinai after Moses requested to see God's glory, his essence, "the LORD passed before him, and proclaimed, 'The LORD, the LORD, a God merciful and gracious, slow to anger and abounding in steadfast love and faithfulness' " (Ex 34:6). These two characteristics are at the core of God's being.

Psalm 25:10 says, "All the paths of the LORD are steadfast love and faithfulness, for those who keep his covenant and his testimonies." Psalm 26:3 repeats the theme: "For thy steadfast love is before my eyes, and I walk in faithfulness to thee." In Psalm 40 we read "I have not concealed thy steadfast love and thy faithfulness from the great congregation. . . . let thy steadfast love and thy faithfulness ever preserve me" (40:10-11).

Proverbs says, "Do not let kindness and truth leave you; bind them around your neck, write them on the tablet of your heart" (Prov 3:3 NASB). Remind yourself of them, memorize them, know them; because if you have mercy and truth, then you have direction for your life. The prophets tell us the same. "He has told you, O man, what is good; and what does the LORD require of you but to do justice, to love kindness, and to walk humbly with your God?" (Mic 6:8 NASB). Justice and judgment, executing God's law, come under the heading of truth. Kindness and mercy are forms of his love. Micah is not alone. Hosea (2:19; 12:6) and Zechariah (8:19) proclaim the same theme.

In the New Testament Christ condemns the Pharisees for ignoring what is truly important. "Woe to you, scribes and Pharisees, hypocrites! for you tithe mint and dill and cummin, and have neglected the weightier matters of the law, justice and mercy and faith" (Mt 23:23). John introduces Christ by twice highlighting these as the center of Christ's person and work. "The Word became flesh and dwelt among us, full of grace and truth. . . . grace and truth came through Jesus Christ" (Jn 1:14, 17). Two other New Testament writers pick up the theme as well—Paul in Ephesians 4:15 and Peter in 1 Peter 1:22.

The Reluctant Missionary

The problem we have with these two themes is our tendency to absolutize them, to turn them into abstract principles rather than living realities. When we do this, of course, we are likely to polarize the two or to emphasize one over the other. "Love is all that matters. We must be sure all our thoughts and actions are in love." This thinking creates license. Others might say, "But if truth is not preeminent, how can you say you even know love is important? Truth must come first." This thinking creates legalism.

Jonah offers us an example. This reluctant missionary refused God's call to go preach judgment to Nineveh, the capital of Israel's enemy, Assyria. Why? Not because he was afraid of persecution but, in his own words, because "I knew that thou art a gracious God and merciful, slow to anger, and abounding in steadfast love, and repentest of evil" (Jon 4:2). In his head he knew God was both truth (he was to preach judgment) and love (God would forgive Ninevah). But Jonah had failed to integrate these in his own life. He wanted Israel's enemy destroyed. He did not want to give them a chance to repent.

His understanding was so limited, in fact, that God had to show him his judgment and mercy twice—once by putting him in the belly of the great fish and then getting him out; then by comparing Jonah's concern for a plant and God's concern for Ninevah.

Opposing or separating truth and love represents a false dichotomy because both truth and love come from God, who is a unity. It is in God as a unified *person* that they are joined.

We too often assume that if we have a comprehensive and consistent collection of propositions about God, that we will then have a clear concept of God. This is not so because God is a person who will not be reduced to mere propositions. We must also know him in his actions and in our experience. This is a very Hebrew notion. To be real, truth must be more than an idea; it must also be action consistent with that belief. In God's personality, truth and love are consistently expressed to us. In him we have both and so avoid both legalism and license.

Yet God is infinite. "How can we who are finite adequately express truth and love in full unity?" some may respond. We are able to express them because we too are persons. Admittedly, we cannot do so as fully as God. God is unchanging and we are changing. Yet we by his Spirit are moving toward God, becoming like him.

The Confessing King
David saw this process clearly in Psalm 5. "For thou art not a God who delights in wickedness; evil may not sojourn with thee. The boastful may not

stand before thy eyes; thou hatest all evildoers. Thou destroyest those who speak lies; the LORD abhors bloodthirsty and deceitful men" (Ps 5:4-6). How we agree with David! That's exactly what God is like, we say. But think a minute.

This is the David who on several occasions recognized that he was wicked. "Evil may not sojourn with thee." David knew his own proud nature. "The boastful may not stand before thy eyes." David realized he had made some terrible mistakes in how he brought up Absalom. David was also so bloodthirsty that God would not allow him to build the temple. "The LORD abhors bloodthirsty and deceitful men." David is not talking about some abstract person in Psalm 5. He is saying, "God, you will not tolerate any of these things—and I am all of these things!"

Yet in the next verse he says, "But I through the abundance of thy steadfast love will enter thy house." David says in essence, "God, I know you are absolute truth into whose presence I cannot come, but I also know that because you are absolute love, I can enter in."

In verse 8 David then says, "Lead me, O LORD, in thy righteousness." David shifts from God's absoluteness to his own finiteness and imperfection, and anticipates the fuller truth and love God is going to put in him. As we approach other value systems, other cultures, we must come humbly recognizing our own limitations and faults. We must see that God cannot have us in his presence but that he is also changing us into his likeness. This can also prevent arrogance on our part because God is working the same process in other cultures.

Like Jonah, we condemn the city because it is our enemy. Our pride blinds us to the fact that people in the city also have partial truth and love which God is making more complete. Indeed, by learning about other cultures, we can then learn about the truth and love God has given them which we do not yet possess. The result? The whole church is strengthened as its view of God becomes more complete. This is one of the great benefits of missions. But if we absolutize our culture and box God inside it, we will not be enriched. Rather we will die—if God does not cut us off first.

The isolationist, provincial mindset has captured much of the missionary thinking of the church. "You go over there and do missions, and we'll stay here and take care of our own little secure selves. But don't let what is happening over there affect us." I ran into this when under the African Inland Mission I helped bring the mission field within thirty miles of some of our supporting churches. Some could not handle it. That mission field was too close, and they did not like it. They would not support it. Much of the money that we got to operate the ministry in Newark came from outside of New York and New Jersey. People from Los Angeles were glad to support our urban ministry in Newark. (But make sure you do not ask them to get involved in Los Angeles!)

Light and Love: 1 John

I began to work out the interrelationship of truth and love through a study of the first letter of John. I will highlight some of my findings, but it is certainly worth thorough study by anyone who wants to understand how God's absoluteness is lived out in our finiteness.

After a brief introduction, John begins with God's absoluteness: "God is light" (1 Jn 1:5). The next two verses say we must not only believe that but live it as well. How is that possible if we are finite? "The blood of Jesus his Son cleanses us from all sin" (1:7). God's love makes it possible for us to walk in truth. The result is fellowship (1:7), harmony and unity among God's people.

But if we are arrogant enough to claim that we have all truth, that there is no darkness in us, "if we say we have no sin, we deceive ourselves, and the truth is not in us" (1:8). Indeed, the very act of admitting our falsehood is the necessary prerequisite for receiving truth. "If we confess our sins, he is faithful and just, and will forgive our sins and cleanse us from all unright-eousness" (1:9). God is not expecting us to be absolute truth; he is absolute truth. But God does expect all of us to live up to the truth that he has revealed to us.

This applies directly to what you have been reading in this book. You may have begun to hear some things that burden you. You may be beginning to say, "I am responsible for so many things." But God does not expect us to be instant crosscultural experts. He does, however, want us to begin changing. So ask yourself, "How much of this, Lord, do you want me to apply this month?" And then begin to do it. Begin to activate the truth God has given you. God is not expecting us to love all the people of the world. But he is expecting us to love those people with whom he has brought us in contact.

By living consistently with what we know to be true, we confirm that we know the one God. "By this we may be sure that we know him, if we keep his commandments" (2:3). Not only this, "But whoever keeps his [God's] word, in him truly love for God is perfected" (2:5). This equation of truth and love is repeated in 2:8-10.

While the last half of chapter 2 goes on to emphasize the theme of truth, John rolls back in chapter 3 to the theme of love. Chapter 4 focuses on truth and 5 deals primarily with love. Thus the book's structure, with its intertwining of the two themes, reinforces their essential unity. I want to point out only a few more specific verses.

"See what love the Father has given us, that we should be called children of God; and so we are. The reason why the world does not know us is that it did not know him" (3:1). In the world, people are all tied up in themselves, creating their own gods. They do not understand us because their attention is focused on themselves rather than on God. Even so, "it does not yet appear what we shall be, but we know that when he appears we shall be like him, for we shall see him as he is. And every one who thus hopes in him purifies himself as he is pure" (3:2-3). Our present truth and love are being transformed. We are in the process of moving toward God.

"This is the message which you have heard from the beginning, that we should love one another, and not be like Cain who was of the evil one and murdered his brother. And why did he murder him? Because his own deeds were evil and his brother's righteous. Do not wonder, brethren, that the world hates you" (3:11-13). We are back in Genesis, contrasting the line of Seth and the line of Cain. So we marvel not that the line of Cain hates us when we show God's love to one another.

For many years we thought of our country as a Christian nation. The church had control over large sections of society. Hospitals are still named St. Mary's, St. Luke's and the like because they were under the control of the church. A hundred years ago most of our private universities were church institutions.

But the church is no longer in control of such enterprises. So we should seriously question whether we are manifesting God's love by simply, for instance, donating funds to a public tutoring program. Such involvement is not wrong if we are doing so as a fellowship of people who love God, one another and the world. But I question if we are manifesting God's love by volunteering as an individual to teach in a secular tutoring program. How does that differ from what non-Christians are doing? If, however, we undertake such a project as part of the body of Christ, we can show God's love to the world. In this way, God's truth is clearly revealed. Our love for each other, which the world cannot reproduce, carries truth to the world.

This is what John Perkins's wholistic ministry, Voice of Calvary, is doing in Mississippi. As they begin to help people develop economically, as they confront the establishment with justice, they are leading people toward truth. They can begin to sense when people are ready to accept the gospel. Of course some individuals have a special gift of evangelism. But we all need to become more involved in the broader process of communicating truth corporately to the world. After a person comes to a personal confrontation with truth, he or she will still continue to move toward truth. Only once they come to know Christ, we call it discipleship.

When the body of Christ as a body is strong, then it can begin to redeem a culture as a whole. Individually, the truth God gives us is finite. It is finite collectively, too, but far less so. And if a group of Christians in one culture can begin showing love to a group of Christians in another culture, the truth is magnified and the world is changed.

"What about doctrinal differences? We cannot fellowship with people whose ideas are semipagan." John has an answer for that too. "Beloved, do not believe every spirit, but test the spirits to see whether they are of God; for many false prophets have gone out into the world. By this you know the Spirit of God: every spirit which confesses that Jesus Christ has come in the flesh is of God, and every spirit which does not confess Jesus is not of God" (4:1-3).

That is an awfully broad statement. Are you going to accept anyone who says that Jesus Christ is come in the flesh? In my experience, this has actually proven to be an adequate division line. If someone believes and lives in light of the fact that Jesus Christ is Lord and also man, that Jesus Christ is God but he came in the flesh to provide a way back to God, then that person has a fairly good grasp of what Christ and Christianity is all about. Some of the implications of these statements for our lives are taken up in the next chapter.

Beyond believing Jesus is human and Lord, of course, there can be some tremendous differences. But Christianity is Christ. Our unity is in him and in nothing else. "We know that the Son of God has come and has given us understanding, to know him who is true; and we are in him who is true, in his Son Jesus Christ. This is the true God and eternal life" (5:20).

17
True
Discipleship

▼▼▼▼▼▼▼▼▼▼▼▼▼

A FEW YEARS AGO A LEADER OF A CHRISTIAN ORGANIZATION TOLD ME ABOUT a plan he was developing to evangelize the world by computer. It was a rather detailed and well-thought-out plan. People would ask the computer questions, and answers would flash on the screen. Of course, thanks to the computer, the answers would come in a tremendous variety, almost personal. But they would be standard answers from the Word of God whose intent was to remove the problems these people faced so they could receive Christ. This would then be followed by a three-step plan of salvation. For example, after all the response cards from an evangelistic meeting had been collected, they could be put into the computer and answers would be ready before anyone left the meeting. Then people could accept Christ in a small side room that had computers available for them to use.

Today we find impersonal, group-imposed standards in every aspect of our culture. The Western world is pitted against true discipleship. Because a large percentage of our population has reached a high standard of living through a rather sophisticated technology, individual standards have had to be eliminated and replaced with group standards.

For example, morally, some acts are not considered wrong, but getting caught is. Many people are a little dishonest with their income tax. Few actually stay within the speed limit. And a man thinks, if she's willing—why not? In other words, if everybody else does it, I can do it.

Success too is measured by group standards. Much of our lives is aimed at trying to find out what the present "in" standard is. Since this can be frustrating if it is up to the individual to find out what the group wants, we begin to develop institutions to reinforce our successes. We have programmed education; we have mass media.

The Urbana Student Missions Conventions are massive undertakings. I understand the need for efficient operation, or nothing would happen. But I found it quite revealing (and a little humorous) to be in line with thousands of others, an amoebic blob waiting to register. Everything was running smoothly and steadily until I was foolish enough at one point to say, "I am different." Immediately the computer rejected me, and I was pushed out of the line into a small room with a closed door. It was some hours before my problem could be sorted out. Because I was an individual, I was a problem. This is the society that we live in.

The church has also fallen into the grip of society. We too have impersonal, group-imposed standards. If my church has three hundred people, and all the churches in my conference or district or neighborhood have two hundred, then I am successful. If all the youth groups in my area have twenty young people, and my group has twenty-five, I am successful. If all the evangelism teams are converting one person a month and my team is converting three, I am successful. If all the churches in my area are giving $2,000 a year to missions, and we are giving $3,000 a year to missions, we are successful. We measure success by growth. We have established standards and percentages for what we consider growth.

To achieve this end we have institutionalized the church. To educate our youth we have established the Sunday school. To create fellowship for our youth we have established youth clubs. We have institutionalized prayer to Wednesday night, and worship to Sunday morning. And we have determined who is a good Christian and who is not by group standards. Anybody can look into the church and tell whether or not that sixteen-year-old boy is a good Christian. Does he attend youth fellowship? Does he bring a Bible to church? Does he please the elders of the congregation by not rocking the boat?

"Who Do You Say That I Am?"

One of my purposes in this book has been to enlarge your vision of who Jesus is. This is important because if we are to follow Jesus (one of the most basic definitions of discipleship), we must know who he is. Luke 9 gives us this chance to step back from urbanization and ethnicity and culture to put our discussions in a larger setting. The person of Christ, then, can give us proper direction in contrast to the artificial standards often imposed on us.

Luke has arranged his material following the same principles John followed in chapter 4 of his Gospel. History is important, and so facts are not changed. Rather, they are arranged differently on different occasions to teach larger lessons. In this way people are taught both history and important truths for their lives.

In chapter 9, Luke is about at the midpoint of Jesus' ministry. So he brings together some episodes to help his readers start drawing conclusions about who Jesus is.

The chapter begins with Jesus giving the Twelve a task. "And he called the twelve together and gave them power and authority over all demons and to cure diseases, and he sent them out to preach the kingdom of God and to heal" (9:1-2). After giving a few more instructions, it says, "Now Herod the tetrarch heard of all that was done, and he was perplexed, because it was said by some that John had been raised from the dead, by some that Elijah had appeared, and by others that one of the old prophets had risen. Herod said, 'John I beheaded; but who is this about whom I hear such things?' And he sought to see him" (9:7-9). This is followed in verse 10 by, "On their return the apostles told him what they had done."

It is a bit odd that Luke would drop this interlude about Herod right in the middle of the story of the disciples being sent out and then coming back. I believe Luke is using the words of Herod to raise a question: Who is this Jesus? Because of the context, however, it is not an academic question to be answered in a void. Rather it becomes a question of how Jesus' identity affects discipleship. Who Jesus is, implies Luke, should alter the way we follow him, the way we carry out the tasks he has given us to do. And especially if we are to be his witnesses, we had better know who he is.

Once the apostles return, Jesus takes them apart to Bethsaida (9:10). But the crowd follows and gathers, and Jesus becomes so absorbed with the crowd that he teaches them all day (9:11). "Now the day began to wear away;

and the twelve came and said to him, 'Send the crowd away, to go into the villages and country round about, to lodge and get provisions; for we are here in a lonely place' " (9:12). But their concern for the crowd is really an excuse to get rid of them. They had come to tell Jesus all that they had done, and they had not yet had a chance. Jesus, sensing their spirit, turns to them and says, " 'You give them something to eat.' They said, 'We have no more than five loaves and two fish' " (9:13). So Jesus fed the multitude. This is Jesus' way of saying that the disciples are not really ready to do his work because they do not know who he is. He is a person concerned with people and the needs of people. The disciples were mostly concerned with reporting on their accomplishments, their successes.

The question is again raised in the following verses. "Now it happened that as he was praying alone the disciples were with him; and he said to them, 'Who do the people say that I am?' And they answered, 'John the Baptist; but others say, Elijah; and others, that one of the old prophets has risen' " (9:18-19). These are the same possibilities Herod worked with. All the answers are biblical, yet they are all wrong. So Jesus asked, " 'But who do you say that I am?' And Peter answered, 'The Christ of God.' " Peter began to perceive who Jesus really was, but his understanding was not complete, as later events showed. He had trouble living out the implications of Jesus' identity.

What are these implications? There are implications first for Jesus himself and then for those who would follow him:

"The Son of man must suffer many things, and be rejected by the elders and chief priests and scribes, and be killed, and on the third day be raised." And he said to all, "If any man would come after me, let him deny himself and take up his cross daily and follow me. For whoever would save his life will lose it; and whoever loses his life for my sake, he will save it. For what does it profit a man if he gains the whole world and loses or forfeits himself? For whoever is ashamed of me and of my words, of him will the Son of man be ashamed when he comes in his glory and the glory of the Father and of the holy angels. But I tell you truly, there are some standing here who will not taste death before they see the kingdom of God." (9:22-27)

This is one of the strongest statements in Scripture on what it means to follow Jesus. But it is in the context of needing to know who Jesus is before you can follow him.

The next paragraph picks up this theme too. "Now about eight days after these sayings he took with him Peter and John and James, and went up on the mountain to pray. And as he was praying, the appearance of his countenance was altered, and his raiment became dazzling white. And behold, two men talked with him, Moses and Elijah, who appeared in glory and spoke of his departure" (9:28-31). Who do the people say he is? Some say he is Moses; some say he is Elijah. The transfiguration makes it explicit that this is not who Jesus is.

"And a voice came out of the cloud, saying, 'This is my Son, my Chosen; listen to him!' " (9:35). Who Jesus is, on the other hand, is also made explicit. Jesus is the Son of God. The progression has been who the people say Jesus is, who the disciples say he is, who Jesus says he is and finally who the Father himself says Jesus is. Intertwined with this also is the theme of what it means to follow such a person.

On the next day, they came down the mountain and were met by a man whose son had a demon. He tells Jesus, "And I begged your disciples [who were not on the mountain with you] to cast it out, but they could not" (9:40). This is in stark contrast to verse 1, "He called the twelve together and gave them power and authority over all demons." Though Peter had said Jesus is Christ, and he and James and John went with Jesus to the top of the mountain, there were still the other disciples whose understanding was not as developed. They could not use the power that Jesus had already given them. Jesus' response is, "O faithless and perverse generation, how long am I to be with you and bear with you?" (9:41). Jesus can give you all the power in the world, but if you don't know who he is, you cannot use it.

So once again Luke lifts up the question, " 'Let these words sink into your ears; for the Son of man is to be delivered into the hands of men.' But they did not understand this saying, and it was concealed from them, that they should not perceive it" (9:44-45). Despite Jesus' attempts to drag them along, to see him in a larger context, they still did not fully know who Jesus was. We too, as I hope this book has been encouraging us to do, must be asking ourselves whether or not we have the large vision of Jesus he wants us to have. In the last chapter I spoke of a value system that causes us to follow the light that God has put in front of us, that calls us to be faithful to that which he is revealing to us. As we obey that call, God then gives us more light to follow. More truth. More love. In so doing he expands our understanding of himself and of the world around us.

Beyond Possibility

As we saw with Peter in Acts 10—11, our culture tends to define possibility and impossibility for us.

Jesus also likes to take us out to the ends of our culture and say, "That's what you believe is possible? Let me show you what is really possible." And he leads us into the realm of the seemingly impossible—and that is faith. He takes us across the boundary of what our culture says cannot be done and does it. Jesus is not bound by our culture; he is beyond it. If we accept our culture's definition of who Jesus is, we do not know who he is. He is much larger than that. Because none of us know what our culture is doing to us, we have an obligation to find out.

A friend of mine, Dave, who graduated from Rutgers engineering school several years ago, had been working for a large corporation. The first month there somebody asked him to go out and buy coffee for the whole crew.

"Who's going to pay for it?" he asked.

"Just put in an expense form for mileage to cover the cost."

"I can't do that. That's not what it's for."

"Well, you had better do it," came the answer.

He was firm, however, so they got somebody else to do it.

Dave never got a promotion for the rest of that summer even though all the others did. Of course he noticed this and began asking about it. He discovered that this firm wanted people at the top who had submitted themselves to a system, people who had become corrupted and were therefore corruptible, people whom the company could control in this way. Unless you were willing to do what you were told, there was no promotion. The main means for moving up was to so identify yourself with the system that by the time you got ready for management, you would have been so bought out by that system (you would already have done so many deceitful things) that you could no longer expose what they were doing in the home offices. Great corruption from tiny misdeeds grows.

Dave, however, stuck it out, working honestly within the system that tried to mold him. He did get a choice promotion eventually—to a position in which the company had to have someone who was scrupulously honest!

Our culture tries to mold us in other ways. In the seventies one friend of mine was making $20,000 a year (a good salary then!) and was hurting because the recession cut back on his ability to make money through investment. Because he anticipated that extra income beyond his $20,000 salary, he was not able to keep up with the standard of living to which he had become adjusted. So at $20,000 a year, he found himself to be poor. Poverty, however, is relative. Poverty is defined for us by our culture. But society should not dictate the standard of living for Christians. Only God's Word should do that.

Every day we are being bombarded by mass media which define for us what is possible and impossible. Our family came home from the mission field with three children. We were making $7,500 a year. The first year we were home I put $1,400 in savings because we did not have any need for it. We had brought our African standard of living with us. The second year we put $200 in savings. The third year we could not pay the bills at the end of each month. Our culture had molded us into its own image. With ten years of living in a poverty culture, we suddenly found that even our Christian friends were putting pressure on us to get a better car, to have a TV, to enjoy this or that. We were being caught in a trap. So we began to cut some of these nonessentials that people will tell you are essential ("Oh, I couldn't *possibly* live without that!") and free up our money for God's glory.

It is not too early to confront the limits of your culture even while in college. Those on residential campuses could approach the school administration with a proposal to spend your third year of study in an urban context. Some administrators will look at this like going overseas for a year of study. They could easily make the arrangements with another institution to transfer credits. This could give you in your final year a new awareness of what the world around you is like and begin to give you an education that is more representative of the world as a whole.

Six Signposts of Discipleship

While it is essential to know who Jesus is before we can follow him, Jesus is willing to allow us to follow him at any level of understanding. He then wants to bring us into a larger vision of him. At the end of Luke 9 we find six signposts on the road of discipleship.

> And an argument arose among them as to which of them was the greatest. But when Jesus perceived the thought of their hearts, he took a child and put him by his side, and said to them, "Whoever receives this child in my name receives me, and whoever receives me receives him who sent me; for he who is least among you all is the one who is great." (9:46-48)

The disciples were arguing about who was the greatest, and Jesus says that is not leadership, that is not discipleship, that is not the kind of people he wanted following him. The first signpost is childlike humility, openness, curiosity and enthusiasm—not worldly jockeying for power and status.

Second, "John answered, 'Master, we saw a man casting out demons in your name, and we forbade him, because he does not follow with us.' But Jesus said to him, 'Do not forbid him; for he that is not against you is for you' " (9:49-50). How many times have we sought to condemn other Christians because they were not using our methods! But those who follow Jesus are not to be concerned with who else is following Jesus. We have no right to condemn, to cut down, to criticize or to negatively question the work of others just because they are different, just to build ourselves up. It can be legitimate to give critique as part of the body, to build one another up. But true discipleship has only one enemy.

The third signpost of discipleship emphasizes much of what has already been said in this book.

When the days drew near for him to be received up, he set his face to go to Jerusalem. And he sent messengers ahead of him, who went and entered a village of the Samaritans, to make ready for him; but the people would not receive him, because his face was set toward Jerusalem. And when his disciples James and John saw it, they said, "Lord, do you want us to bid fire come down from heaven and consume them?" But he turned and rebuked them. And they went on to another village. (9:51-56)

As we saw in John 4, Jews and Samaritans were antagonistic toward each other. Samaritans even harassed pilgrims on the road to Jerusalem. The disciples responded in kind. But Jesus' plan went far beyond those cultural boundaries. Jesus saw that the disciples still had a heart full of racism. They wanted to destroy and burn out the Samaritans in revenge for a discourtesy. Jesus rebuked them, saying, "Let's simply go to another village."

How patient we are in explaining the gospel over and over to a friend or relative. But we preach the gospel once in the city, are rebuked by some angry young Black person who has all kinds of reasons to reject us, and we immediately pack up and leave because "These people don't want to hear the gospel." Whole ministries have been torn out of a city because of a lack of commitment. Every summer people come into cities, pass out tracts and then scatter. We fear the city. We fear Blackness, ethnicity, the ghetto. The disciples had the same ignorance and fear. Fear that turns to rejection is not the kind of discipleship that Jesus has in mind.

Discipleship is not seeking worldly status; it is not cutting down other Christians; it is not racism. Luke gives three more signposts in the last six verses of chapter 9 which emphasize the priority of discipleship. "As they were going along the road, a young man said, 'I will follow you wherever you go.' And Jesus said to him, 'Foxes have holes, and birds of the air have nests; but the Son of man has nowhere to lay his head' " (9:57-58). If we are going to follow Jesus, we are not going to have any fringe benefits. They may come our way, but they are not guaranteed. If you decide to follow Jesus, that is your priority. Discipleship is a lack of material concerns.

Next, "To another he said, 'Follow me.' But he said, 'Lord, let me first go and bury my father.' But he said to him, 'Leave the dead to bury their own dead; but as for you, go and proclaim the kingdom of God' " (9:59-60). This is not a treatise on Christian burial or on how to take care of your relatives. This is a treatise on discipleship. The death of a father, particularly in cultures where the extended family is important, changes the entire relationship of the oldest son to the community. He now becomes the patriarch, the head of the family line. You can be sixty years old, but if your father is still alive you are a nobody. When your father dies, you become somebody. In our culture, this is still seen in royal succession. Charles is simply a prince playing games. But if his mother dies tomorrow, he suddenly becomes a mature, responsible King of England.

It may be that this disciple is saying, "Let me go back and wait till my father dies so I can have some authority and some wealth. Then I'll come and follow you." Or he may be saying, "My father has just died. I've got to go back and accept his inheritance, his responsibilities." In either case, Jesus is saying that getting such wealth or taking such responsibility is not that important if you are going to follow him, because you are going to give it all up anyway.

Even if we take this at a basic level (he simply wants to bury his father and pay his respects), following Jesus is still a more important activity and calling in life.

Lastly, "Another said, 'I will follow you, Lord; but let me first say farewell to those at my home.' Jesus said to him, 'No one who puts his hand to the plow and looks back is fit for the kingdom of God' " (9:61-62). The point is not that we can't shake hands and say goodby. Rather, the custom in that culture was to go back and put one's affairs in order (to arrange who was going to feed the chickens, and who was going to plant the wheat in the spring, and who was going to harvest it in the fall). Then he would follow Jesus. But he would follow Jesus with the thought that maybe things were not going right back there. As soon as some rain clouds gathered, he might wonder if those kids know enough to bring the harvest in now. Or if the market changed a bit and he saw that now was the time to sell the pigs, he might start thinking to himself, "How can I get word back to them?" And Jesus does not want that kind of dual loyalty. Once you put your hand to the plow, you keep moving.

He Must Increase

In these six points is a definition of discipleship. While the call is ultimately to total discipleship, I also see patience on Jesus' part. "You can pick up at any level of understanding, follow me, and I will begin to teach you who I am." On several occasions throughout the ministry of Jesus, the crowd following him got large. When he intensified his teaching, many dropped off. We too need a sensitivity to call people to follow Jesus from their current understanding. But then we should bring them a fuller vision of who Jesus is and keep repeating, "Are you still willing to follow Jesus now that you've discovered more of who he really is?" Indeed, this is the question we should be asking ourselves.

Before closing, I want to go on to Luke 10. "After this the Lord appointed seventy others, and sent them on ahead of him, two by two, into every town and place where he himself was about to come" (10:1). A very similar opening to Luke 9. But when the seventy came back, they "returned with joy, saying, 'Lord, even the demons are subject to us *in your name!*' And he said to them, 'I saw Satan fall like lightning from heaven' " (10:17-18). In Luke 9:10, however, notice the shift of emphasis: "On their return the apostles told him what *they had done*."

Our culture tells us to measure success by our accomplishments. In Luke 9 the apostles fell into the same trap. But after all the events of Luke 9, after finding out more and more of who Jesus is, the disciples have a totally different outlook. They now emphasize who Jesus is. We too will have broken the bonds of culture and moved into the realm of seeming impossibility when we thrill to what God is doing. The word of God has made us free—free from our cultural accretions and free from Satan who is the ruler of this world. We are free from the institutions and all the propaganda. We will not only be liberated from sin, but liberated in our ability to build a lifestyle that meets the task of true discipleship.

The same can happen in the church. We need a community that reinforces us to live with Jesus. His values of truth and love are beyond the realm of the culturally possible. They inhabit the realm of what Jesus considers normal. Just as Jesus through the power of the Holy Spirit took the early church in Acts 1—11 step by step beyond their cultural limitation—out of Jerusalem, out of Judea, out of Samaria to the uttermost parts of the earth—so he is calling us to bring disciples out of the whole world into his church. This is true discipleship.

Appendix A

▼▼▼▼▼▼▼▼▼▼▼▼▼

Reaching
the
Campus

AS AN URBAN SPECIALIST FOR INTER-VARSITY CHRISTIAN FELLOWSHIP, I HAVE
tried to apply the model for ministry found in this book to the campus. Just
as with the rest of our world, colleges and universities have been profoundly
influenced by urbanization.

In the 1800s and early 1900s nearly all universities had residential
campuses. Students lived together in a community separate from the rest of
society. Such schools aimed to lift the student out of a provincial worldview
to a more cosmopolitan and sophisticated value system. Students expected
to graduate with new priorities in life as well as new intellectual directions.
Rarely did students return after graduation to the old community life they
came from. Instead, they adopted a new culture.

In the United States this was part of the American Dream. You gave up
your old culture and took on a new one. In this way education became the
tool of the establishment. Anthropologically, this is a normal process. Education exists to conserve culture and pass on its values.

Today such schooling is epitomized by the Ivy League schools. Yet now,
unlike during the 1800s, these schools no longer dominate the university

landscape. With urbanization has come the community commuter college. Instead of aiming to change the value orientation of students and move students into a new culture, commuter schools allow students to remain in their home communities and help them to be productive there. Because these students have no intention of leaving their communities, it is not surprising that they choose not to live on campus. Their primary orientation, unlike that of residential-school students, is not to the college community but to their home.

Because of urbanization, the primary community which students go back to is not necessarily their geographic community. It is more likely to be their ethnic community, their kinship community, their professional community (in the case of continuing-education students) or a volunteer association such as their church. These groups set the values and agendas which students take with them to campus. While residential students are open to almost any influence imposed by their schools, commuter students come to campus to find what fits their predetermined interests and concerns.

Commuter students may change some of their values as part of their academic experience, but the pressures from the school to change are minimal. Greater influence is often exerted by peers from their home community or isolated professors crusading for particular causes. The campus as a whole limits both its value judgments on others and its concern for conformity. Unlike residential schools, commuter schools have no clear value system to pass on.

InterVarsity (which traces its roots to student groups active at Oxford and Cambridge over a hundred years ago) has traditionally worked on residential campuses. Christians from diverse church and social backgrounds came to the campus, made new friends and together developed a close evangelizing fellowship. Thus, many grew to be dedicated postcollege Christians. This was often an effective ministry because college administrators (concerned to build a new culture) were suspicious of outside influences. An indigenous group which developed from within was far less threatening to them.

With the rapid growth of commuter colleges, InterVarsity has had to face the challenge of reaching these as well. Unfortunately, the strategy used to reach residential schools is seldom effective in this new environment. When an urban campus is spread across a city and thus does not form a cohesive, geographic whole, how can an indigenous community be formed? When students do not even think of themselves primarily as students, how can an indigenous *student* community be formed? How can friendship evangelism take place on campus when students make most of their friends off campus?

Another problem is that in the city a rule of survival is to never be alone.

The need for community goes beyond social needs to one of self-preservation. Thus, urban students do not easily give up their group commitments. Calling a student to commitment to Christ without providing a community for protection and support may not be rational. Most successful urban ministries know the need to incarnate the gospel in a visible community. How can we take seriously existing student commitments and build a new, strong, visible community at a commuter school?

I do not know the full answers to these questions. But I believe we can begin to answer them by adopting an urban rather than a rural mindset. A rural strategy would require that the campus be the prime focus of our ministry. An urban strategy would follow the lines of communication within each cultural stripe. Our task, then, is to find and become involved with the different communities students belong to. In that setting we are more likely to win their trust and the trust of their communities.

To reach commuter schools with large Black populations, for example, we need to build especially strong relations with Black churches and pastors in the area. Since community is important to survival in the city, Black Christians may go to church four or five times a week. To reach such students, it will be helpful to go back to their community, to their church, and attend there regularly. Thus Blacks will not feel threatened that you are trying to tear them out of their church community. Likewise, Black pastors will not feel as though you are trying to steal their students. In New York City a whole group of students showed up at the InterVarsity meeting because their pastor told them to.

One InterVarsity staff member discovered that about half the Black students he was in touch with were teaching Sunday-school classes. So he gave a seminar in teaching Sunday school. The students thus saw that he had their interests and concerns in mind. He was trying to increase their contribution to the community that they cared for most.

The same can be done with pastors by trying to help them reach their goals. When I began to do this I found warm support and a willingness to think together about collegians. At the Center for Urban Theological Studies (CUTS) in Philadelphia I took some courses at night. This was very broadening as I sat with urban Christians, all of whom had ministries. It also gave me entrance as a white person into the African-American church, to the Hispanic Christian body and to other ethnic people. CUTS became a mediator for InterVarsity as we thought through together how to serve the commuter and urban students at Temple and Community College of Philadelphia. By applying the mission principle of going to the present church in the city, it was possible to network with it and students. We did not want to pull the church's leadership away. We wanted to come alongside and provide resources to the church in the city. This we began to do.

Reversing the flow of communication can also build greater trust. Establish relationships with African-American or Asian or Hispanic pastors and ask them to come on campus with you to help you reach ethnic students. They can help you overcome racial barriers, and you can help them expand the ministry of their church into a new setting. Their commitment to college work will increase not only because of their involvement but also because this can provide a new channel for more people coming into their church. Thus both church and school are strengthened.

Initially, the result of this strategy may be the development of separate, parallel communities on one campus—a Chinese Christian community, a nurses' Christian community, a Baptist Christian community and so on. But we must not leave matters there. Christ calls us to be one body. Our unity may begin along the lines of the Antioch model (Acts 13:1-3)—a leadership team made up of representatives of each major group. From there we can work to develop unity and cooperation among the group as a whole.

In addition, we will want to foster cooperation among several schools in a given area. A special interest group from one school might help begin or develop similar groups at other schools. Special areawide seminars or conferences might also be offered for Hispanic Christians or Jewish Christians, for example.

Lastly, because there is no one campus community, building Christian unity (which is so essential) will not be easy. First, it will require a higher degree of input from InterVarsity staff than they give to residential campuses. Second, it will take a longer period of time to establish a solid group. In New York City, for example, it has taken about five years on most campuses.

Residential schools in urban settings can no longer be isolated from the realities of the city. In the past there were options to be an InterVarsity group in a capsule. Now urbanization demands involvement. That is why the urban projects of InterVarsity in Chicago, Atlanta, Philadelphia, Buffalo, New York and Los Angeles, to name a few, are vital training grounds and discipling truth for staff and students.

If the urban campus movement is to be an indigenous movement, support both in prayer and finances must come from the communities to which we are preparing leaders to return. But to develop this support means we must first make contributions to the prime needs of those communities.

Appendix B

▼▼▼▼▼▼▼▼▼▼▼▼▼▼

Study Guide
for Individuals
or Groups

Andrew T. Le Peau

Introduction and Instructions for the Leader

Let's face it. Fear is one of the main reasons we don't like to cross cultures—with Christ or without him. Whether it's a subtle grinding in our stomachs or screaming rage, fear in its many forms holds us within our cultural walls. We are threatened by differences—not enriched by them.

A small-group setting can provide a supportive community for discussing and acting on this potentially uncomfortable material. The aim of this study guide is to help such a group understand the ideas in this book and to identify ways we should change in response to them.

There are fourteen studies in this guide and an optional fifteenth study for those particularly concerned to reach the campus. It can be used in a Sunday-morning class or a weeknight series.

Each study is structured in three parts. First, a *purpose* states the main aim of each discussion. The *discussion* section helps group members clarify what the authors are saying, respond to their ideas and consider particular ways the book may be applied. Finally, several *activities* are suggested.

The discussion section is designed to fit a 45- to 60-minute time slot, giving the leader an outline of questions to ask during each study. A lecture is not encouraged. The goal is to allow people to talk. The questions are designed to help you keep your group working steadily through the content of an entire chapter so that everyone will benefit from the Hoplers' ideas and have a chance to respond to their full presentation.

You should flesh out the discussion by using follow-up questions such as, "Why do you say that?" "Have any of the rest of you ever felt that way?" "Can you give an example?" or "What else does the author say on this point?" Also, give one-sentence summaries frequently to remind people of where they have been and where they are going.

Do everything you can to encourage balanced discussion. When someone who talks a lot finishes a statement, invite further comment by saying something like, "Does anyone want to add to that?" or "Does someone have another idea?" Doing this will encourage quieter people to make contributions.

At the same time, don't be afraid of silences. If the group is working together, silences can be periods of creative effort. If a silence goes too long, rephrase your question. If someone is continually dominating or silent, talk with him or her privately about it. You will find other helpful principles for leading in James Nyquist and Jack Kuhatschek's *Leading Bible Discussions* (IVP), especially chapter seven.

You may find the number of questions in the guide impossible to cover in the time you have. If this proves true, handle some by summarizing the portion of the text they cover and then proceed to the next question. Keep discussion brief for questions which ask you to evaluate the Hoplers' content, or use only the evaluation question that seems most likely to be of interest to your group. Decide beforehand and mark which questions you can or will omit. At the same time emphasize that group members are free to challenge any idea the Hoplers set forth. You don't want to beat people down with their conclusions.

As a discussion leader, you will need to take time (probably between two to three hours) to "make the study your own." Read the chapter(s) carefully. Write a brief answer to each question; then go back and, wherever necessary, put the questions into words and phrases you feel comfortable using. Make sure, however, you don't stray from a question's intent. All the questions are written so you can ask them directly to the group. Make notations on how much time you'd like to spend on each group of questions so you don't get bogged down. Finally, mark which questions you can skip, or summarize their answers if time starts running out.

The activities will take different amounts of time depending on the nature of each activity. Some offer ideas for further discussion; some involve further study or research by individuals or the group; some suggest outings for the group, like going to a concert.

Some activities can be undertaken as part of your normal discussion period while some will require a separate time together. This may mean (depending on which activities you choose) that you could have as many as twenty-eight group meetings—fourteen one-hour discussions and fourteen activities also including discussion. But this number can be reduced by occasionally meeting for two hours—one for discussion and one for an activity—or by skipping some sessions.

We do not suggest that you do all the activities with each study. Select one or two that fit your group best. Involve the group as much as possible in the decision of which activity to select. Allow individuals to choose activities, if appropriate, and then report their findings to the group at the next meeting. Remember that discussion time for the activities is in addition to the forty-five to sixty minutes suggested for the discussion section itself.

As the leader, you will want to evaluate the activities ahead of time—in fact, at least two studies ahead. Say, for example, that you are preparing to discuss chapter three. At that time you will not only want to review the activities for chapter three but for chapter four as well. In this way, if you wish, the group can assign individuals to do research ahead of time for chapter four and then make a presentation at the same time as your discussion of chapter four.

Also tell members to read the appropriate chapter(s) prior to each session. Encourage them to underline and ponder significant passages.

To summarize what has been said so far and to add a little more, here are the ground rules to be explained to the group before beginning your first study:

(1) This is a discussion. Everyone's contribution is valuable.

(2) No one will be forced to comment though everyone is encouraged to.

(3) No one's feelings are to be criticized.

(4) People are free to disagree with what the authors say.

(5) Members should stay on the topic under discussion, and the leader will bring the group back if it strays too far.

(6) Everyone is expected to read the appropriate chapter or chapters before the session.

(7) At the end of each discussion, we will decide as a group which activities we will do for that chapter or for the next chapter. We will decide who will do what, when and where.

(8) The leader will begin and end on time.

Finally, as a leader, do not forget to pray for the people in your group throughout the week. And encourage them to pray for each other as well. The

Holy Spirit is interested in working in our lives to bring them into conformity with the character of Christ. Prayer is one way of freeing the Spirit to work, and it reinforces our own openness to have him work in us. Prayer will bring you closer together even while you're apart. And, as Thom Hopler says, the unity we have despite our differences can be a mighty witness to the world.

1. "How Much Did You Pay for Your Wife?" (Chapter One)
Purpose
To begin to understand how our culture affects us.
Discussion
1. To help us get to know each other better, let's each introduce ourselves, list the places we have each lived in for a year or more, and mention briefly what we each expect from studying *Reaching the World Next Door* together.

2. What four ways does Hopler mention to explain what culture is (pp. 14-16)?

Give an example of a mental road map in your life.

3. What are some values that give direction to your life? How do they guide you?

4. List some things that our society generally considers impossible.

Do you think these are also impossible in God's view?

5. How does Hopler illustrate that Western culture may not be more civilized than African culture (pp. 16-17)?

Do you know of any weddings like those Hopler describes?

If so, what were they like and why were they that way?

6. How, on pages 17-18, does Hopler suggest the church has been affected by cultural blindness?

These issues will be discussed more fully in the coming chapters. But for now, what is your reaction? Do you agree or disagree with Hopler? Explain.

7. On pages 18-20, Hopler mentions some of the issues and influences which have affected his thinking. What are some of these?

8. Summarize what you see to be the main purpose of this book.
Activities
1. List some of the heroes, important places and days, and key historical events for a subculture of which a group member is a part (church, college, company or the like). How is the importance of these shown in the subculture? Why are they important?

2. See a movie that highlights different cultures and discuss it. Some possibilities include *The Chosen* (Jewish), *Long Walk Home* (Black), *A Great Wall* (Chinese), *Witness* (Amish), *Cry Freedom* (South African), *A Cry in the Dark* (religious vs. secular) and *El Salvadore* or *Missing* (Latin American).

3. As a group, attend an artistic event outside your culture (a concert, play, foreign film or art-gallery exhibition). Afterward discuss what you learned of that culture's mental road maps, system of values or limits of possibility.

2. Building the Family: Genesis (Chapter Two)

Purpose
To understand how the teaching on families in Genesis interrelates with culture as a whole and our culture in particular.

Discussion
1. What do you most appreciate about the family you grew up in? Why?

2. Why, according to Hopler's view of Genesis 1—2, are we corporate beings (pp. 23-25)?

Does this mean that God did not create each of us as complete and whole people? Explain.

Do you think society tends to be more individualistic or more corporate? Explain.

3. In what four ways did sin break down relationships God had established (p. 25)?

How did God begin to rebuild these relationships (p. 26)?

What does this tell us about God?

4. How does the family of Cain contrast with the family of Seth (pp. 27-28)?

5. In Genesis 1—11, what were some of the ways God protected man from himself and kept him from self-destructing?

What are aspects of our culture that keep us from destroying ourselves and each other?

6. What five principles regarding the family does Hopler draw out of Genesis 12—50 (pp. 29-32)? Explain each in a sentence.

Which, if any, of these five principles were broken in your own family life? How has it affected your family?

Which of the five principles would you say is most needed in our society? Explain.

7. How, according to pages 33-34, should our witness in the world be affected by the teaching of Genesis on the family?

How can you apply this teaching in the next week?

8. How does the story of Beth illustrate the principle that God's time frame is not the same as ours (pp. 34-36)?

Do you agree that Beth should not have been encouraged to immediately stop living with Lou? Why or why not?

9. What specific situations are you involved with where our society's moral priorities may be at odds with God's priorities? (If you aren't involved in any, why is that so?)

What do you think your response should be?

Activities

1. Have one person or several from the group research their roots, develop a family tree and then explain it to the group.

2. In groups of four, have each person share his or her family background using the following format:

(a) Describe your family (the community you grew up in, how the head of the household operates and so on).

(b) Describe your family economically. (Where does the money come from, where is it kept and what is it spent on?)

(c) What kind of work do your parents do (blue collar, white collar)?

(d) How are your parents seen or involved in the community?

(e) Where do you fit in the family?

(f) How aware is your family of the culture it is in?

3. The Impact of a Minority: Daniel (Chapter Three)

Purpose

To see the impact a minority can have on the larger community.

Discussion

1. What minority groups are you a part of (in regard to race, religion, age, sex, economic class, politics, employment, ethnic origin and so on)?

As a member of such a minority, how is it difficult for you and your group to have an impact on the larger society?

2. After having been an influential people in Egypt, how did Israel end up as a suppressed people in Babylon (pp. 37-38)?

3. Why did Daniel and his friends stand above the best of Babylon (pp. 38-39)?

In what specific ways can obedience to God help us stand above society?

4. According to Daniel 3, how did the Jews end up with substantial influence in Babylonian society (pp. 40-41)?

5. What were the results of Nebuchadnezzar's finally turning to Yahweh (pp. 41-42)?

6. According to Daniel 5, why was Daniel able to maintain his power even though Babylon was overthrown by Persia (p. 44)?

7. Read Jeremiah 29:4-7, found on page 46. In what ways can you "seek the welfare" of the community in which God has placed you?

How are you likely to meet opposition or persecution as you try to influence your society?

How will you cope with such opposition?

8. What can we learn from past and present Jewish and Black communities about influencing society at large as a minority group?

Activities

1. Read *The Autobiography of Malcolm X* and discuss what it feels like to be a member of a rejected minority group.

2. Invite several members of an ethnic minority not already represented in your group to have a meal with you and to discuss how they relate to the larger culture.

3. Spend some in-depth time with a foreign student and listen to him or her talk about how he or she feels about being away from home.

4. The Center of History: Jesus Christ (Chapter Four)

Purpose

To consider how the life and work of Christ can strengthen us to go beyond our cultural limitations.

Discussion

1. How did God work through each of the empires of Babylon, Persia, Greece and Rome to prepare the world for Christ (pp. 48-50)?

2. How has your culture been prepared for Christ?

What, therefore, are the most likely avenues through which the gospel can be spread?

In what specific ways could you work through one of these avenues to spread God's word?

3. In what four relationships did Christ demonstrate a redeemed life (pp. 51-52)?

How did he demonstrate this kind of life in each case?

4. Which of these four relationships is in most need of reconciliation and healing *in your life*? Explain.

How can Christ's life help you in this area?

5. Which of these four relationships is in most need of reconciliation and healing *in society*? Explain.

How can you live your life to demonstrate redemption most effectively in the area of society's greatest need?

6. What limitations did Christ impose on himself when he became human (p. 52)?

What limitations do we have as humans?

What further limitations does our culture place on us?

7. How was Christ able to overcome his human limitations and resist the

temptations of Satan (p. 53)?

How does this offer hope to us?

8. Why, in Hopler's view, did Jesus emphasize building community more than evangelism (p. 54)?

Christ returned to the Father to send his Spirit. How does this affect your unity with other Christians? Be specific and practical.

Activities

1. Research the current state of the natural environment and formulate biblical principles for how society should relate to the environment. (Consider such topics as nuclear energy, abortion, dieting and overeating, family planning, waste disposal or use of energy.)

2. Consider the issue of self-acceptance. Have each person list what he or she likes and dislikes about himself or herself. How will these likes and dislikes affect your ability to relate to those in other cultures? (This activity is meant to spur discussion of how self-acceptance affects our relationships with those from other cultures. It should not be allowed to develop into a discussion of one another's weaknesses.)

5. Reaching an Oppressed and Open People: John 4 (Chapter Five)

Purpose

To see that our contact with other cultural groups can and should be built on what we hold in common with them and on the truth God has already given them.

Discussion

1. What are some groups (racial, religious, social, economic) of people with whom you feel uncomfortable?

Why do you think you feel this way?

Why are differences in other people so threatening to us?

2. How did many Jews feel about Samaria (p. 56)? In John 4:4, how did Jesus show that his attitude was different from most other Jews?

3. What, according to John 4:5, is common in the heritage of Jews and Samaritans?

What do you have in common with one of the groups you mentioned earlier?

4. What are the two parallel story lines that run through John 4:7-27 (pp. 57-58)?

How did Jesus' reaction to the woman contrast with the disciples' probable reaction to the townspeople?

5. Hopler points out that the woman was possibly a prostitute (p. 58). How

do you respond to the idea of talking with prostitutes about the gospel?

How is Jesus able to set aside her social stigma and show that he is interested in and concerned for her as a person?

6. In John 4:19-24, Jesus deemphasizes the Jews' theological differences with the Samaritans and emphasizes the basics they have in common (p. 59). What secondary issues should you deemphasize when speaking with those from a religious background different from yours?

What primary issues should you keep in mind?

7. In crossing cultural boundaries, why can it be important to acknowledge honestly the faults, failings and weaknesses of your own culture, as well as its strengths (p. 60)?

8. How do the two parallel story lines shift in John 4:28-38 (p. 61)?

Why does Jesus rebuke the disciples?

9. Why can we be confident that every group we go to with the gospel will already have some truth we can build on and learn from (pp. 62-63)?

Think back to the group or groups of people you mentioned at the beginning with whom you feel uncomfortable. How can you find out what truth they already have?

Activities

1. At a social gathering of any kind, list all the cultural differences you see (language differences, taste preferences, fashion distinctives, economic diversities and so on).[1] Which made you uncomfortable? Why? (Allow 5 to 10 minutes for each person with a list. For example, allow 15-30 minutes for group discussion if three members made lists.)

2. Interview someone from a group with which you are uncomfortable (see question 1 above). Ask about his or her culture and try to discover as many similarities with yourself as possible. (Allow 5 or 10 minutes for discussion for each person who interviewed someone.)

3. Go to a foreign restaurant as a group and order from a menu in a language you do not know. Afterward, discuss how you felt about the experience.

6. Dividing Power, Multiplying Disciples: Acts (Part One) (Chapter Six)

Purposes

To see how the early church became and grew as a group of diverse people.
To identify ways our Christian community can be the same.

Discussion

1. Why is unity such a desirable goal for Christians?

How can this desire also be a source of division among Christians?

2. What were some of the differences between the Diaspora Jews and the Palestinian Jews (pp. 65-66)?

How then was the church able to get such a multicultural start at Pentecost (pp. 67-68)?

3. This multicultural beginning for the church soon drifted into a segregated situation. Why (pp. 68-69)?

How did the problem surface in Acts 6:1?

4. How did the apostles solve the problem (p. 69)?

What results came of their action (p. 70)?

5. What minorities are in your Christian community? How could they be given independent power within your fellowship?

Do you believe they should be given such authority and responsibility? Why or why not?

6. Why were some of the Hellenistic Jews so upset with Stephen even though he gave a basically Hellenistic interpretation of the Scripture (pp. 72-73)?

7. In Acts 7:2-43, how did Stephen show that the law had little to do with Palestine (pp. 73-76)?

How did he defend his position on the temple in 7:44-50 (pp. 76-77)?

In what ways might our interpretation of the Bible be culturally limited? (If you don't know, how could you find out?)

How could a less limited view offer a broader base for unity with others?

Activities

1. Interview several people who are second-generation immigrants. Discover how they feel about their home country and how they feel about their adopted country.

2. Interview several first-, second- and third-generation immigrants regarding their feelings about their homeland and their adopted country. Discuss what patterns, if any, distinguish the attitudes of one generation from another.

3. Investigate services (both public and private) to recent immigrants in your community. (For example, is there bilingual education in the schools? Do government employees who deal with immigrants speak two or more languages? Do banks and utility companies have service representatives who speak appropriate foreign languages?)

7. Unified but Not Uniform: Acts (Part Two) (Chapter Seven)

Purpose

To understand how God's people can and should be both diverse and united.

Discussion

1. How was Paul affected by Stephen and his message—both immediately and in the long run (pp. 79-80)?

2. The thinking of other apostles was not so profoundly affected as Paul's. How did the Holy Spirit overcome this barrier in Acts 10—11 (pp. 81-83)? Why did the Spirit lead in such a step-by-step fashion?

3. The Palestinian Jews (and even the Judaizers in the church) said one had to be circumcised to be in a right relationship with God. What does your Christian fellowship say is necessary to be a Christian?

Would the requirement(s) automatically eliminate those in some groups (in certain denominations, for example)?

4. Are there certain actions a person could do which would automatically make it impossible for that person to be a Christian? If so, what are they?

Is there a broader definition of what it means to be a Christian that would be more in tune with Acts 10—11? What would it be?

5. Hopler notes that "the Hellenistic Jewish Christians from Jerusalem went into Greek areas but only spoke to other Hellenistic Jews about Jesus" (p. 83). Have you noticed a similar tendency in yourself to offer the gospel only to people whose culture you know well? Explain.

What will be necessary for you to be able to go to those in different settings or with different values?

6. How was Barnabas able to help reconcile the Jewish and Gentile Christians in Antioch (pp. 84-85)?

7. How does Acts 13 indicate that the Christians in Antioch achieved unity with diversity (pp. 86-87)?

Would a similar structure (integrated leadership representing several homogeneous subgroups) be valuable in your church or fellowship? Explain.

8. How was the debate at the Council of Jerusalem resolved (pp. 89-90)?

9. Why, according to Hopler (pp. 90-91), does the church need to fulfill both its "prophetic" role (going out into the world) and its "priestly" role (calling God's people to be faithful)?

To which side does your church or fellowship give the most emphasis? How could the imbalance, if any, be corrected?

10. Looking over Hopler's conclusions on pages 91-93, what strikes you as being most crucial? Explain.

Activities

1. Each person can study a book of the Bible not highlighted in *Reaching the World Next Door* to learn what it says about culture and report his or her findings to the group. Some possibilities are Exodus, Judges, Jonah and any of the Gospels.

2. Discuss with missionaries the problems in separating one's culture from

the presentation of the gospel.

3. Attend a church service outside your denomination or culture (perhaps Pentecostal, Roman Catholic or Black) and afterward discuss what your culture can learn from that expression of Christianity.

8. Rural Christians in an Urban World (Chapter Eight)
Purpose
To understand how the church has and can use the overall trends in history to expand.
Discussion
1. What was the main thing you learned from part one, chapters two to seven, of *Reaching the World Next Door*?

Why do you consider this important?

2. Now look at figure 1 on page 98. How did each wave threaten the church?

How was the church able to use each wave to expand?

3. Hopler says that the era of colonialism is ending and a new era of technology and urbanization is rising (pp. 100-102). Do you agree or disagree with this assessment? Explain.

4. How does a geographic frame of reference differ from a functional one (pp. 103-4)? Give examples.

5. Think of five or six people who are your best friends. What would you say is the primary reason you got to know each of these people and have remained so close? (For example: you went to school or church together; you played on the basketball team together; you are cousins; you work together or have similar jobs.)

6. What are other examples of how our society exhibits a functional frame of reference?

7. In what ways has Christianity tended to be geographic-oriented rather than function-oriented?

How has your fellowship group in particular been geographic- rather than function-oriented?

8. What would be the value, if any, of becoming more function-oriented for (a) the church at large and (b) your Christian group?

How could you become more function-oriented?
Activities
1. Survey ten people in the immediate geographical location you live in to discover how much they relate to one another and how much they relate to others outside the locale. Report your findings to the group.

2. Read Peter Wagner's *Our Kind of People*. Discuss the pros and cons of

Wagner's proposal. Do you think his proposal is biblical? Why or why not?

9. Networks of Communication (Chapter Nine)

Purpose
To explore how networks of communication function and how they can be influenced.

Discussion
1. Indicate which group within each of the following pairs you believe has more influence—university administrators or students and faculty; politicians or voters; pastors or churchgoers; union leaders or union members; executives of advertising firms or consumers.

Did you tend to pick those with formal authority or those in the grassroots? Why?

2. On page 110 Hopler says, "Our rural mindset blinds us to the importance of [human communication networks]. . . . Our orientation is toward impersonal power structures and institutions. These are really what matter, aren't they?" Do you agree that society in general places greater value on the structures? Explain.

How does the article by Hitt illustrate Hopler's point?

3. How, according to Hopler, do we normally view the flow of communication (and influence) within government (p. 114)?

How does the example of the Newark public school (pp. 114-15) indicate that influence within the government does not always flow from the top down?

What are some other examples you know of government being influenced strongly from outside forces?

4. From your own experience or what Hopler says on pages 115-17, how do professions seek to mold the values of their members?

Why is it so difficult to resist such influences?

How does Hopler suggest we influence these networks of communication for Christ (pp. 117-18)?

5. The third major communication network Hopler discusses is kinship. How much influence does your extended family have in your life? Explain.

On page 119 Hopler says, "I used a slogan during my four years of ministry in Newark: Every person is a doorway to a family, and every family is a gateway to a community."

What is meant by this?

How might you use this strategy?

6. What are volunteer associations (pp. 122-23)? Why do people join them?

7. What volunteer associations do you belong to?
Which others could you or would you join?
How could you use these to expand Christ's influence?

Activities

1. Invite a professional to discuss his or her professional community using the eight characteristics identified by William Goode (p. 000). Try to discover how true these characteristics are of this person's profession.

2. Go to a local government agency with a problem to find out what would have to be done within the system to get the problem resolved.

3. View and discuss *Four Families,* a sixty-minute film available from New York University Film Library, 26 Washington Place, New York, NY 10003, for a rental fee. (Give desired show date and alternate dates. Also try to give a street address, not a box number.) The film compares patterns of family life in India, France, Japan and Canada.

4. Join a volunteer association. Report on the friendships you develop and on your opportunities for ministry.

10. Dynamic Ethnicity (Chapter Ten)

Purpose

To understand how ethnicity has affected us and how it should affect our witness.

Discussion

1. What is your ethnic makeup?
How do you feel about it?
How do you feel about jokes that make fun of your ethnic background?

2. How, according to Hopler, did the unbalanced melting pot develop in the United States (pp. 126-27)?

3. Look at figure 4 (p. 131). Do you agree with the way Hopler has rated the level of influence the eight groups have had on the American value system? Why or why not? How, if at all, does figure 4 illustrate your own experience?

4. The first two nonvolunteer immigrant groups Hopler mentions are Native Americans and Puerto Ricans (pp. 133-34). Why have their values generally been rejected by the American melting pot?

5. Why have Blacks found it difficult to assimilate to American culture (p. 134)?
What is society's general attitude now toward Blacks (pp. 135-36)?

6. Consider the quote from *Time* on page 137. Why do many Blacks oppose legalizing gambling?
What other factors does Hopler mention which indicate that society's

stance toward Blacks is a desire to control them rather than accommodate or help them?

7. What third alternative to government solutions and criminal solutions does Hopler propose (p. 139)?

8. Hopler says that three issues must be considered seriously to make this third alternative possible. Regarding the first, how do lines of communication in ethnicity affect our witness?

How should our witness be changed because of this (pp. 140-41)?

9. Regarding the second issue, how should ethnicity affect our view of missions (pp. 141-43)?

What specifically should you do?

10. Regarding the third issue, how should the dynamic ethnicity presented in chapter ten affect our attitude toward our own values (pp. 143-45)?

Activities

1. Visit an urban ministry in your area to discover how they are responding with the gospel to the city. (See your pastor for leads on whom to contact.)

2. Read *Bury My Heart at Wounded Knee* by Dee Brown and report to the group.

3. Go to a local welfare office and go through the process of signing up for aid. What obstacles did you encounter? How long did you have to wait? Were you forced to miss work or classes? How did you feel?

4. Talk with a missionary about how his or her agency is facing the issue of appointing more minorities.

11. Urbanization and Community (Chapters Eleven and Twelve)
Purpose
To understand the ways our world has been urbanized and how we can minister in and through community.

Discussion

1. What kind of urban experiences (in the broad sense) have you had—positive and negative?

2. What system of values is generated through advertising (pp. 150-51)?

3. What role have media (television, radio, movies, music, magazines and so on) played in urbanization (pp. 151-56)?

4. Consider a recent major event or controversy in the news. On the whole would you say that news coverage has had a beneficial effect or a harmful effect? Explain.

5. Why is reconciliation important in a media-saturated, urbanized culture?

6. In chapter twelve, the author considers the importance of community when crisis hits. What are ways in which the Christian community has

ministered to you in times of need?

7. The author describes ways in which communities can be built. How might this be done among those who are in need around you?

8. What are the advantages and disadvantages of moving into the city for the sake of ministry (pp. 160-64)?

9. When might it be appropriate to help a family move out of the city (p. 165)?

10. The author says God is more interested in changing our character than our situations. What do you think this means?

Explain whether or not you agree and why.

Activities

1. Select a half-dozen magazine ads and describe the values you believe are communicated by each.

2. Have two or three people take an afternoon for a driving tour of the different parts of the city with an urban guide and report back your impressions to the rest of the group.

3. Contact Christian Community Development Association (P.O. Box 459, Angels Camp, CA 95221; 209/728-1485) for information on ways to assist in community development and ways to educate churches to become involved in development work in their own neighborhoods.

4. Investigate the InterVarsity mission project in your area. Call 608/274-9001.

12. Black Culture and the Black Church (Chapters Thirteen and Fourteen)

Purpose

To understand the dual natures of Black culture and the Black church.

Discussion

1. If you are Black, how would you say that you have been influenced by the white culture? If you are not Black, how have you been influenced by the Black culture?

2. How, according to the author, are Blacks in America in tension from a dual heritage (p. 167)?

3. Why is there a controversy about whether African-Americans have a dual culture or whether their culture has no roots in Africa?

4. What case does the author make for there being a distinct link to African culture (pp. 168-71)?

5. Hopler says that the notion of "Black is beautiful" is debatable to some. How do you view Black culture—positive and worth encouraging, negative and in need of change, or both?

6. Summarize the dual heritage of the Black church discussed in chapter fourteen (pp. 174-76).

7. What constructive role has the Black church played in the Black community over the years (pp. 175-76)?

8. How could 23 million Black evangelicals in America be largely invisible to white Christians (p. 177)?

9. What are some of the contributions the Black church can make to the church as a whole (pp. 178-79)?

10. In what practical ways do you think these contributions could actually be brought to the wider church?

Activities

1. For an excellent history of Christianity among Blacks in America, read *The Negro Church in America* and *The Black Church Since Frazier* by Franklin E. Frazier and C. Eric Lincoln (published by Schocken Books) and report to the group.

For a shorter reading project, select articles from the *Dictionary of Christianity in America* such as "Black Religion," "Black Theology," "Black Catholics," "Black Colleges," "African Methodist Episcopal Church," "National Baptists," "William Seymour," "Richard Allen" and others.

2. Get to know a Black Christian and attend church with them.

13. Keys to Reconciliation (Chapter Fifteen)

Purpose

To see the importance and difficulty of reconciliation among races.

Discussion

1. How do you tend to handle conflicts and disagreements? Do you avoid them or dive into them? Try to give a specific example.

2. The author suggests that people get to know those from other ethnic groups by visiting them on the home turf (p. 181). Why can this be a good place to start the process of reconciliation?

3. James Baldwin's pact with his friend Budd Shulberg is quoted on page 181. What would be the cost of following this in your marriage, family or church? How would it be even more difficult to do across races?

4. What is the difference in learning *about* someone from another culture and learning *from* someone from another group?

5. Do you agree or disagree that slavery and racism of decades past are still important issues that need to be dealt with by Americans? Explain.

6. Describe an injustice or wrong that you experienced from a school authority, a government official, a church leader or in another situation. What are you feelings about this occurrence?

7. When seeking to help someone who has experienced injustice, why is it important to see things through their eyes?

8. Why is it difficult for whites to see the continued importance of slavery and past injustices in the current experience of Blacks?

9. On page 184, the author says, "What happened in our country to American Blacks, free or slave, happened to all of us. Our attitudes have been shaped by historical events and how they have been presented to us." Do you agree or disagree? Explain your answer.

10. The author gives some examples of how she spoke truth without love (p. 185). What makes it so hard to balance the two?

11. Likewise the author points out ways in which the religious leaders of Jesus' day knew the truth but didn't do it—like knowing where the Messiah would be born but not going there (pp. 186-87). What are some current examples of us knowing the truth but not doing it?

12. The professor from USC (p. 189) said that reconciliation before the Civil War could have been so powerful that it might have prevented World War I. What potential power for good do you see in reconciliation between races?

Activities

1. Visit a friend from another race at his or her church. Take the opportunity to get to know their family and friends there.

2. Read *More Than Equals* by Spencer Perkins and Chris Rice (IVP) or *The Coming Race Wars?* by William Pannell (Zondervan). Report to the group.

14. Christ Beyond Culture (Chapters Sixteen and Seventeen)

Purpose

To discover the basics of Christianity which can help us follow Christ beyond our cultural walls.

Discussion

1. Why is it important to have a firm grasp on the most basic biblical values before encountering another culture (p. 194)?

2. Hopler says the two key values are truth and love (p. 194). What two or three biblical values do you believe are most important? Why?

Why does Hopler believe truth and love are most basic (pp. 194-95)?

3. What problems can arise if we separate truth and love or emphasize one over the other (pp. 195-96)?

What benefits come from holding the two together?

4. What do we learn about truth and love from 1 John (pp. 198-99)?

When, according to Hopler's view of 1 John 4:1-3, should doctrinal differences interfere with our ability to have fellowship with others (p. 200)?

What do you think of his analysis? How might you need to change your views and actions because of this?

5. Look now at chapter seventeen. How has the church in general been affected by impersonal, group-imposed standards (pp. 201-2)?

How has your fellowship in particular been affected?

6. Hopler suggests that the remedy for the bad effects of such standards is to look to Jesus as a guide for discipleship. How does Luke 9:22-27 connect Jesus' identity with the kind of disciples we should be (pp. 204-5)?

How are we trying to save what we have, to maintain our values and to conserve our culture rather than losing them for Christ's sake?

7. Hopler gives two examples on pages 206-7 of culture trying to bind us. What other limits does our culture impose that Christ would take us beyond?

8. What are the six signposts of discipleship (pp. 208-10)? Explain each briefly.

Which of these is most important for you as you seek to become a true disciple? Why?

Activity

1. Study Ephesians, Galatians or Romans 12—15, analyzing Paul's arguments for maintaining unity and handling differences among Christians.

Optional Study: Reaching the Campus (Appendix A)

Purpose

To help students and faculty understand how Hopler's model for ministry can be applied to their campus.

Discussion

1. How do residential and commuter campuses differ (p. 213)?

What do you believe to be the most significant difference? Why?

2. How does Hopler's description apply to our campus?

3. What strategy is usually used to reach a residential campus?

Why is this strategy seldom effective with commuter schools?

[For those on a largely residential campus:] How has urbanization (that is, the development of communication along functional lines rather than geographical ones) affected residential schools?

4. What suggestions does Hopler give for reaching commuter schools (pp. 214-15)?

Which ideas could we apply on our campus?

5. What else could we do to follow various groups of students back to their primary communities and build relationships there?

6. What suggestions does Hopler give to unify Christians in different cultural groups on campus?

How could we unify the Christians in different cultural groups on our campus?

Activities

1. Divide a page into five columns. In the first column list all the functional groups (freshmen, sophomores, graduates, international students, night-school students, ethnic groups, clubs, faculty, majors and so on) and all the geographic groups (dorms, apartments, city students, suburban students, fraternities and so on) on campus.

In the second column indicate the numbers in each and in the third column the percentage each represents of the total school population. (This could require a fair amount of research. If so, assign different parts of the list to different people to investigate.)

In the fourth column note the number in our Christian fellowship from each of the groups listed and in column five the percentage each represents of the total number in our group.

What groups are our fellowship most successful in reaching? Why is this so?

What groups are we least successful in reaching? Why?

Write out a few specific steps we can take in the next six months to begin to reach the three major groups our fellowship is missing most.

2. Read *The Impossible Community* (IVP) by Barbara Benjamin and discuss how the experiences of Brooklyn College might apply to your campus.

3. Ask Black, Asian or other ethnic staff or students to share their honest impressions of your campus group's cultural sensitivity.

4. Read *Ministering Cross-Culturally* by Sherwood G. Lingenfelter and Marvin K. Mayers (Baker). Discuss value patterns and apply them to your campus.

Notes

Introduction

[1] Floyd McClung, "The Urban World," in *Target Earth*, ed. Frank Caleb Jansen (Kailzia-Kona, Hawaii: University of the Nations, 1989), p. 74.
[2] Thom Hopler, "Learning from Foreign Missions," in *Urban Mission*, ed. Craig Ellison (Lanham, Md.: University Press of America, 1974), p. 178.

Chapter 1. "How Much Did You Pay for Your Wife?"

[1] Arthur Glasser in *World Vision*, quoted in *HIS*, January 1971, p. 17.
[2] Eugene Nida wrote forty years ago,

Polygamy is generally no longer treated by informed missionaries with shocked denunciations, but with an appreciative understanding of the numerous problems. More and more missions are sympathetic to permitting polygamists to become church members (but not to hold office) if such persons became polygamists before becoming acquainted with the gospel. Rather than have unwanted widows turned out to prostitution, churches have acted as sponsors of such women in arranging marriages. An awakened consciousness as to the need of educating women is changing the prevailing practice of concentrating some 90 per cent of the educational budget on training boys and men. Rather than oppose harmless but "strange" customs approved by the people, missionaries are learning to wait and work with cultural developments.

Eugene Nida, *Customs and Cultures* (New York: Harper & Brothers, 1954), pp. 264-65.

Chapter 2. Building the Family: Genesis

[1] Derek Kidner, *Genesis* (Downers Grove, Ill.: InterVarsity Press, 1967), p. 78.
[2] This is not controverted by the ultimate dismissal of Hagar and Ishmael in Genesis 21:8-21. In regard to 21:8 Kidner says,

Sarah spoke more truly than she knew; but the sequel shows how different was God's Spirit towards the outcasts from hers—a fact to be remembered in discussions of His sovereign will. At the close (20-21) the natural affinities of the pair are emerging, to confirm the wisdom of the parting. The story is the complement of chapter 16, where all the parties had acted on impulse and had been recalled to live together another fourteen years or more (*cf.* 17:25). Now, with the two sons born and circumcised, God's time has ripened; *cf.* another slow maturing in 15:16. (Kidner, *Genesis,* p. 140)

[3]I do not mean to imply that marriages by choice are morally superior to marriages by arrangement. Rather, I believe God is emphasizing through the story of the patriarchs that love in marriage is a key element no matter how it may have begun.

Chapter 3. The Impact of a Minority: Daniel
[1]Richard R. DeRidder, *The Dispersion of the People of God* (Kampen, Netherlands: J. H. Kok, 1971), p. 60.
[2]Ibid., pp. 77-83.
[3]Others identify Darius as being Cyrus himself. For a full discussion see Joyce Baldwin, *Daniel* (Downers Grove, Ill.: InterVarsity Press, 1978), pp. 23-28, 119.
[4]Ronald S. Wallace, *The Lord Is King* (Downers Grove, Ill.: InterVarsity Press, 1979), p. 86.

Chapter 4. The Center of History: Jesus Christ
[1]DeRidder, *Dispersion,* p. 73.
[2]Ibid., pp. 71-72.
[3]Ibid., p. 10.
[4]In Ephesians 5:31-32 Paul indicates that the reverse is also true: we learn about the church through marriage. Genesis 2:24, he says, refers to Christ and the church. The community God intends is one built with the same kind of commitment and unity as marriage. The deterioration of marriage and the prevalence of divorce is tied to the deterioration of the church in the West.

Chapter 6. Dividing Power, Multiplying Disciples: Acts (Part One)
[1]Joachim Jeremias suggests the population of Jerusalem swelled from approximately 25,000 to 150,000 at Passover. Joachim Jeremais, *Jerusalem at the Time of Jesus* (Philadelphia: Fortress, 1969), pp. 77-84.
[2]F. F. Bruce, *New Testament History* (Garden City, N.Y.: Doubleday, 1972), pp. 220-22.
[3]"Probably one synagogue is meant, although five, four, three and two have been understood by various commentators. . . . *Freedman* (Gk. *libertinoi*). Probably Jewish freedmen or descendants of freedmen from the various places mentioned." F. F. Bruce, "The Acts of the Apostles," in *The New Bible Commentary: Revised* (Grand Rapids, Mich.: Eerdmans, 1970), p. 980.
[4]Bruce, *New Testament History,* p. 218.
[5]Paul explains the true place of circumcision and the true meaning of Judaism in the book of Galatians.

Chapter 7. Unified but Not Uniform: Acts (Part Two)

[1] Paul elaborates on this in 1 Corinthians 8 and 10 and Romans 14:1—15:6, where he stresses Christian liberty with responsibility.

[2] While prophets certainly engaged in calling Israel to obedience (as the priests did), I use the term *prophetic* to highlight the prophets' role in emphasizing that God was not a local deity tied to geographic Israel. Rather they clearly saw and spoke of the need to view him as a universal God who was sovereign over all nations.

Chapter 8. Rural Christians in an Urban World

[1] Kenneth Scott Latourette, *A History of Christianity* (New York: Harper & Row, 1975), 1:xxi.

[2] Ibid., p. 330.

[3] Ibid., p. 936.

[4] Ibid., p. 414.

[5] Ibid., p. 457.

[6] Ibid., p. 404.

[7] Ralph D. Winter, *The Twenty-five Unbelievable Years, 1945 to 1969* (Pasadena: William Carey Library, 1970), pp. 11-13.

[8] Ibid., p. 14.

[9] Kenneth Little, "Some Aspects of African Urbanization South of the Sahara," Module 5, 1971, in *McCaleb Modules in Anthropology* (Reading, Mass.: Addison-Wesley, 1971), p. 5-1.

[10] Advertisement, "The Think-Tank Bank," *Wall Street Journal,* 3 February 1976.

[11] Richard L. Meier, *A Communications Theory of Urban Growth* (Cambridge, Mass.: MIT Press, 1962), p. 13.

[12] F. Stuart Chapin, "Selected Theories of Urban Growth and Structure," in Internal Structure of the City, ed. Larry S. Bourne (New York: Oxford, 1971), pp. 141-53.

[13] Paul Craven and Barry Wellman, "The Network City," *Sociological Inquiry* 43, no. 3-4, (1973):76.

[14] Meier, *Communications,* p. 13.

[15] Ibid., p. 14.

Chapter 9. Networks of Communication

[1] Russell T. Hitt, "New York City: Spiritual Power Failure," *Eternity,* November 1977, pp. 37-39, 55.

[2] Amos H. Hawley, *Urban Society: An Ecological Approach* (New York: Ronald Press, 1971), p. 9.

[3] William J. Goode, "Community Within a Community: The Professions," *American Sociological Review,* April 1957, p. 194.

[4] See Kamir Olson's article on Canadian Jim Hunter, "His Pulpit: A Ski Slope," *Teen Power,* 30 November 1975, pp. 2-3, 6.

[5] Editor's note: Mafia involvement was confirmed several years later through a report

by the Pennsylvania Crime Commission entitled "Organized Crime's Infiltration of the Pizza and Cheese Industry." See James Coates, " 'Pizza Wars' Bring Death to Mozzarella Mobsters," *Chicago Tribune,* 24 August 1980, section 1, p. 6.

Chapter 10. Dynamic Ethnicity
[1]U.S. Department of Justice, Immigration and Naturalization Service, *1969 Annual Report on the Commission of Immigration and Naturalization* (Washington, D.C.: U.S. Government Printing Office, 1969), p. 61.

[2]Ibid., p. 62.

[3]John W. Wright, ed., *The Universal Almanac 1993* (Kansas City, Mo.: Andrews and McMeel, 1992), p. 281.

[4]David D'Amico, "Evangelization Across Cultures in the United States," *Review & Exposition* 90, no.1 (Winter 1993): 84; quoted in "The Invisible Minority," *Urban Mission,* June 1993, pp. 3-5.

[5]"A Surging New Spirit," *Time,* 11 July 1988, p. 47, quoted in "The Invisible Minority."

[6]U.S Census Bureau, *Commerce News,* 12 June 1991, p. 10; quoted in "The Invisible Minority."

[7]D'Amico, "Evangelization," p. 85, quoted in "The Invisible Minority."

[8]Wright, *The Universal Almanac 1993,* p. 299.

[9]Nathan Glazer and Daniel Patrick Moynihan, *Beyond the Melting Pot* (Cambridge: The M.I.T. Press, 1963), p. 311.

[10]Ibid., p. 310.

[11]Sgt. Stacey Koon, quoted in the *Los Angeles Times,* 16 May 1992, quoted in William Pannell, *The Coming Race Wars?* (Grand Rapids, Mich.: Zondervan, 1993), p. 40.

[12]Pannell, *Race Wars,* pp. 40-41.

[13]"The 'Irregular Economy,' " *Time,* 19 February 1973, pp. 80-81.

[14]Mark Olson, "White Follies, Black Shackles," *The Other Side,* June 1979, p. 18.

[15]Ibid.

[16]Glazer and Moynihan, *Melting Pot,* p. 290.

Chapter 11. Urbanization: Bane or Blessing?
[1]Kenneth Little quoted in Aylward Shorter, *The Church in the African City* (Maryknoll, N.Y.: Orbis, 1991), p. 13.

[2]Lewis Mumford quoted in Shorter, *African City,* p. 13.

[3]Shorter, *African City,* p. 13.

[4]William Ecenbarger, "There's No Escaping Us, America Is Everywhere You Want to Be," *Philadelphia Inquirer,* 7 March 1993, p. 18.

[5]Ibid., p. 32.

[6]Ibid.

[7]Os Guinness quoted in Marshall Shelley and Bob Moeller (interviewers), "When Foundations Tremble," *Leadership,* Spring 1993, p. 136.

[8]Ibid.

[9]"A Statement by the National Committee of Negro Churchmen," 31 July 1966, quoted in C. Eric Lincoln, *The Black Church Since Frazier* (New York: Schocken Books, 1974), p. 176. Emphasis in the blocked quote is mine.

[10]Leonard Sweet, "Target the Trends," *Leadership,* Spring 1993, pp. 21-22.

[11]James Montgomery Boice, "Exposition not Entertainment," *Leadership,* Spring 1993, p. 27.

[12]Eugene Peterson, "Return to the Timeless," *Leadership,* Spring 1993, p. 22.

[13]William Pannell, *The Coming Race Wars?* (Grand Rapids, Mich.: Zondervan, 1993, pp. 82-83.

[14]Anita Hill quoted in Jill Nelson (interviewer), "No Regrets," *Essence,* March 1992, p. 56.

[15]Kenneth Little quoted in Shorter, *African City,* p. 7.

[16]William J. Broad, "Doing Science on the Network: A Long Way from Gutenberg," *The New York Times,* 18 May 93, pp. C-1, C-10.

[17]Larry Smarr quoted in ibid, p. C-10.

[18]Eugene Nida, "Why Are Foreigners So Queer? A Socioanthropological Approach to Cultural Pluralism," *International Bulletin of Missionary Research,* July 1981, pp. 102-6.

Chapter 12. The Key of Community

[1]William Ecenbarger, "Whispers from the Wall," *Philadelphia Inquirer,* 9 May 1993, p. 24.

[2]"Operation Neighbor," *Urban Family,* Fall 1992, p. 19.

Chapter 13. The Controversy of Black Culture

[1]W. E. B. DuBois quoted in Janet E. Hale-Benson, *Black Children: Their Roots, Culture and Learning Styles* (Baltimore: Johns Hopkins University Press, 1986), p. 21.

[2]Ibid., p. 183.

[3]Tom Mboya, *The Challenge of Nationhood* (London: Heinemann Educational Books, 1970), pp. 221-22.

[4]Ibid., p. 223.

[5]Ibid., p. 225.

[6]Harold Dean Trulear, "Hope Reflected in Black Church Heritage," address given at the IVCF Black Student Leadership Conference in Atlanta, 1992.

[7]Thomas Jefferson quoted in Benjamin Quarles, "What the Historian Owes the Negro," *Saturday Review,* 3 September 1966, quoted in Molefi Kete Asante and Kariamu Welsh Asante, *African Culture* (Trenton, N.J.: African World Press, 1990), p. 165.

[8]Hale-Benson, *Black Children,* p. 178.

[9]Ibid., p. 180.

[10]Ibid., p. 39.

Chapter 14. Black Church Power

[1]M. R. Sawyer, "Black Religion," in *Dictionary of Christianity in America,* ed. Daniel G. Reid, Robert D. Linder, Bruce L. Shelley, Harry M. Stout (Downers Grove, Ill.: InterVarsity Press, 1990), p. 161.

[2]Kristin A. Goss, "Helping Black Churches Heal Cities," *The Chronicle of Philanthropy,* 6 October 1992, p. 15.

[3]Ibid., p. 16.

[4]Letters section, *Christianity Today,* 8 March 1993, p. 10.

[5]Sawyer, "Black Religion," p. 161; and C. Eric Lincoln and Lawrence H. Mamiya, *The Black Church in the African-American Experience* (Durham, N.C.: Duke University Press, 1990), p. 407.

[6]Vernon Grounds, foreword to William Pannell, *The Coming Race Wars?* (Grand Rapids, Mich.: Zondervan, 1993), p. 1.

[7]Ibid., p. 108.

[8]Ibid., p. 109.

[9]I am grateful to Barbara Brown for these thoughts.

[10]See Sherwood G. Lingenfelter and Marvin K. Mayers, *Ministering Cross-Culturally* (Grand Rapids, Mich.: Baker, 1986).

[11]Clarence L. James, *The Black Church and the Black Male* (Atlanta: Youth Leadership Development Programs, 1990), p. 3.

[12]Ibid.

[13]Carl Ellis Jr., *Malcolm, the Man Behind the X* (Chattanooga, Tenn.: Accord, 1993), p. 68.

Chapter 15. Keys to Reconciliation

[1]James Baldwin quoted in William Pannell, *The Coming Race Wars?* (Grand Rapids, Mich.: Zondervan, 1993), p. 19.

[2]Letters to the Editor, *Ebony,* March 1993, p. 13.

[3]George Caywood, interview, *HOPE ,* May-June 1993, p. 26.

Chapter 16. One in Christ in Truth and Love

[1]John Perkins, *A Quiet Revolution* (Waco, Tex.: Word, 1976), p. 33.

[2]See, for example, Ps 25:8-10; 85:10-13; 100:5; 115:1; Prov 16:6, as well as those mentioned in the text.

Appendix B. Study Guide for Individuals or Groups

[1]Adapted from Marvin K. Mayers, *Christianity Confronts Culture* (Grand Rapids, Mich.: Zondervan, 1974), pp. 28-29.

Suggested Reading

Christian Social Responsibility

Bockmuehl, Klaus. *Evangelicals and Social Ethics*. Outreach and Identity 4. Translated by David T. Priestly. Downers Grove, Ill.: InterVarsity Press, 1979.

Gladwin, John. *God's People in God's World: Biblical Motives for Social Involvement*. Downers Grove, Ill.: InterVarsity Press, 1979.

*Perkins, John. *Let Justice Roll Down: John Perkins Tells His Own Story*. Glendale, Calif.: Regal, 1976.

_____. *A Quiet Revolution: The Christian Response to Human Need—A Strategy for Today*. Waco, Tex.: Word, 1976.

Sider, Ronald J., ed. *Cry Justice: The Bible Speaks on Hunger and Poverty*. Downers Grove, Ill.: InterVarsity Press, 1980.

_____. *Rich Christians in an Age of Hunger*. 3rd ed. Dallas: Word, 1990.

Culture

Kraft, Charles H. *Christianity and Culture: A Study in Dynamic Biblical Theologizing in Crosscultural Perspective*. Maryknoll, N.Y.: Orbis, 1979.

*Mayers, Marvin. *Christianity Confronts Culture: A Strategy for Crosscultural Evangelism*. Grand Rapids, Mich.: Zondervan, 1974.

*Nida, Eugene A. *Customs and Cultures: Anthropology for Christian Missions*. Pasadena: William Carey Library, 1954.

_____. *Message and Mission: The Communication of the Christian Faith*. Pasadena: William Carey Library, 1960.

*Niebuhr, H. Richard. *Christ and Culture*. New York: Harper & Row, 1951.

Osseo-Asare, Francislee. *A New Land to Live In: The Odyssey of an African and American Seeking God's Guidance on Marriage*. Downers Grove, Ill.: InterVarsity Press, 1977.

_____

*Indicates books to be read first in each category.

Samovar, Larry A., and Richard E. Porter, eds. *Intercultural Communication: A Reader.* Belmont, Calif.: Wadsworth, 1972.

Winter, Ralph D. *The Twenty-five Unbelievable Years: 1945-1969.* Pasadena: William Carey Library, 1970.

General Ethnicity

*Benjamin, Barbara. *The Impossible Community.* Downers Grove, Ill.: InterVarsity Press, 1978.

Glazzer, Nathan, and Daniel Patrick Moynihan. *Beyond the Melting Pot.* 2nd ed. Cambridge, Mass.: MIT Press, 1970.

Handlin, Oscar. *The Newcomers: Negroes and Puerto Ricans in a Changing Metropolis.* Cambridge, Mass.: Harvard University Press, 1959.

*Marden, Charles, and Gladys Meyer. *Minorities in American Society.* New York: D. Van Nostrand, 1978.

Novak, Michael. *The Rise of the Unmeltable Ethnics.* New York: Macmillan, 1972.

Black Ethnicity

Asante, Molefi Kete, and Kariamu Welsh Asante. *African Culture: The Rhythms of Unity.* Trenton, N.J.: Africa World Press, 1990.

The Autobiography of Malcolm X. New York: Ballantine, 1976.

Banks, William L. *The Black Church in the U.S.A.* Chicago: Moody, 1972.

*Bennett, Lerone, Jr. *Before the Mayflower: A History of Black America.* Chicago: Johnson, 1969.

Blackwell, James. *The Black Community.* New York: Harper & Row, 1975.

Ellis, Carl F. *Malcolm: The Man Behind the X.* Chattanooga, Tenn.: Accord, 1993.

Franklin, John Hope. *From Slavery to Freedom: A History of Negro Americans.* New York: Alfred A. Knopf, 1967.

Frazier, Franklin E. *The Negro Church in America.* New York: Schocken Books, 1963.

*Hale-Benson, Janice E. *Black Children: Their Roots, Culture and Learning Styles.* Baltimore: The Johns Hopkins University Press, 1986.

James, Clarence L. *The Black Church and the Black Male.* Atlanta: Youth Leadership Development Programs, 1991.

King, Martin L., Jr. *Why We Can't Wait.* New York: New American Library, 1964.

Kotlowitz, Alex. *There Are No Children Here.* New York: Doubleday, 1991.

Lincoln, C. Eric. *The Black Church Since Frazier.* New York: Schocken Books, 1963.

Martin, Elmer P., and Joanne Mitchell Martin. *The Black Extended Family.* Chicago: University of Chicago Press, 1978.

*Perkins, Spencer, and Chris Rice. *More Than Equals.* Downers Grove, Ill.: InterVarsity Press, 1993.

Salley, Columbus, and Ron Behm. *What Color Is Your God?* Downers Grove, Ill.: InterVarsity Press, 1981.

Woodson, Carter G. *The Mis-education of the Negro.* Trenton, N.J.: Africa World Press, 1933.

Urbanization

Abrahamson, Mark. *Urban Sociology.* Englewood Cliffs, N.J.: Prentice-Hall, 1976.

*Bakke, Ray. *The Urban Christian.* Downers Grove, Ill.: InterVarsity Press, 1983.

Ellison, Craig, ed. *The Urban Mission.* Grand Rapids, Mich.: Eerdmans, 1974.

Fava, Sylvia, ed. *Urbanism in World Perspective: A Reader.* New York: Harper & Row, 1968.

Frenchak, David, and Sharrel Keyes, ꝛds. *Metro-Ministry.* Elgin, Ill.: David C. Cook, 1979.

*Greenway, Roger S., and Timothy Monsma. *Cities: Mission's New Frontier.* Grand Rapids, Mich.: Baker, 1989.

*Mumford, Louis. *The City in History: Its Origins, Its Transformations and Its Prospects.* New York: Harcourt Brace Jovanovich, 1961.

Southall, Aidan, ed. *Urban Anthropology: Cross-Cultural Studies of Urbanization.* New York: Oxford University Press, 1973.

Warren, Rachelle, and Donald I. Warren *Neighborhood Organizers' Handbook.* South Bend, Ind.: University of Notre Dame Press, 1977.